HORSE
COLOR
EXPLORED

Over 150 Breeds,
Types, and Variations

Vera Kurskaya

TRANSLATED BY
DR. MICHAL PROCHAZKA

First published in 2017 by
Trafalgar Square Books
North Pomfret, Vermont 05053

Disclaimer of Liability

The author and publisher shall have neither liability nor responsibility to any person or entity with respect to any loss or damage caused or alleged to be caused directly or indirectly by the information contained in this book. While the book is as accurate as the author can make it, there may be errors, omissions, and inaccuracies.

Trafalgar Square Books encourages the use of approved safety helmets in all equestrian sports and activities.

Library of Congress Cataloging-in-Publication Data

Names: Kurskaya: Vera, author.

Title: Horse color explored: over 150 breeds, types, and variations / Vera Kurskaya; translated by Michal Prochazka, PhD.
Other titles: 880-01 Масти лошадей. English

Description: North Pomfret, Vermont: Trafalgar Square Books, 2016. | Includes index.

Identifiers: LCCN 2016024680 (print) | LCCN 2016040655 (ebook)
ISBN 9781570767319 (pb) | ISBN 9781570768101 (kindle) | ISBN 9781570768118 (epub)

Subjects: LCSH: Horses—Color. | Horses—Genetics.

Classification: LCC SF279.K87 2016 (print) | LCC SF279 (ebook) | DDC 636.1/0821—dc23

LC record available at https://lccn.loc.gov/2016024680

COVER PHOTOS:

Front (left side, from top to bottom): Natal Clasi, a Brazilian Warmblood owned by Vivian Hill, Stonybrook Farm, photo by Vivan Hill; Painted Patchen, a Thoroughbred bred by Patchen Wilkes Farm LLC, photo by KS Veitch Photography; Twilight Reemarkable, owned by Lisa Estridge, Palisades Appaloosas (www.palisadesapps.com), photo by Lisa Estridge; Zippos Millenium Bug, an American Quarter Horse owned by Heidi Trimber, photo courtesy of Carolyn Shepard; California Champagne, an American Paint Horse owned by Michele Jorgenson, photo by Carolyn Shepard

Front (main): Photo courtesy of Yeguada Paco Marti

Back: Left top photo of PKR Primavera Brio, a Morgan owned by John Hutcheson, Gab Creek Farm (www.gabcreekfarm.com), photo by Laura Behning (www.brookridgemorgans.com); middle top photo by Olga Yeremeeva; right top photo of Aktepel, an Akhal-Teke owned by Amrita Eldine Ibold, Sweet Water Farm Akhal-Teke (www.akhalteke.cc), photo by Amrita Eldine Ibold; author photo by Polina Lurye

Cover design by RM Didier | Book design by Brian P. Graphic Arts | www.brianpgraphics.com
Typefaces: Body set in ITC Franklin Gothic and ITC Slimbach

Printed in China

10 9 8 7 6 5 4 3 2 1

Contents

Preface

think my story is an unusual one. I am a Russian horsewoman, and I study horse colors, their variations, and the genetic mechanisms controlling them. I have always been interested in colors in a general sense, paying attention to those around me all the time. Surely, this linked to my love of horses and led to an interest in *horse colors*. But for a very long time my curiosity remained unsatisfied because of the lack of literature on the subject in my country.

When I was a teenager, I also dreamed of being a professional show jumper. But at the age of 20 an injury meant I couldn't continue riding horseback any more. What could I do to keep horses in my life? I started reading every equine book and magazine I was able to get my hands on, and eventually, I came across an article about horse color genetics. I learned of a mysterious champagne color that existed but was not, however, well described. I was intrigued. I did my best to find information about the color, discovering there was a group of colors controlled by the *Champagne* gene. As I searched for the details, I was drawn deeper and deeper into the world of horse color—and I am absolutely sure it *is* an entire world! I started a blog explaining horse colors to others who felt an interest in the subject. People began to ask for my help in identifying colors and in predicting foals' colors. Time passed, and some years after I first started my blog, I felt I had accumulated enough information to do what hadn't yet been done: a specialty horse color book in Russian. And I felt the need to write it myself.

The first edition of my book was published in 2011, and it was so popular all the copies were sold in two months. A year later I published a revised version—and now you have an English edition in your hands.

More than 10 years have passed since the moment I started to study horse colors, and many things have changed for me. My published book has led to clinics at equine exhibitions, and what was a hobby at first grew into scientific work. I started my own research concerning the rare Silver gene in horse breeds originating in Russia. By 2015 I had discovered the Silver gene mutation and silver colors in Soviet Heavy Draft and Byelorussian Harness breeds. I can say that because of my work, the Soviet Heavy Draft stallion Ratoborets 2011 (Reketir—Rezonerka) became the first Russian horse registered in the studbook as *silver bay* (see p. 28). Such discoveries are very important for the rare or threatened horse breeds, as they can increase interest and thus the breeds' chance of survival.

My research continues today. As of 2016, I became a post-graduate student at the Russian State Agricultural University named after K.A. Timiryazev, the oldest and the best agrarian university in my country. My thesis, of course, is devoted to my favorite subject—horse color identification.

I am so glad that my book is now published in the English language. When I first began studying horse color, most of my sources were in English because of lack of information in Russian. That is why my first aim was to tell something new to my native horsemen. Now I hope to say something new to English-speaking horsepeople around the world.

Writing and publishing a book is never an easy matter, and I am grateful to all the people who helped me with this process. I thank my husband for his patience, faith, and support. Thank you to Yevgeniy Matuzov for his interest in horse color genetics and generous support of my Silver gene research, and to Tatyana Zubkova for her Dun gene research, which is really important for the conservation of Russian Don and Budyonny breeds.

I especially thank Dr. Michal Prochazka, who respected my book enough to be so kind as to translate it into English. The English edition you are holding in your hands now would have been impossible without his participation.

I also thank Barbara Kostelnik for the effort she puts into her website devoted to rare horse color dilutions and for her kind help with the DNA test for the Iberian stallion Oro Mafiozo (see p. 37), Lee Patton and Holly Zech for their contribution to Oro Mafiozo's test, and Yelena Volkova for her questions, which were always very difficult to answer, but I did my best, and they made me go out of my comfort zone and move far forward.

I thank all the owners, breeders, breed associations, and photographers from around the world who helped provide the photos for this book, and of course, I thank Trafalgar Square Books for making my book available for English-speaking horse people.

Vera Kurskaya

CHAPTER 1:
Introduction to Horse Color

What Is Horse Color?

To begin, it is necessary to offer my own definition of *horse color*. A horse's "color" is genetically determined as the sum of color characteristics of the entire integument (natural outer covering of the animal), including hair, skin, hooves, and eyes.

I must emphasize that, first of all, we must both consider and come to understand the genetic approach to horse color. Second, it is important not to limit ourselves by paying attention to the horse's hair (coat) color only. Of course, you need to look at the horse in order to determine his color, but simultaneously, for a precise determination, you must also understand the genetic mechanisms of the formation of color, special features of pigment production, and how pigment is distributed over the body. (The latter especially helps during determination and differentiation of colors connected with the admixture of white hair.) Finally, an analysis of a horse's ancestry helps further when faced with unresolved questions regarding color and pattern.

The color in horses and other mammals is stable over the course of the animal's entire life. Changes that can modify the color characteristics of the hair cover (coat) of an individual horse during his lifetime are simply variations in one and the same color. While it is difficult to determine "final" coat color in a foal, specific diagnostic regularities (characteristics) can be observed, even at a very young age. In fact, color is a *combination* of several signs and characteristics. This is true regarding any color, even if its description seems deceptively simple. For example, pigmentation of hooves must be considered in coat color determination, since in certain cases Appaloosa color can be verified only with the help of a visible pattern of stripes on the horse's hooves.

COLOR VARIATIONS

Each color has its own variations, which are called *shades* and differ from each other in terms of the color nuances of hair. Unfortunately, many horse people completely overlook this aspect: While figuring out a horse's color, they try to find a photograph that exactly corresponds to his exterior appearance. Finding two animals that completely match each other in all details is extremely difficult, if not impossible, so many people, in the end, cannot determine the color of their horses and remain confused. This is the wrong way to go about color identification, since the majority of colors can be described with the help of several characteristics, regardless of variations in shade (see p. 68 for more on color shades).

TYPES OF HAIR

In horses, the hair on the body can be divided into several categories:

- *Body* (soft, short).

- *Guard* (mane, tail, feathers, and also "beard" on the lower jaw, although usually meant only to describe the hair of the mane and tail, which serves for the protection from insects, sun, and cold).

- *Tactile* (whiskers, eyebrow).

Color Terms

The nomenclature I'll rely on for colors is influenced by the traditional names long prevailing in the Russian color science and practice, and in equestrian pursuits, supplemented to reflect popular usage in the world at large. American geneticist Dr. Dan Philip Sponenberg (2009) stated that "the ideal nomenclature of the names of colors of horses can be that, in which each unique name of color corresponds with the specific genotype, and each specific genotype has a unique name of the corresponding color. Such precise connection between the genotypes and the colors is absent from all systems and nomenclatures. This happens sometimes for biological reasons, but it is much more frequent for cultural and historical reasons." As an example, "red" coat color in the English language is a single category, and all variations are built on the basis of the word "chestnut." But there are *three* concepts of chestnut in the Russian language—"red," "brown," and "flaxen chestnut"—and there are also three in Spanish.

Classification of Colors

Dr. Sponenberg (2003) separates the *base colors* black, bay, and red, and Dr. Anne Bowling (2000) calls the base colors black (including bay) and red, with both scientists relying on genetics. In principle, both their versions are accurate, since black and bay are determined by identical alleles of the *Extension* gene (see pp. 14

and 108 for more on this). In this book, I basically adhere to Dr. Sponenberg's classification—with small changes and refinements. I divide horse colors as follows.

BASE COLORS

- Bay
- Black (including dominant black)
- Seal brown
- Chestnut (including red, brown, and flaxen chestnut)

DILUTED COLORS

Colors determined by cream dilution:
- Buckskin
- Smoky black
- Smoky seal brown
- Palomino
- Double cream

"Wild" colors determined by the *Dun* gene:
- Bay dun
- Grullo
- Brown dun
- Red dun

Silver colors:
- Silver bay
- Silver seal brown
- Silver black (including silver dapple)

Champagne colors:
- Amber champagne
- Classic champagne
- Sable champagne
- Gold champagne

Pearl colors:
- Bay pearl
- Black pearl
- Seal brown pearl
- Chestnut pearl

Mixed diluted colors (colors determined simultaneously by combinations of different dilution genes):

- Dun and cream
- Dun and silver
- Cream and silver
- Cream and champagne
- Cream and pearl
- And others

COLORS DUE TO ADMIXTURE OF WHITE HAIR

- Gray
- Roan
- Spotted
- Appaloosa-spotting patterns (Leopard complex)

To summarize, there are four base colors, plus genes controlling all remaining colors. Figuratively speaking their "actions" are superimposed on the four base colors. I also introduce a separate category I call *color phenomena: countershading, rabicano, pangaré, brindle, gloss of body hair, false dun,* and *giraffe marks,* as well as characteristics of the horse's coat where the genetic nature is not proven or the characteristics do not remain stable over time. Examples include *dapples*, the phenomenon of *"Catch A Bird,"* and *frosty.*

A Very Basic Introduction to Genetics

You can't learn about horse color without learning at least a little bit about equine genetics.

HOW IT ALL BEGINS

Genetic information that determines the traits of a living organism is stored in the nucleus of a cell. Using a microscope, it is possible to observe oblong structures in the nucleus during certain time periods in the life cycle of a cell. These structures, called chromosomes, contain *deoxyribonucleic acid* (DNA), which is the direct carrier of hereditary information. The molecular building blocks of DNA are the four nucleotides known as *adenine, thymine, cytosine,* and *guanine.* A DNA molecule has two strands aligned with each other (like the tracks of a train), forming the familiar double helix. Segments of DNA are called *genes.* They are essentially the ingredients for the recipe to make a living thing and determine the kind of "products" the cell will manufacture and the characteristics they determine—for example, eye or hair color.

SO...WHAT'S SO IMPORTANT ABOUT GENES?

The DNA sequence of an organism and the presence or absence of proteins that code for certain traits is called *genotype*; their external manifestation (the organism's observable traits and characteristics) is *phenotype*. Most multicellular organisms obtain half of their chromosomes and genes from each parent. Horses have 32 pairs of chromosomes for 64 in total, and each gene normally exists in the same place on the same chromosome—this location is called the *locus*. The locus is the physical site on the chromosome where one form of a gene can be found. The different forms of genes that determine possible phenotypes are known as *alleles*. The alleles for a gene normally will be found in the same place on a chromosome from one parent as on the same chromosome from the other parent. As one locus is paired with another locus, the horse has two *allelic* genes matched from the series of alleles possible for a specific characteristic.

Alleles may be represented by a pair of letters: one letter denoting the allele donated by one parent and a second letter indicating the allele contributed by the other parent. If both alleles from both parents are identical, the animal has a *homozygous* genotype with two identical alleles at this locus (for example, AA or aa), but if they are different, then the individual is *heterozygous* (Aa or aA). When one of the alleles in a heterozygote completely determines the phenotype even when the second allele is present, the suppressing allele is said to be *dominant* and the suppressed allele is *recessive*. This phenomenon is called *complete dominance*. The completely dominant allele is designated by a capital letter (A), and the corresponding recessive allele is designated by a lowercase letter (a). In this scenario, the individual with the genotype "AA" has the same phenotype as individual with the genotype "Aa"—the recessive gene is hidden. But, while it doesn't "show" in the individual, it could emerge as observable in offspring. This plays an important role in the probabilities of the inheritance of any trait.

When individuals with the genotype "AA" and "Aa" are *phenotypically different*, and the trait encoded by allele "A" is more weakly expressed in the heterozygous "Aa" individual than in the homozygous "AA" individual, then the allele "A" is designated as *incompletely dominant*. In this case the heterozygous individual has a phenotype that can be an intermediate phenotype (that is, an "average") between individuals with the genotype "AA" and "aa."

A LITTLE ABOUT TRAITS

Now let us discuss genes that can amplify, weaken, or otherwise modify the action of *other* genes. Such genes are called *genetic modifiers*. An organism's phenotype can be formed by the action of two or more of these *non-allelic* or *complementary* genes, which in combination create an effect other than what the genes would on their own. Examples in horses are the genes *Extension* and *Agouti*, the first of which codes for the production of black pigment, and the second of which distributes the black pigment throughout the horse's body. Another genetic modifier is a gene that masks the expression of non-allelic genes, called *epistatic*.

Traits in living organisms are divided into *quantitative* and *qualitative*. Quantitative traits can be measured—that is, they are the kind of trait where how much you have can vary: body weight, height, and the thickness of bones, for example. Quantitative traits are usually not the product of one gene, but instead are coded by several pairs of genes and have a so-called *polygenetic inheritance*.

Qualitative traits, on the other hand, are usually *monogenetic* or influenced by a single gene. The phenotype is either/or—that is, you have one variant of the gene or another that dictates *how* it manifests. Pigments and blood type are examples.

When it comes to genes working nicely together (or not), there are other terms to become familiar with and to aim to understand:

- *Penetrance* is the ability of a gene to show itself phenotypically. It can be either *complete* (manifested in each individual that carries the gene) or *incomplete* (not phenotypically expressed by all carriers).

- *Pleiotropic action* is when one gene is responsible for two or more phenotypic traits.

- Some genes can lead to serious deviations from the norm, such as decreasing its viability (*sub-lethal effect*) or even leading to death (*lethal effect*). The loss of an animal due to an unfavorable genotype can occur either at the early stage of embryogenesis or sometime after its birth.

- Some genes located on the same chromosome can be *linked* and transferred together to offspring. Their pattern of inheritance differs from that of *unlinked* genes.

- A *mutation* is a change in the DNA sequence of a cell or its locus. The extent of mutations can range from a single or few nucleotides to entire chromosomes. Mutations lead to variation and ultimately the formation of alleles. The allele that exists in its original "normal" form in the species is called *wild*. Other alleles of the same gene are the product of mutations involving the wild allele.

With a basic grasp of the vocabulary I've introduced in this first chapter, you'll be able to now appreciate the genetics of horse color as much as you appreciate the myriad colors themselves. In the next chapter we'll examine over a hundred colors, how they manifest, and the genetic influences at play. Throughout you will find references to the color photographs you can view in the Color Photo Reference sections.

Horse Color
Photo Reference

For the images that follow, I have tried to provide the color and likely *or* proven (tested) expressed alleles for horse breeds from all over the globe. An asterisk (*) designates a position in a genotype that can be occupied by any allele, either dominant or recessive. A question mark (?) means I am not certain but feel secure suggesting such a variant. I must thank the many owners, breeders, breed associations, and photographers who contributed to this photographic reference section.

PHOTO 1

Color: Black

Expressed alleles: E* aa

Breed: Russian Saddle Horse

PHOTOGRAPHER: VERA KURSKAYA

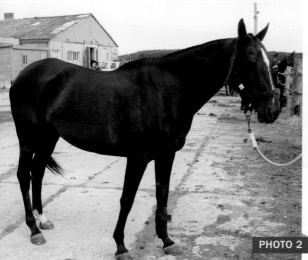

PHOTO 2

Color: Faded black. An example of rather weak fading: the horse has a brownish shade on the girth area, trunk, flanks, and groin.

Expressed alleles: E* aa

Breed: Argentine Polo Pony

PHOTOGRAPHER: VERA KURSKAYA

Color: Bay with a barely visible star.

Expressed alleles: E* A*

Breed: Trakehner-Budyonny cross

PHOTOGRAPHER: VERA KURSKAYA

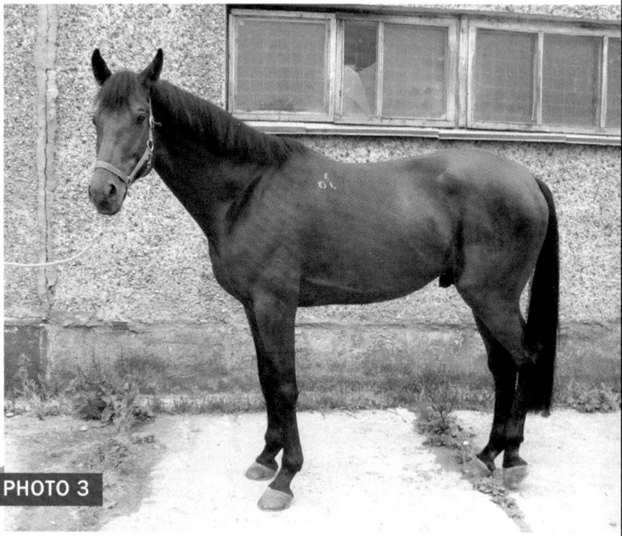

PHOTO 3

Color: Dark red bay with countershading.

Expressed alleles: E* A*

Breed: Unknown

PHOTOGRAPHER: KSENYA ABRAMOVA

PHOTO 4

Color: Dark red bay with countershading, a star and short blaze, right front leg with white fetlock, left rear white fetlock, right rear white sock. Note the countershading is stronger than in Photo 4.

Expressed alleles: E* A*

Breed: Unknown

PHOTOGRAPHER: KSENYA ABRAMOVA

PHOTO 5

PHOTO 6

Color: Dark bay with countershading, star, snip on the muzzle, front legs white to the fetlocks, and white socks on hind legs. Countershading strongly expressed on the frontal parts of the body: the neck, shoulder, withers, chest, and upper front legs are almost completely black.

Expressed alleles: E* A*

Breed: Unknown

PHOTOGRAPHER: KSENIYA ABRAMOVA

PHOTO 7

Color: Bay with a light tail, small star, and uneven white coronet on both front and right rear legs. The tail is light due to horse's young age (one year). Slight countershading is evident.

Expressed alleles: E* A*

Breed: Hanoverian

PHOTOGRAPHER: VERA KURSKAYA

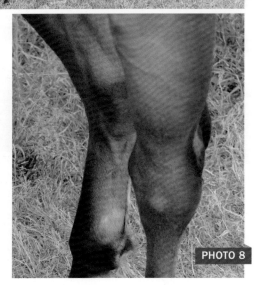

PHOTO 8

Detail: The legs of a "Wild" bay: The black hair barely rises above the horse's fetlock joints.

PHOTOGRAPHER: POLINA LURYE

Color: Seal brown with a star.

Expressed alleles: E* A^{t}* (?)

Breed: Latvian Horse

PHOTOGRAPHER: GREGORY SOLOVIEV

PHOTO 9

Color: Chestnut, star, turning into a blaze and extending to the nostrils and lower lip, with one white sock on left hind leg.

Expressed alleles: ee**

Breed: Argentine Polo Pony

PHOTOGRAPHER: VERA KURSKAYA

PHOTO 10

Color: Chestnut, white sock on right hind leg.

Expressed alleles: ee**

Breed: Unknown

PHOTOGRAPHER: KSENIYA ABRAMOVA

PHOTO 11

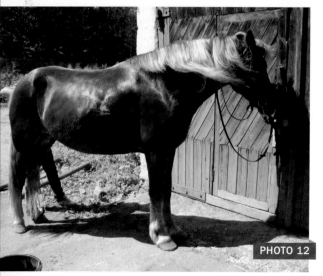

PHOTO 12

Color: Dark Chestnut with flaxen mane and tail. In addition to white, the mane and tail of this horse also contain a significant amount of red hair.

Expressed alleles: ee**

Breed: Unknown

PHOTOGRAPHER: ANASTASIA GRECHKO

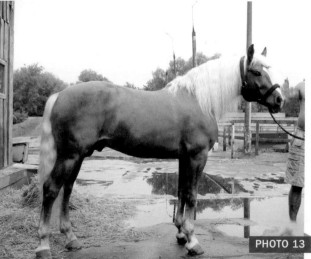

PHOTO 13

Color: Flaxen chestnut with a star turning into a blaze, white socks on the front legs, and a snow-white mane and tail. The lower part of legs lightened on all four legs. Overall the coat is light red or ochre color.

Expressed alleles: ee**

Breed: Haflinger

PHOTOGRAPHER: VERA KURSKAYA

PHOTO 14

Color: False red dun, blaze extending to lower lip, and white stockings on left front leg and right hind leg. The mane and tail are almost black.

Expressed alleles: ee** nd1*

Breed: Russian Don

PHOTOGRAPHER: VERA KURSKAYA

Color: The same horse as in Photo 14. Although the mane and tail almost appear black, there aren't other traits—black tipped ears, for example—characteristic for the bay color.

Expressed alleles: ee** nd1*

Breed: Russian Don

PHOTOGRAPHER: VERA KURSKAYA

PHOTO 15

Color: Liver chestnut.

Expressed alleles: ee**

Breed: Russian Trotter

PHOTOGRAPHER: VERA KURSKAYA

PHOTO 16

Color: Dark buckskin with uneven white markings on the hind legs. This is an example of a dark shade, similar to bay. But you can see how the horse's coat is more yellowish (see Photo 3 for comparison).

Expressed alleles: E* A* C^cr C

Breed: Akhal-Teke-Heavy Draft cross

PHOTOGRAPHER: VERA KURSKAYA

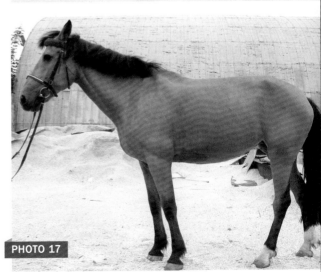

PHOTO 17

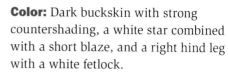

PHOTO 18

Color: Dark buckskin with strong countershading, a white star combined with a short blaze, and a right hind leg with a white fetlock.

Expressed alleles: E* A* C^{cr} C

Breed: Akhal-Teke

PHOTOGRAPHER: VERA KURSKAYA

PHOTO 19

Color: Dark buckskin with strong countershading, a star, and hind legs with white socks just above the fetlocks. The countershading is strongly expressed. The color can be determined in small areas on the barrel, chest, nose, underbelly, and the insides of the legs, which have a yellowish tint.

Expressed alleles: E* A* C^{cr} C

Breed: Akhal-Teke

PHOTOGRAPHER: VERA KURSKAYA

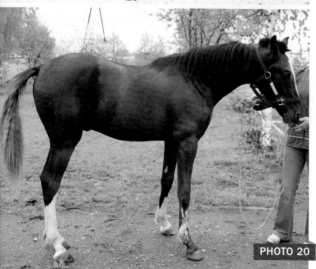

PHOTO 20

Color: Smoky black (?), with a star turning into a blaze. The tail is lightened, which is typical for smoky black, not faded black.

Expressed alleles: E* aa C^{cr} (?) C

Breed: Orlov Trotter

PHOTOGRAPHER: OKSANA BUYEVICH

CHAPTER 2:
Horse Colors

Base Colors

As I mentioned in Chapter One: Introduction to Horse Color, in this book I am working with four base colors in horses: bay, black, seal brown, and chestnut. They are called "base colors" because any individual horse must have one of them; they are the basis for color effects of additional genes.

BLACK

Black color (Photo 1) is evident in the hair on the horse's torso, head, legs, and also the mane and tail. The skin is dark gray, the eyes dark or hazelnut, the horn on hooves is pigmented, and the eyelashes are black. *Faded black* color usually develops under prolonged exposure to external factors such as excessive sunshine, harsh weather conditions, or increased sweating, but it may also develop spontaneously (Photo 2). The tips of faded black hair acquire a dirty-brown color, and the extent can vary. The head and legs of the faded black horse are always darker than the body, since the hair on these places is very short and less subjected to noticeable discoloration in comparison with longer hair on the body. In order to distinguish faded black from *seal brown* (see p. 12), it is necessary to look at the horse's head, in particular the region around the muzzle and the eyes. If in these places the hair is reddish or dark brown, then the color is seal brown. Note: There are also so-called *non-fading black* horses but they are less common. Such horses do not become faded, even when exposed to the effects of external elements.

Black foals are usually born ashy color and the legs and stomach are lighter than the remaining areas of the body.

Black horses are less common than *bay* (see p. 12) or *chestnut* (see p. 13). This color is the preferred color in Friesians. Some breeds where black color is frequently encountered include: the Percheron, Shire, Russian Saddle Horse, Russian Trotter, Kabardin, Vladimir Heavy Draft, Karachai, and the Kladruber. At the same time, it is rare in other breeds—Arabians, for example.

BAY

Bay horses have red or brown color of the trunk, and parts of the head, legs, mane, and tail are black (Photos 3–7). The tips of the ears and outer rims are also black. The skin and hooves are pigmented, eyes hazel, and eyelashes dark brown. The separation of the shades of bay is sometimes difficult and very subjective.

A *light bay* horse has light brown body hair. It is encountered rarely, and may be difficult to visually distinguish from *buckskin* (see p. 17). Dapples are observed in such horses more frequently than in the usual bay.

A bay horse with a dark or almost black torso is called *dark bay*. Dark brown and black hairs are mixed on the torso, and the brightest are concentrated above the nostrils, around the eyes, into groin, on the stomach, on the upper inside of the legs, and on the torso near the elbows. Let me emphasize that the expression "brightest" in this context is relative—in the case of dark bays it can be brown or dark brown, as long as it is "brighter" than the hair on the trunk. This color is characterized by dapples and can be confused with faded black (see p. 11). The two can be distinguished by the color of hair around the eyes: in the black horse, it will be black, while in the dark bay there is a brown or reddish ring in this place.

Bay without countershading, with a saturated reddish tone of body hair, is called *red bay*. This color is fairly rare. Bay with an expressed golden gloss of body hair is called *golden bay*. It occurs in the Akhal-Teke breed, and less frequently in Budyonny and Karabakh horses.

Sometimes you may encounter the so-called *"Wild" bay* color. On this horse the zone of black hair on the legs is restricted to the lower part, below the hocks and knees (Photo 8).

Bay foals have a red or light brown trunk and pale, almost white legs, with hardly noticeable dark hair below the hocks and knees. These areas become dark with age. The underbelly of a bay foal is also whitish.

Bay is the most common color in the world and is inherent to the majority of breeds. Some where it is found frequently include: the Arabian, Thoroughbred, Shire, Clydesdale, Paso Fino, Peruvian Paso, Kabardin, German Sport Horse, Latvian Horse, Vladimir Heavy Draft, French Trotter, and it is characteristic of the Cleveland Bay.

SEAL BROWN

Seal brown color (Photo 9) is described as black or dark color of the body and guard hair with a brown or tan area around the muzzle, eyes, groin, near the elbows, on the underbelly (especially in the girth region), and sometimes on the upper inside of the hind legs. These markings can be present in different horses at different intensities and in different combinations, and most frequently it is possible to observe on the horse's muzzle and near the eyes. In fact, people frequently confuse seal brown with dark bay (see p. 12), and even experienced horse breeders can make errors. In addition among some horsemen circulates a myth that seal brown color does not exist, and such horses are simply very dark bay or strongly faded black horses.

In order to accurately determine seal brown color, it is necessary to remember the following characteristics:

- Brown areas usually have rounded or oval outlines, clearly separated against the black or dark background. In dark bays, on the other hand, there is a smooth transition between the red, brown, dark brown, and then black color. It is especially easy to examine this on the muzzle above the nostrils.

- Brown areas have a relatively bright, reddish color, but are seldom light red.

Unfortunately, color determination in this case is complicated by the fact that the seal brown color also can have *shades*, as observed in bays. The characteristics described above are accurate only for the darkest and most typical versions of seal brown. In addition, the skin and hooves are pigmented, the eyes dark hazel, the eyelashes black or dark brown. Foals are usually born looking similar to bay foals, but with noticeably darker legs. The horse develops the color's characteristic phenotype only after baby hair is shed. Seal brown color is common in German Sport Horse breeds, Thoroughbreds, Standardbreds, and Russian Trotters.

CHESTNUT

Chestnut color is a relatively uniform red or brown color of the trunk, legs, mane, and tail (Photos 10 & 11). Shades can range from very light red, to close to apricot, to dark, to almost black (dark red and dark brown). The mane and tail in chestnut horses are usually of the same color as the body, but it is not unusual to see horses with brighter or darker guard hair. The skin and hooves are pigmented, the eyelashes red, eyes hazel.

Dark (liver) chestnut horses have dark orange or brown color of body hair. The mane and tail can be the same tone as the body or brighter (yellowish or even flaxen), or sometimes darker. *Standard (average) chestnut* horses are orange or red-colored. Guard hair can be the same tone as the body hair, or lighter or darker. *Light chestnut* horses have light carrot or almost yellow color of the body hair. This nuance is characteristic for the Akhal-Teke and Russian Don horses, and also for many draft breeds. The mane and tail are typically brighter than the body hair.

Chestnut horses with a whitish or almost white hair in the mane and tail are called *flaxen chestnuts* (Photos 12 & 13). The mane and tail usually change shade with seasons and can become lighter or darker, depending on the individual animal. I discuss flaxen chestnuts and specific information about heredity in more detail on p. 39.

It is extremely rare to encounter chestnut horses with brown, dark brown, or black color of the mane and tail, and it may be indicative of *false* red dun (see p. 26 and photos 14 & 15). This version of chestnut color is characteristic of the Karabakh, Russian Don, and Budyonny breeds. In addition, many Russian Don and Budyonny horses develop a golden gloss to their hair.

The darkest version of chestnut color is called *liver chestnut* (Photo 16). The mane and tail can be yellowish, the same shade as the horse's torso, or almost black. This color can be distinguished from dark bay by the body and legs—they are black in a bay (see p. 14). There is also a very rare shade of dark liver chestnut color, which can be confused with black. In this case the tail and mane can range from white, to vivid red, to the same color as the horse's trunk. This color can be found in Morgan horses, for example. Such horses can be identified as chestnut with the aid of DNA analysis.

The hair of chestnut horses can also fade; in such cases, a horse may look like he is covered with dust.

Chestnut foals are born red color with whitish legs and underbelly. Guard hair is often light. The foals become darker with age.

Chestnut color is common, surpassed in frequency only by bay. It is prevalent in the Arabian, Thoroughbred, Hanoverian, Budyonny, and Karabakh breeds, and some breeds have a characteristic chestnut shade, including Suffolk Punch and Russian Don horses. Chestnut color is encountered extremely rarely in Friesians, Percherons, Cleveland Bay, Orlov Trotters, Exmoor ponies, and Andalusians.

INHERITANCE OF BASE COLORS

Base colors in horses (black, bay, seal brown, and chestnut) are controlled by two genes: *Extension* and *Agouti*. The gene corresponding to the Extension locus is called MC1R (melanocortin-1 receptor). The "Wild" allele of this gene, designated "E," is dominant and codes for the intact, normal receptor for the melanocyte-stimulating hormone. Upon binding of the hormone, the receptor leads to the synthesis of the black pigment *eumelanin* in melanocytes.

A recessive allele of the receptor is designated "e," and in the homozygous state the horse can produce only a defective receptor. As a result the melanocyte-stimulating hormone cannot activate the production of black pigment and the cells switch to synthesize the red/yellow pigment *pheomelanin*.

Thus, genotype "EE" or "Ee" determines the presence of black hair, and genotype "ee" produces red. A DNA test is available to test for the "e" (red factor) allele. With the aid of this test it is possible to determine if there is a chance to obtain foals with red color—for example, from a black horse. The absence of the "e" allele in the genotype (EE) means that a horse is homozygous for the dominant allele; the presence of allele "e" in a single copy (Ee) indicates that the horse is heterozygous. A horse homozygous for the recessive "e" allele (ee) can only have a chestnut base color.

The dominant allele "A" of the gene *Agouti* codes for an Agouti-signaling protein (ASIP), which is an antagonist of the melanocyte-stimulating hormone, neutralizing its action in some areas of the body. In these areas there isn't any black pigment production and the hair is red. In sections in which Agouti-signaling protein is not produced (the mane, tail, lower part of the legs, and ear rims), the pigment synthesis is switched to the black eumelanin and the hair in these locations is black. Thus, dominant allele "A" leads to the formation of the bay color. The recessive allele "a" of Agouti results in the lack of production of ASIP, and in a homozygous state (aa) does not suppress the synthesis of black eumelanin throughout the entire integument. Therefore an "aa" horse, which also has the genotype "EE" or "Ee," will have a black base color. A phenotype effect of the Agouti gene appears only in the presence of allele "E," and directs the synthesis of eumelanin in necessary quantities. The Agouti gene has no effect in an "ee" homozygous horse because there is only the red pigment produced.

At present there is a DNA test for the "a" allele. It is possible to determine with this test, whether, for example a bay horse can produce a black foal. Interactions of the genes and alleles of Extension and Agouti are summarized below.

Table 1.

Agouti	Extension	Color
AA, Aa	EE, Ee	Bay
aa	EE, Ee	Black
AA, Aa	ee	Chestnut (often)
aa	ee	Chestnut (rare)

However there are additional alleles in these loci. An allele of Agouti designated "A^t" is responsible for the seal brown color and has an intermediate phenotypic effect between "A" and "a." There is a hierarchy of domination (A > A^t > a), and a DNA test developed in 2009 helps breeders to distinguish the seal brown color from dark bay. Interactions of this allele with others in Agouti and Extension are summarized in the following table.

Table 2.

Agouti	Extension	Color
AA^t	EE, Ee	Bay
A^{t}A^t, A^{t}a	EE, Ee	Seal Brown

DNA tests show that the "A^t" allele is encountered much more frequently than it was thought previously. In the United States, Dr. Michal Prochazka (the translator of this text) detected this allele and developed the DNA test, but as of writing the information has not been published yet. Based on my research, "A^t" has been found in several breeds, including: the Thoroughbred, Quarter Horse, Paint Horse, Arabian, Morgan, American Miniature Horse, and in some British ponies. This allele was also found in six Przewalski horses.

The existence of another allele "A$^+$" has been proposed, which is responsible for the "Wild" bay color. However, again as of writing, it has not been confirmed.

The Extension locus also has a third allele "e^a," which is recessive and present only in Black Forest Horses. In the homozygous state it leads to the formation of chestnut color—that is, phenotypically it is analogous to allele "e." This can introduce confusion with the analysis of the red factor "e," because a chestnut horse homozygous for the allele "e^a" can be erroneously identified as homozygous for "E." However, chestnut offspring will be produced upon crossing with another chestnut horse.

BODY DISTRIBUTION OF PIGMENT

Once I was asked why in horses pigment is frequently located on the periphery of the body. Apparently, it can be explained by the lower body temperature in these areas. An illustrative example is the color pattern in Siamese cats, which is characterized by a dark nose, ears, paws, and tail. The reason for this distribution of pigment is a temperature-sensitive form of *tyrosinase*, which facilitates the synthesis of dark pigment in the sections of the body with a reduced temperature. In horses, the existence of such a form of tyrosinase and its effect on the color has not yet been proven. However, Bowling and Ruvinski (2000) suggested that the reason for the outlying distribution of pigment in horses is indeed a biochemical mechanism, connected with a reduced temperature on the periphery of the body.

DOMINANT BLACK

Scientists have been examining the so-called *dominant black color,* which presumably may be controlled by a separate allele "E^D". So far its location is not known, but in the opinion of some experts, it can be located in the Extension locus. Similar phenomenon of the inheritance of dominant black color has been described and studied in other animals.

The presence of this allele leads to the formation of black color even in genetically bay horses. As a result the carrier of this allele has a black color that cannot be distinguished from ordinary black horses (EE aa or Ee aa). Thus, allele "E^D" is epistatic with respect to allele "A."

A foal with dominant black is similar to bay: brown with darker guard hair rather than the ashy color typical for ordinary black foals. The phenotype of the foal carrying dominant black becomes darker with age.

Diluted Colors

Next we will discuss color modifications determined by dilution mutations. Currently there are several separate dilution genes (for example, *Cream, Silver, Champagne, Dun*), and each has its own biochemical and molecular mechanism of action. More often it is possible to view color dilution as a weakening of pigmentation, and the molecular mechanisms of the action of some of these genes/mutations are still unclear.

COLORS DETERMINED BY CREAM DILUTION

Buckskin

A *buckskin* is a bay horse with one Cream Dilution allele (C^{cr}). Buckskin horses have a sandy yellow color of trunk, neck, and head, while the mane, tail, and lower parts of the legs are black (Photo 17). The nuances of body color are broad—from pale yellow or almost white to dark yellow. The lower part of the legs sometimes appears brown rather than black. The skin is pigmented but can be somewhat lighter than in a bay horse; the eyes are hazel or amber. Dapples are frequently observed.

I distinguish three varieties of the color, depending on the bay base: *light buckskin, average buckskin,* and *dark buckskin.* Light buckskin horses are characterized by sandy, sometimes almost white coloring of body. Average buckskin horses have a standard yellow body color, and as a rule, dark buckskins can have a significant amount of dark hair, concentrated on the upper back (countershading) in contrast to the lighter abdomen (Photos 18 & 19). The parts closer to the darker area tend to show dapples.

Newborn buckskin foals are typically light in color, tending to darken after they shed their baby hair. The lower part of the legs can be diluted or black, and with time the black zone tends to extend almost to the knees and elbows.

This color is encountered in many breeds: Lusitanos, Quarter Horses, Miniature Horses, Shetland Ponies, Welsh Ponies, Connemara Ponies, Australian Ponies, and Kinsky horses, for example. Light or dark buckskin color (with visible countershading) is common in the Akhal-Teke breed, and the Byelorussian Harness Horse frequently features very light-colored horses with an almost white trunk. Very rarely is the buckskin color found in Orlov Trotters, and only very recently was it discovered in Thoroughbreds.

Smoky Black and Smoky Seal Brown

In some countries the *smoky black* color is not considered its own entity and is not recorded in breeding documents, and rarely is referenced in the literature. Visually this color is difficult or even impossible to distinguish from faded black (see p. 11). Smoky black horses can have smoke-colored hair, and in such cases the shade is uniform over the entire body. The main difference between the smoky black and faded black horse is that in a smoky black animal there is almost no difference between the color of the neck and head. The skin and hooves are pigmented, and the eyes can be a walnut color, causing this color to sometimes be called "yellow-eyed black."

The smoky black color is on a very rare occasion similar to dark bay or seal brown. In such cases a precise determination of color can be accomplished by an analysis of pedigree data and by performing appropriate DNA tests. For example, if one of the parents of a black horse is *double cream* (cremello or perlino—see p. 20), then the horse in question must be smoky black. It can also help to study the offspring of the particular horse mated with horses of colors *not* connected to Cream. If a questionable "black" horse mated with a bay or red produces a buckskin or palomino foal, then the horse must be smoky black. Similar logic would apply if this "black" horse produces a double cream dilute (cremello or perlino) foal.

Smoky black foals are born looking similar to regular black—ashy, sometimes with silvery nuances (Photo 20). Also at a young age they frequently have broad darker bands, which run from the spine parallel to the ribs. The eyes are dark blue and the ears are frequently light inside with black edges. Young smoky black horses can for some period of time acquire dark brown shade. Smoky black horses that have a noticeable dark coffee shade are frequently seen in the Akhal-Teke breed, but this color is also encountered in other breeds carrying the Cream Dilution in their gene pool.

Sponenberg (2009) also mentions a very rare color he refers to as *smoky seal brown*. This color is most commonly encountered in Morgans and Quarter Horses, although in principle it can be encountered in any breed where the Cream Dilution gene is present. Smoky seal brown horses are visually *not* different from faded black. Their bodies are almost black but with the expressed red nuances around the muzzle and eyes that are characteristic for seal brown color (see p. 12). The legs as a rule are black. So far the only registry using appropriate names for genetically seal brown horses that are also carriers of dilution genes is the International Champagne Horse Registry (www.ichregistry.com). In almost all other registries, such horses are recorded as brown, dark bay, or black.

Palomino

Palominos are horses with chestnut base color, carrying one Cream Dilution allele. They appear bright pale yellow with white mane and tail (Photo 21). The skin is dark gray, although it can be somewhat brighter than the skin in chestnut horses, and the hooves are pigmented. Palomino eyes are typically brown color and only rarely hazel or amber. Eyelashes are yellow or light red.

In palominos the hair has a light red color with the characteristic cream tone, but the determination of shades requires practice. *Dark palominos* have saturated honey-red color and can be mistaken for chestnuts with flaxen manes and tails. *Light palominos* are characterized by a sandy colored body, and the mane and tail are practically always white (Photo 22). Sometimes a palomino can be so light that you mistake him for a cremello, but the main difference is the pigmented skin (see p. 20).

There is a special version of light palominos with sooty countershading. Such horses show a significant admixture of dark brown hair concentrated along the spine and extending downward to the sides. Bright, contrasting, yellow dapples and admixture of dark hair in the mane and the tail are frequently present (Photo 23). From a distance, some of these horses appear dirty yellow. This shade is so unique that in Australia it has its own name: *lemonsilla*. In other places it is common to designate such horses simply as dark palominos. The extremely rare countershading against the light background is expressed so strongly that such horses look practically completely dark brown, and the mane and tail have a significant admixture of brown and dark yellow hair, or they can be almost completely dark brown. This horse can be erroneously labeled "brown," and a precise color identification is, in such cases, possible only through DNA tests (or less reliably by pedigree analysis). It should be noted that many palomino horses noticeably change color tone according to the season.

Palomino foals are usually born very light cream or almost white-colored, sometimes with pink skin, which becomes darker in the course of time.

Palomino color is commonly found in the Quarter Horse, Akhal-Teke, Lusitano, Kinsky, and Byelorussian Harness Horse, but rarely in the Thoroughbred, among others. In spite of wide belief, this color is *not* characteristic for heavy draft horses of European and Russian origin; those registered as palomino are usually, in reality, light chestnuts.

Double Cream Dilution

Horses homozygous for the Cream Dilution gene (*double cream*) are characterized by light-beige color, varying from pale cream or almost white to saturated yellow (Photo 24). The skin is pink and eyelashes yellow or reddish. The eyes are most often blue, although you can also find golden, green, and greenish-blue with amber specks. In old literature on the subject, this color was not differentiated from light palomino (see p. 19).

In the past double cream diluted color was considered the manifestation of albinism, but this is incorrect. Albinism assumes the *absence* of any pigment in the hair and skin. White marks on the nose and legs are clearly visible in double cream diluted horses, consistent with the *presence* of pigment. The mane and tail could be the same color as the body, but it can also be brighter (white), or darker. When present, dapples on these horses have a light coffee color. The intensity of the color can be of an average shade, or light or dark.

Regardless of their base color, double cream horses all have the same name in the Russian language: "Isabell." However, there are distinctive terms used in the United States and elsewhere, depending on the base colors: *cremello* (chestnut base), *perlino* (bay base), and *smoky cream* (black base). Barbara Kostelnik (2008) uses *brown cream* for homozygous cream combined with the seal brown base. In reality, all these terms are names based on genotypes. In the United States the opinion exists that it is possible to make a conclusion about the genotype of a horse from the *shade* of the color. It is believed that in cremello horses, the mane and tail can be white, pale cream, or reddish; in perlino the mane and tail are light brown or ashy, as well as the lower part of the legs; and in smoky cream there is a light ashy tone of the body, mane, and tail. However, studies have not revealed a precise correlation between these nuances of hair color and the genotype of double cream horses.

Foals are born very light, almost white, with pink skin and light blue eyes. Sometimes, when grown a little more, the foal's coat can have a light golden tinge. Double cream horses are vulnerable to the sun and frequently suffer from burns on the nose, and sometimes also from skin cancer. Their eyes are sensitive to the bright sunlight. Long sun exposure can cause their skin to become spotty, as they develop reddish pigmented areas (so-called "pumpkin color"), and sometimes can even become gray, especially around the eyes. Because of the sensitivity to sun, this color was actively selected against by breeders in different parts of the world, Australia or Turkmenistan, for example.

Double cream dilute colors are relatively rare, and as might be expected are found in breeds in which other variants of Cream Dilution occur (palomino, buckskin, smoky black). Examples include the Lusitano, American Saddlebred, Tennessee Walker, Icelandic Horse, Miniature Horse, Paso Fino, Peruvian Paso, Quarter Horse, Welsh Pony, Australian Pony, Shetland Pony, Kinsky, Akhal-Teke, and Byelorussian Harness Horse.

Inheritance of Colors Determined by Cream Dilution

The Cream Dilution mutation is located in the MATP (membrane-associated transporter protein) gene on the twenty-first chromosome. This gene is responsible for the synthesis of a protein, which participates in the process of pigment formation and melanocyte differentiation. This protein is also found in large quantities in melanoma tumor cells.

The mutation of MATP is designated "C^{cr}," while the "Wild" allele that does *not* influence the color of the animal is designated by "C" or "Cr." The "C^{cr}" allele is incompletely dominant, and in the heterozygous state it causes dilution of pheomelanin-pigmented regions without an effect on eumelanin colored areas. However, observations show that the regions pigmented with eumelanin also show the action of this gene, although it is not always clearly noticeable. An example can be the brownish coloring of the lower part of the legs in some buckskins, or the brownish shades sometimes encountered in smoky black horses. In some cases the "C^{cr}" gene in the heterozygous state lightens up the iris color in the eye, which then becomes hazel or amber. A horse homozygous for "C^{cr}" shows strong pigment dilution not only in the hair, but also in the skin and the iris of the eye (Photo 25). The colors caused by Cream Dilution are summarized in Table 3 (see p. 22).

A DNA test for "C^{cr}" is available, and it is especially useful to determine the smoky black color, which as mentioned earlier, in the majority of cases cannot be distinguished visually from black. Based on the results of this test, the breeder will know if a particular horse can produce certain diluted colors caused by this mutation, and plan appropriate breeding. Tests of Agouti and Extension further help to determine the precise genotypes in double cream dilutes.

Table 3.

Base Color	C^{cr}/C	C^{cr}/C^{cr}
Bay	Buckskin	Perlino
Black	Smoky Black	Smoky Cream
Chestnut	Palomino	Cremello
Seal Brown	Smoky Brown	Perlino

COLORS DETERMINED BY THE DUN GENE

"Primitive" Markings

The color determined by the Dun gene (Dn$^+$ allele) in combination with the bay base color is genetically close to the color of the ancestors of the domestic horse, as well as contemporary wild representatives of the species. They are also typical for aboriginal species. Including this group of colors in the category of dilutions is only relative: The main characteristic of the color *dun* is the presence of the so-called "Wild" or "primitive" markings. The dilution of hair is only an additional feature, and it is not present or obvious in all cases.

The following primitive markings are seen in horses with the Dun gene:

- The *dorsal stripe* is a dark stripe that runs along the horse's spine from the withers to the dock of the tail. Its main characteristic is clearly defined boundaries (Photos 26 & 27). It is possible to liken it to a wide line drawn on the horse with a fat-tipped marker. Sometimes you can also see short transverse stripes, which is called *fishboning* (or *barbs*) due to the similarity with a fish's spine. Occasionally in horses with strong color dilution you can also find a zigzag-shaped or discontinuous dorsal stripe.

- *Zebra bars* or *zebra stripes* are short, dark, transverse stripes on the horse's legs, located in or above the region of the knees and hocks (Photo 28). Zebra bars are frequently present only on the backside of the legs.

- Often on the backside of the lower part of the horse's legs, you will see a line of *lighter hair,* known by some as a *zipper* (see Photo 109).

- *Cobwebbing* or *lacing* is a net of dark lines, which converge in the center of forehead of some dun horses, resembling a cobweb. This marking rarely involves the eye area.

- Many dun horses have dirty yellow, pale yellow, or even white strands of hair concentrated on the edges of the mane (Photo 29). Sometimes there can be so much *frosting*, as it is called, that the mane looks white. Although the latter scenario is rare, it can create difficulty in determining the color of the animal. Frosting is frequently dark in summer and becomes more noticeable in winter.

- Frequently in addition to frosting in the mane, there is also light hair in the tail (*light guard hair*). It can be white or pale yellow and is located along the sides of the tail dock, concentrated at the base (see Photos 26 & 27).

- *Dark ear rims and white tips* are present in almost all dun horses, spanning the perimeter of the ears (see Photo 29). In contrast to the bay and brown horses, this primitive marking is wider and has clearer boundaries.

- When the lower part of the horse's head, from the eyes to the nostrils, is darker than the forehead, neck, and body, he is said to have a *mask* (Photo 30). This is most noticeable when the horse is observed from a distance, and in bay- or black-based horses. It can be less obvious when the horse has white head markings.

- Many horses have more or less noticeable darkening on the withers and shoulders in the form of a *stripe* or *shadow* ("wing") perpendicular to the spine with poorly defined boundaries (Photo 31).

- A noticeable concentration of *dark hair* is often found on the neck near the mane.

- A *ventral stripe* along the horse's underbelly resembles the dorsal stripe (see p. 22), but it runs down the middle of the abdomen parallel to the spine.

Of all the primitive markings described here, the dorsal stripe is the only one "required" for the categorization of dun color. Zebra bars on the legs are common, but they may not be always noticeable against dark background hair. The remaining markings I've mentioned are encountered in different combinations and can be poorly visible. The color of primitive markings varies and depends on the color of a particular horse. They are usually the color of the horse's guard hair.

Bay Dun

Like the bay base color on its own, the Dun gene in combination with bay (*bay dun*) has many shades. The horse's body color can vary from brownish red to almost yellow with light reddish or ochre tinges (Photo 32). The mane and tail and lower legs are black or sometimes dark brown. In dun horses, the tips of black hair frequently lose their color, and therefore the tail and mane can appear "rusty" due to sun exposure. Primitive markings are black or, less frequently, brown-colored.

The following distribution and color of markings is most often observed: The mask is dark red or brown, and cobweb markings and any other admixture of dark hair on the body is black. The dorsal stripe and zebra bars can be either of these two colors. The hooves and skin are pigmented, the eyelashes reddish, and the eyes hazel, or sometimes light hazel or yellowish. Some horses show the *pangaré* trait (sometimes called "mealy") with lighter hair along the flanks, belly, inner legs, muzzle, and around the eyes (Photo 33 and see p. 72).

It is possible to find bay dun horses with a color that is practically indistinguishable from the usual bay color. Bay dun color is the most common "Wild" color and is often seen in Quarter Horses. It is also frequently encountered in such breeds as Vyatka and Bashkir Horse, as well as other aboriginal horses. The color is rare in some breeds, such as the Andalusian and Lusitano.

Grullo

Grullo (sometimes called *grulla*) is a color resulting from a combination of the Dun gene with the black base (Photo 34). These horses have ashy, grayish body color, sometimes with a distinctive bluish tone. All the body hairs have the same color—a major distinction from the gray and the black *roan* colors (see p. 44). The mane and tail are black, and the head is dark or almost black because of either cobwebbing or a mask, which when present together are superimposed on each other. The lower part of the legs is black, or sometimes dark ashy with a tone close to the body color, just darker. Primitive markings are black. The skin and hooves are pigmented, the eyes are hazel or (rarely) light hazel.

The grullo color can be subdivided based on its shades. *Dark grullos* are almost black, sometimes with an inconspicuous brownish tinge on the body, while the mane, tail, head, and lower parts of legs are black. Primitive markings are difficult to observe against such a dark background, and the horse can be mistaken for black or faded black (see p. 11). This color shade is very rare. *Light grullos* are characterized by a pale ashy color to the body hair and black or dark ashy guard hair (Photos 35 & 36). The eyes can be dark-blue with a blue ring around the iris, especially at a very young age, and from a distance they may appear hazel. Some breeders of Quarter Horses consider this trait an indication that the horse is carrying the Cream Dilution gene.

Sometimes the body hair can have a light yellowish tone, which according to some Polish scientists studying the Konik breed, becomes stronger in winter (2004). It is true that the overall color can change its tone depending on the season, and it tends to be most noticeable in horses that live outdoors. Mares are usually lighter than stallions. Interestingly, frosting is more often observed in the mane and tail of horses with this light shade of grullo.

Color: Palomino with a broad blaze and white stockings on the right front leg and hind legs.

Expressed alleles: ee** C^{cr} C

Breed: Byelorussian Harness Horse

PHOTOGRAPHER: GREGORY SOLOVIEV

PHOTO 21

Color: Light palomino with a star turning into a blaze and white coronets on all legs.

Expressed alleles: ee** C^{cr} C

Breed: Arabian-Orlov Trotter cross

PHOTOGRAPHER: IVAN FEDYAKIN

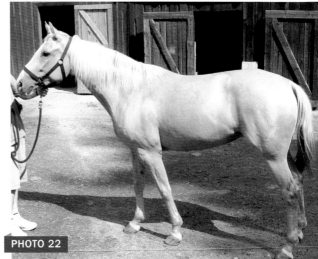

PHOTO 22

Color: Dark palomino with countershading.

Expressed alleles: ee** C^{cr} C

Breed: Shetland Pony

PHOTOGRAPHER: VERA KURSKAYA

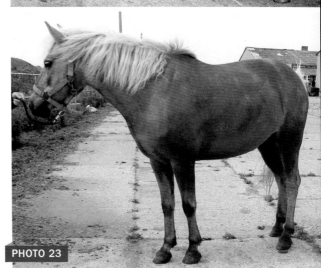

PHOTO 23

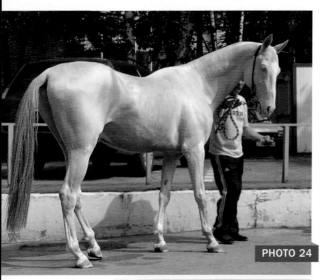

PHOTO 24

Color: Double cream dilute with a star turning into a blaze.

Expressed alleles: **** C^{cr} C^{cr}

Breed: Akhal-Teke

PHOTOGRAPHER: OLGA YEREMEEVA

PHOTO 25

Detail: Double cream dilute with "wall" or "china" eye.

Expressed alleles: **** C^{cr} C^{cr}

Breed: Akhal-Teke

PHOTOGRAPHER: OLGA YEREMEEVA

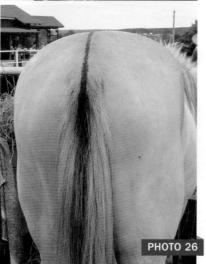

PHOTO 26

Detail: A dorsal stripe on the rump and visible white/light hair in the tail.

PHOTOGRAPHER: VERA KURSKAYA

Detail: A red dorsal stripe along the rump, extending into the tail.

PHOTOGRAPHER: VERA KURSKAYA

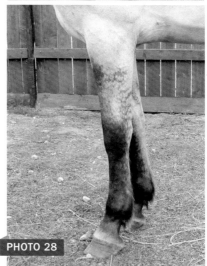

PHOTO 27

Detail: Zebra "bars" or "stripes."

PHOTOGRAPHER: VERA KURSKAYA

PHOTO 28

Detail: The dark rim of an ear and "frosting" in the mane.

PHOTOGRAPHER: VERA KURSKAYA

PHOTO 29

PHOTO 30

Detail: A "mask" on the head of a dun horse. Note also the darkening on his ears.

PHOTOGRAPHER: VERA KURSKAYA

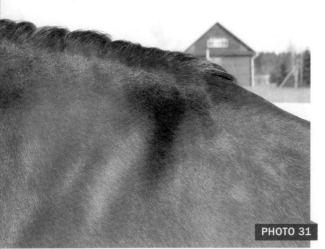

PHOTO 31

Detail: A distinct "wing" shape on the neck (right side) of a bay dun horse. This marking is barely visible on the other side of the same horse.

PHOTOGRAPHER: VERA KURSKAYA

PHOTO 32

Color: A bay dun—note, the hooves of this horse are pigmented normally but stained with soil from the arena.

Expressed alleles: E* A* Dn^{+*}

Breed: Vyatka Horse

PHOTOGRAPHER: VERA KURSKAYA

Color: A bay dun with pangaré ("mealy") color around the eyes, muzzle, and groin. This horse is a darker color than the horse in Photo 31, but in summer the horse does lighten, although maintaining a reddish-brown or ochre shade.

Expressed alleles: E* A* Dn⁺*

Breed: Unknown

PHOTOGRAPHER: VERA KURSKAYA

PHOTO 33

Color: Grullo with a mask, black legs with zebra bars, ears with dark rims, and a slightly shaded neck.

Expressed alleles: E* aa Dn⁺*

Breed: Unknown

PHOTOGRAPHER: VERA KURSKAYA

PHOTO 34

Color: Light grullo with a noticeable mask on the head, black legs with zebra bars, ears with dark rims, and a slightly shaded neck.

Expressed alleles: E* aa Dn⁺*

Breed: Unknown

PHOTOGRAPHER: VERA KURSKAYA

PHOTO 35

PHOTO 36

Color: A light grullo with a dorsal stripe, mask, black ear rims and tips, and dark legs.

Expressed alleles: E^* aa Dn^{+*}

Breed: Heck horse

PHOTOGRAPHER: ANNA MURATOVA

PHOTO 37

Color: Red dun with a dorsal stripe, a mask on the head, dark wings on the shoulders, dark hair on the lower part of the legs with zebra bars. Slight frosting of the mane and tail.

Expressed alleles: ee^{**} Dn^{+*}

Breed: Byelorussian Harness Horse

PHOTOGRAPHER: MARINA DMITRENOK

PHOTO 38

Color: A light bay dun, and an example of how the dun color often manifests in Norwegian Fjords. You can clearly see the black hair in the central part of the mane (called the midstol), with white frosting on the edges, a small mask on the face, and characteristic lightening of the legs.

Expressed alleles: E^* A^* Dn^+Dn^+

Breed: Norwegian Fjord

PHOTOGRAPHER: OLGA YEREMEEVA

Color: A dunskin with a yellowish shade, zebra bars on the legs, a facial mask, and with sparse strands of lighter frosting visible in the mane and at the base of the dock of the tail.

Expressed alleles: E* A* C^{cr} C Dn^{+}*

Breed: Bashkir Horse

PHOTOGRAPHER: VERA KURSKAYA

PHOTO 39

Color: A dunskin with a mane that shows strong frosting, zebra bars on the legs (especially the front legs), and a face mask.

Expressed alleles: E* A* C^{cr} C Dn^{+}*

Breed: Byelorussian Harness Horse

PHOTOGRAPHER: VERA KURSKAYA

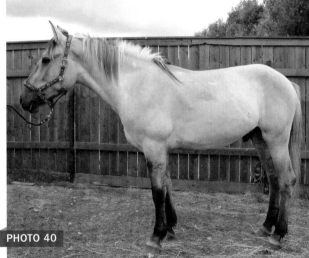

PHOTO 40

Color: A gray horse on a very light dunskin base with strongly expressed frosting in the mane, while the tail is almost completely white. There are zebra bars on the legs, although the rear legs are more pale. Around the age of 12, this horse turned completely white gray.

Expressed alleles: E* A* C^{cr} C Dn^{+}* G*

Breed: Unknown

PHOTOGRAPHER: VERA KURSKAYA

PHOTO 41

PHOTO 42

Color: A dunalino with a star extending into a blaze. There are weak zebra bars on the left hind leg, a head mask, and a slightly noticeable wing on the withers.

Expressed alleles: ee** C^{cr} C Dn^{+*}

Breed: Trakehner-Byelorussian Harness Horse cross

PHOTOGRAPHER: VERA KURSKAYA

PHOTO 43

Color: Smoky grullo with a star and strip, zebra bars on the front legs, and a mask on the face. This color can be confused with a bay dun, light grullo, or buckskin (see pp. 23, 24, and 17). However, any reddish tint is completely absent.

Expressed alleles: E* aa C^{cr} C Dn^{+*}

Breed: Latvian Horse-Byelorussian Harness Horse cross

PHOTOGRAPHER: VERA KURSKAYA

PHOTO 44

Color: Smoky grullo with a white star, dark neck, ear rims, shoulder wings, and a face mask.

Expressed alleles: E* aa C^{cr} C Dn^{+*}

Breed: Unknown

PHOTOGRAPHER: VERA KURSKAYA

Detail: The legs of a silver black horse. Faint webbing is visible close to the hooves.

PHOTOGRAPHER: VERA KURSKAYA

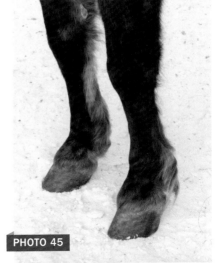

PHOTO 45

Detail: Clear webbing pattern on the leg of a different silver black horse.

PHOTOGRAPHER: VERA KURSKAYA

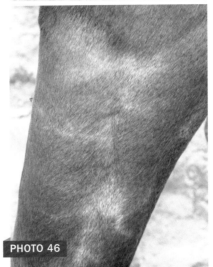

PHOTO 46

Detail: The legs of a silver seal brown horse. The close-up of the hoof shows visible webbing typical for silver horses. The hooves are pigmented, but it is possible to distinguish narrow stripes.

PHOTOGRAPHER: VERA KURSKAYA

PHOTO 47

PHOTO 48

Detail: The mane of a silver black horse in winter Expressed a significant admixture of brown and dark gray hair.

PHOTOGRAPHER: VERA KURSKAYA

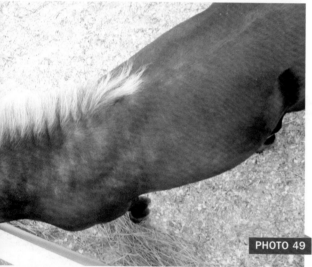

PHOTO 49

Detail: Dapples on the neck and shoulder blades of a silver black horse. Note the blurred boundaries of the dapples.

PHOTOGRAPHER: VERA KURSKAYA

PHOTO 50

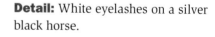

Detail: White eyelashes on a silver black horse.

PHOTOGRAPHER: VERA KURSKAYA

Color: Silver bay.

Expressed alleles: E* A* Z*

Breed: American Miniature Horse (Circle J Sir John Eh owned by Kendra Gale)

PHOTOGRAPHER: CHRISTINE TILLEMAN

PHOTO 51

Color: Silver seal brown. This horse is quite dark with tan markings characteristic of silver seal brown clearly visible around the eyes and muzzle.

Expressed alleles: E* A^t* Z*

Breed: Bashkir Horse cross

PHOTOGRAPHER: VERA KURSKAYA

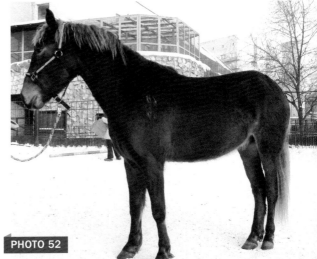

PHOTO 52

Detail: A different look at the tan markings around the eyes and muzzle.

PHOTOGRAPHER: VERA KURSKAYA

PHOTO 53

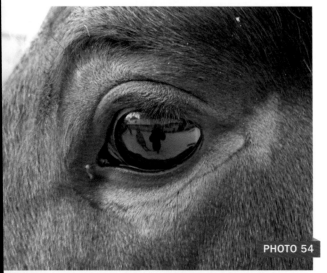

PHOTO 54

Detail: Note that unlike in some silver horses, the eyelashes of this silver seal brown horse are not lightened (see Photo 50).

PHOTOGRAPHER: VERA KURSKAYA

PHOTO 55

Color: Silver black with a small star—photo taken in January. The color is dark, almost black.

Expressed alleles: E* aa Z*

Breed: American Miniature Horse

PHOTOGRAPHER: VERA KURSKAYA

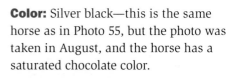

PHOTO 56

Color: Silver black—this is the same horse as in Photo 55, but the photo was taken in August, and the horse has a saturated chocolate color.

Expressed alleles: E* aa Z*

Breed: American Miniature Horse

PHOTOGRAPHER: VERA KURSKAYA

Color: Silver black with a bald face, a white sock on the right front fetlock, and uneven white stockings on hind legs. Note the yellowish hair in the mane closer to the withers.

Expressed alleles: EE aa Zz (confirmed by DNA test)

Breed: Unknown

PHOTOGRAPHER: VERA KURSKAYA

PHOTO 57

Detail: The head of a silver black horse with a very dark coat color, combined with an almost completely white mane, dark eyelashes, and a star above eye level.

Expressed alleles: Ee aa Zz (confirmed by DNA test)

Breed: Unknown

PHOTOGRAPHER: VERA KURSKAYA

PHOTO 58

Detail: An interesting admixture of whitish hair on the neck of the silver black horse from Photo 58. The mane contains strands of white and yellow, but no red.

PHOTOGRAPHER: VERA KURSKAYA

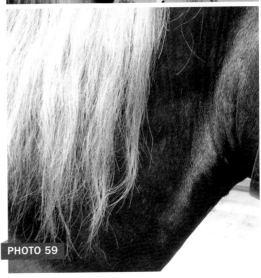

PHOTO 59

PHOTO 60

Color: Silver dapple, possibly combined with gray. There is visible webbing on the left hind leg. This filly is only a year old, and given the fact that her dam is gray, it is possible that over time she will be, too.

Expressed alleles: EE aa Zz (confirmed by DNA test)

Breed: Shetland Pony

PHOTOGRAPHER: ELENA MOLCHANOVA

PHOTO 61

Color: A stunning example of silver smoky black. The horse's body is noticeably diluted to a dark chocolate color. The mane and tail are almost red and resemble those of a faded black horse, but there is a difference: While the mane is almost entirely faded, there is not a visible distinction in shade between the horse's head and barrel.

Expressed alleles: E* aa C^{cr}C Z*

Breed: Morgan (Positively Charmed, owned by Laura Behning, Brookridge Morgans—brookridgemorgans.com)

PHOTOGRAPHER: LAURA BEHNING

PHOTO 62

Detail: The same horse as in Photo 61. Here you can see that the mane is almost entirely red, but the roots are still dark. This is one of the features of silver colors in horses. The pigment gets more and more concentrated in the roots of the mane and tail with age. The most dark hair is on the neck (under the mane), but the head is not the darkest part of the body (another indicator that this horse is not faded black). Also note the horse's amber-colored eye.

PHOTOGRAPHER: LAURA BEHNING

Detail: The whitish blue eye of a newborn champagne horse. which may remain the same in ivory champagne horses, but otherwise changes color over time (see Photos 55 & 56).

Breed: Friesian-Racking Horse Cross (Crixux ZL, owned by Aimee Ziller)

PHOTOGRAPHER: AIMEE ZILLER

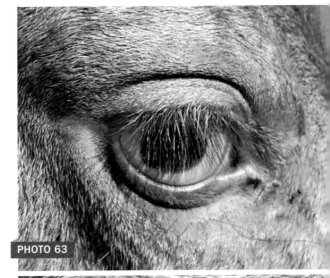

PHOTO 63

Detail: The same champagne foal's eye at one month of age has turned a greenish color.

Breed: Friesian-Racking Horse Cross (Crixux ZL, owned by Aimee Ziller)

PHOTOGRAPHER: AIMEE ZILLER

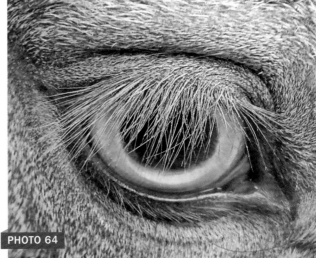

PHOTO 64

Detail: The same foal at 10 months old, showing the amber-colored eye sometimes seen in champagne horses.

Breed: Friesian-Racking Horse Cross (Crixux ZL, owned by Aimee Ziller)

PHOTOGRAPHER: AIMEE ZILLER

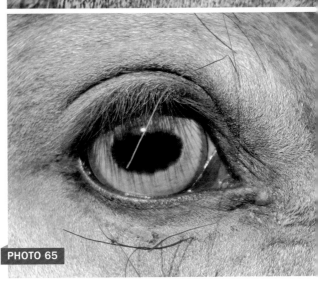

PHOTO 65

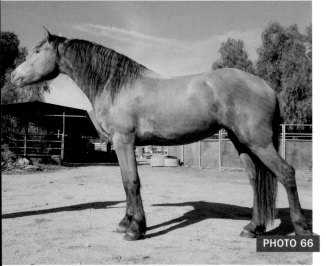

PHOTO 66

Color: Classic champagne.

Expressed alleles: E* aa Ch*

Breed: Friesian-American Saddlebred Cross (Hy-Color Champagne Diva, owned by Aimee Ziller and Bryan Ludens)

PHOTOGRAPHER: AIMEE ZILLER

PHOTO 67

Color: Amber champagne.

Expressed alleles: E* A* Ch*

Breed: Arabian cross (Sweet Champagne, owned by Carolyn Shepard)

PHOTOGRAPHER: CAROLYN SHEPARD

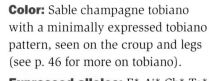

PHOTO 68

Color: Sable champagne tobiano with a minimally expressed tobiano pattern, seen on the croup and legs (see p. 46 for more on tobiano).

Expressed alleles: E* A^t* Ch* To*

Breed: American Paint Horse (California Champagne, owned by Michele Jorgenson)

PHOTOGRAPHER: CAROLYN SHEPARD

Grullo foals are born ashy colored. Light grullos are born yellowish or cream, and very seldomly, light reddish.

Grullo color is common in Polish Konik Horses (up to 95 percent of the breed), Quarter Horses, Vyatka, Heck, and Bashkir Horses. Occasionally it occurs in Norwegian Fjords. Light grullo color is common in Sorraia Horses, Connemara Ponies, and Yakutian Horses.

Red Dun

The body color of a *red dun* horse can have various shades, but as a rule it is lighter than in standard chestnut horses (Photo 37). Primitive markings are of red color. Often the head is darker than the body, showing a mask or cobwebbing. The lower legs, mane, and tail are also darker than the body. The skin and hooves are pigmented.

Dark red duns are almost indistinguishable from ordinary chestnut horses in terms of body color, but they will have noticeable primitive markings. *Light red duns* are almost yellow or sand color and resemble palominos (see p. 19). This color is common in the Norwegian Fjord breed (Photo 38). In 2013, Russian scientist Tatyana Zubkova found examples of light red duns in two breeds where it was not previously considered present: the Budyonny and Russian Don. Their colors were confirmed by DNA analysis.

Other Colors Determined by the Dun Gene

Besides the colors just described, there are others determined by the Dun mutation.

The combination of dun and buckskin (*dunskin*) results in a very light yellow or pale sandy body color with black or dark brown primitive markings (Photos 39–41).

Palomino horses carrying the Dun gene (*dunalino*) resemble light palominos (see p. 19), and their primitive markings have a rusty or dark yellow color (Photo 42). The mane and tail can be practically all white with only the middle part of the tail containing colored hair as a continuation of the dorsal stripe.

One of the rarest colors in this group is double cream dilute (C^{cr}/C^{cr}) combined with the Dun gene. Such horses have a cream body color with a pale caramel dorsal stripe and zebra bars, and also pink skin and blue eyes (sometimes called *wall eyes* or *china eyes*). Dun horses carrying *one* Cream Dilution gene often have light-brown eyes.

Another rarity is the smoky black plus Dun gene color (*smoky grullo*). Visually it is closest to light grullo color with a yellowish tone (see p. 24), but it is impossible to distinguish the two colors without DNA testing. Such horses have dirty-brown or dirty-ashy, yellowish color, lighter toward the underbelly, and the mane, tail, and lower part of the legs are dark brown (Photos 43 & 44). They have a remote resemblance to faded black (see p. 11). Foals are born an ashy color that is lighter than grullo.

These colors are all fairly rare, and when found, are often in the Norwegian Fjord, Quarter Horse, and Bashkir Horse breeds.

Inheritance of Colors Determined by the Dun Gene

The dun colors are controlled by a dominant allele of the Dun gene (abbreviated as Dn^+). This allele is considered the "Wild" version of the gene, while its mutant form (nd2, which means non-dun2) in a homozygous state defines the usual, ordinary non-dun colors. The result of its action is dilution of eumelanin, resulting in bluish or ashy hair color, and pheomelanin, resulting in light red, apricot, or pale caramel. However, the mane, tail, head, and lower part of the legs are diluted to a lesser degree, which may indicate the involvement of a temperature-sensitive biochemical mechanism. An integral part of the action of the Dun allele is the manifestation of primitive markings, and these have an unclear mechanism of formation.

According to a hypothesis made by Nancy Castle (2008), primitive markings are created in *all* horses during embryogenesis. However in color-diluted horses carrying the Dun gene, the markings are visible, whereas in non-Dun-gene horses—due to a darker background—these markings are invisible. Castle bases her theory on the fact that you can observe primitive markings in foals that disappear as the animal ages. In general, the color of a horse darkens with maturity, and it is possible that primitive markings remain present. In support of this hypothesis is the presence of such markings on adult horses that are not dun. Such horses are called *false duns* (see p. 78). The specific mutation of the Dun gene responsible is abbreviated "nd1" (non-dun1). There is a DNA test for the Dun gene. The hierarchy is $Dn^+ > nd1 > nd2$.

Table 4.

Primary Color	Dn^+
Bay	Bay Dun
Black	Grullo
Seal Brown	Brown Dun
Chestnut	Red Dun
Buckskin	Dunskin
Palomino	Dunalino

COLORS DETERMINED BY THE SILVER GENE

The colors of this group (Z) were defined rather recently, at the beginning of the twenty-first century. Understanding the true distribution of these colors is difficult because they are rare, although apparently this dilution *is* present in quite a few different breeds. Color identification in doubtful cases should be guided in part by whether or not a color has shown to be present in a specific breed. Therefore, I feel it necessary to provide a list of breeds in which the Silver gene occurs at the beginning of our discussion. The list includes the: Rocky Mountain Horse, Kentucky Mountain Saddle Horse, Quarter Horse, American Miniature Horse, Morgan, Appaloosa, Missouri Foxtrotter, Virginia Highlander, Paint Horse, Tennessee Walker, Mustang (particularly those found in Oregon, Nevada, and California), Icelandic Horse, Northlands Pony, Australian Pony, Connemara Pony, Shetland Pony, Swedish Warmblood, Finnish Warmblood, Dutch Warmblood, Gypsy Horse, Welsh Pony, Ardennes, Soviet Heavy Draft, and the Byelorussian Harness Horse. It has been determined by DNA analysis that carriers of the Silver gene were also found in the Haflinger breed, but there isn't a visible color effect because this breed occurs only in the red (chestnut) color. Remember that Silver Dilute horses and dark flaxen chestnuts can look similar.

Silver color displays the following characteristics:

- Many silver horses show a characteristic marble pattern on the legs called *webbing*. This has a "rusty" appearance or looks like whitish, irregular, elongated streaks with sharp boundaries (Photos 45–47).

- Ashy or black hair in the mane and tail are found frequently (Photo 48). Silver horses can have yellowish guard hair of a dim, rather dirty shade, but not red or reddish, which would be typical for flaxen chestnuts.

- Striped hooves are found in some silver horses, but they are not always present (see Photo 46). They differ from the striped hooves of appaloosa-spotted horses (see p. 55), because the stripes in silver horses are not black, but dark gray, and do not have sharp borders. Often their stripes are wedge-shaped. Striped hooves can be observed in foals, although in the process of the horse maturing, they may disappear.

- Pronounced seasonal dapples are observed in some silver horses (*silver dapple*—see p. 28), appearing in summer and vanishing in winter (Photo 49).

- Light eyelashes (white or yellowish), while not present on all silver horses, are a reliable characteristic seen on most (Photo 50).

Silver Bay and Silver Seal Brown

Silver bay is often confused with flaxen chestnut (see p. 39)—for example, in the United States these colors have been recognized as separate entities only since 2002. The silver bay horse has a red or brown color to the trunk and a lighter mane and tail—from dark ashy with separate whitish and yellow locks of hair, to almost completely white (Photo 51). Sometimes the same horse can have a dark and smoky tail paired with an almost white mane, or vice versa. The skin and hooves are pigmented.

The main difference between silver bay and flaxen chestnut are the dark legs, resembling the legs of an ordinary bay horse. In flaxen chestnut animals, the lower part of the legs has a red or whitish color. In the silver bay, the color of the lower part of the legs fluctuates from light to dark brown—to sometimes black. In addition, the ears often have black rims.

A horse with the weakest manifestation of the Silver gene does not differ from an average bay, unless the guard hair is mixed with a considerable amount of light hair, making the mane and tail look ashy. The lower part of the legs is almost undiluted, sometimes showing mild leg webbing. This color may also resemble "Wild" bay or dun, but from the first it can again be distinguished by light guard hair, and from the second by a saturated red color of the trunk and lack of primitive markings. When the body hair of this horse is in poor condition, the color can also be confused with red or brown.

Sometimes you may see a horse with brown body hair and black legs, while the mane and tail are diluted, matching the brown body color. However, the most characteristic and recognizable variety of silver bay has a reddish body, a mane and tail that are nearly white or light ashy, and light brown lower legs because of the presence of leg webbing. Separate ashy or black locks remain in the guard hair.

A silver bay foal has light lower legs, similar in appearance to ordinary bay foals, and becomes darker after shedding his baby coat. Silver bay commonly occurs in the Rocky Mountain Horse.

Silver seal brown is very rare (Photos 52–54). It is recognizable by the dark brown, almost black color of the body, sometimes with a bluish tint to it, with characteristic red "burn marks" around eyes, muzzle, near the elbows, on the stomach, and the groin. The guard hair is diluted from dirty red to a whitish color.

Silver Black and Silver Dapple

There aren't well-established English terms designated to represent colors determined by the Silver gene on a black base. It is challenging to divide Silvery black color depending on the degree of dilution, because there are diverse phenotypes depending on the degree of Silver expression. *Silver black* is often a sepia color, usually combined with dapples (Photos 55–59). The guard hair can be from dark brown to light gray or white. *Dark silver black* horses have a black or dark chocolate colored body, and the mane and tail can have a dark yellow color due to the presence of black hair, or sometimes can also be very white. They can be mistaken for dark flaxen chestnuts. Silver black with an almost undiluted body and no dapples is also called *silver chocolate* by some.

This color is characteristic in Rocky Mountain Horses, and according to the Rocky Mountain Horse Association (www.rmhorse.com) it is called *chocolate*. The color is traced to the founding stallion of this breed: "Old Tobe." Today more than 40 percent of Rocky Mountain Horses have the color.

The strongest dilution of the Silver gene results in *silver dapple*, which may remotely resemble *dappled gray* (Photo 60 and see p. 41). Silver dapple horses may also have a sepia shade, which is most common in Shetland Ponies and American Miniature Horses.

Distinguishing silver dapple horses from gray horses with dapples is simple: the head of a silver horse is either *darker* than the body or the *same color*. The head of a gray horse is always *lighter*. You should also look for other traits we discussed on p. 27, such as light eyelashes and leg webbing. White or light eyelashes are found most often in silver black or silver dapple horses.

American Miniature Horses carrying the Silver gene on the black base are often erroneously registered as having the gray, chestnut, or even palomino color. Silver dapple foals with a black base are born rosy cream, light ashy, or the color of a light biscuit, vaguely resembling palominos with gray muzzles. Dapples are absent at this age. The tail and mane of silver black and silver dapple horses sometimes darken with age. In the winter they become browner and dapples disappear.

Other Colors Determined by Silver

The Silver gene dilutes only areas of hair containing eumelanin, and so it has no effect on red hair. The term *silver chestnut* is occasionally used in English writings on the subject of horse color to describe horses with a chestnut base that are *carriers* of the Silver gene. Such horses have the potential of producing silver offspring.

If the Silver gene is present in a horse in combination with other dilution genes, the resulting colors can become difficult to identify when only observing the phenotype. This is especially difficult in the Rocky Mountain Horse, Mountain Pleasure Horse, and the Icelandic Horse breeds, in which many individuals have similar combinations of genes. For example, the mane and tail hair diluted by the Silver gene can be mixed up with frosting, a characteristic of dun colors (see p. 22). In combination with the dun or buckskin, the effect of the Silver gene shows very poorly. For example, a *silver dun* horse looks very similar to a bay dun but also has pale yellow or whitish guard hair; however, the legs are dark, sometimes with leg webbing. I was lucky enough to discover this color in Byelorussian Harness Horses. The *silver buckskin* also looks quite ambiguous. The color ranges from sandy to whitish, and the mane and tail are diluted brown or dirty yellow. This color is found in Icelandic Horses, where some time ago it was mistaken for the Champagne dilution (see p. 32). One more rare combination is *silver grullo*. This horse is externally very similar to grullo—the only difference is an almost-white mane and tail, and sometimes leg webbing.

Silver smoky black determined by the Silver gene plus one Cream Dilution gene appears, on the outside, to be very similar to ordinary silver black with a little more yellowish or brownish shade to the body (Photos 61 & 62). Unfortunately, it isn't always possible to measure this difference by the eye.

There are additional rare combinations, such as *silver dun buckskin*, which can occur in the Icelandic breed. The horse is a light, sandy color, the lower part of the legs is light ashy, and sandy-colored hair is mixed with black and ashy in the mane and tail. Primitive markings are brown.

Inheritance of Colors Determined by the Silver Gene

The Silver gene mutation is dominant, located on the sixth chromosome, and the gene is named PMEL17 (pre-melanosomal protein 17). Two dominant alleles of this gene responsible for silver colors are designated "Z," and the recessive allele that doesn't influence color has the symbol "z." There is a DNA test for two dominant Silver mutations.

The action of the gene on pigment is most noticeable on guard hair and to a lesser extent on the body hair. As mentioned already, it does not affect the color of a red horse. The effect of the Silver gene on horse colors is presented in the table below:

Table 5.

Primary Color	Z
Bay	Silver Bay
Black	Silver Black or Silver Dapple
Seal Brown	Silver Brown
Chestnut	Chestnut
Buckskin	Silver Buckskin
Smoky Black	Silver Smoky Black
Palomino	Palomino
Bay Dun	Silver Dun
Grullo	Silver Grullo

The hypothesis that silver dapple horses are homozygotes, and silver black horses are heterozygous for this mutation could not be confirmed by DNA tests.

Some silver horses have congenital anomalies of the structure of eyes called *anterior segment dysgenesis* (ASD). Scientific literature also uses the name *multiple congenital ocular abnormalities* (MCOA). The phenotypes include:

- Small pupils, which do not react to light or react poorly. (Application of dilating preparations does not have an effect.)
- Abnormally formed pupils.
- Hypoplasia (underdevelopment) of the iris, including its stroma.
- Hypoplasia of iris formed by a pigmentary layer on the top edge of the pupil.
- Abnormal structure of pectineal ligament.
- Cataracts.
- Cysts in the vitreous body.
- Corneal thickening.
- Abnormal arrangement of the eye lens.
- Retinal dysplasia.
- Abnormal circulation of intraocular liquid.
- Defects of the ciliary body, such as small cysts in the junction between the sclera and cornea.
- Cysts of the iris and ciliary body sometimes extending to the peripheral part of the retina.
- Microphthalmia or megalophthalmia (abnormally small or abnormally large eye or eyes).
- Abnormally large eyes.

The majority of the eye anomalies are connected with the forward segment of the eye, and some of them can occur independently, although there are also exceptions—such as the retinal displasia. Heterozygotes for the Silver gene are less affected than homozygotes. The vision of horses with cysts is usually normal. Unlike in normal horses with healthy eyes, the sclera of silver horses is sometimes pink, but not pigmented. Not all horses with MCOA have notable problems with their vision, but there are, of course, exceptions. For example, when cysts of a ciliary body are torn due to an impact, it can lead to the detachment of retina.

Most often MCOA is found in related breeds that originated from horses coming from Appalachia. These include Rocky Mountain Horses, Kentucky Mountain Saddle Horses, and Mountain Pleasure Horses. Similar abnormalities are also observed in other breeds, such as the Morgan, Belgian, Shetland Pony, American Miniature Horse, and Icelandic Horse. Affected horses can display abnormal behaviors due to the problems with their vision. Structural eye abnormalities are the result of a pleiotropic action of the PMEL17 gene. For this reason, since 1998, Kentucky Mountain Saddle Horses are required to pass veterinary inspection for the absence of vision problems before being allowed for breeding (animals with eye anomalies are excluded). The rules are not so strict for the Rocky Mountain Horse. Nevertheless, breeders of Rocky Mountain Horses, including those in Europe, do not recommend breeding carriers of the Silver gene.

COLORS DETERMINED BY THE CHAMPAGNE GENE

Unlike colors due to the Silver gene, champagne colors are absent in breeds in Russia and Europe. They are found in a limited number of breeds: the American Cream Draft, Tennessee Walking Horse, Missouri Fox Trotter, Quarter Horse, Paint Horse, Appaloosa, Rocky Mountain Horse, American Saddlebred, Kentucky Mountain Saddle Horse, Racking Horse, American Warmblood, Miniature Horse, North American Sportpony, and the Mustang.

Horses expressing the Champagne gene have the following features:

- Specific age-dependent change of body color: The majority of foals of other colors is born light and darkens with age. In contrast, champagne foals are born with a dark hair and become lighter with age.

- Color of eyes: Champagne horses are born with light blue eyes that gradually become greenish, then golden, and finally amber or hazel (Photos 63–65). However, the process of pigment accumulation in the iris can stop at any of these stages, and certain animals can have blue, green, or goldish eye color all their lives.

- Speckled skin: Champagne foals are born with pink skin that darkens unevenly over time, developing specks. The skin of champagne horses differs from the skin of double cream diluted horses. It is dark pink, rather than light or bright pink in color. In adult champagne horses the dark, lilac specks are especially noticeable around the eyes, on the muzzle, under the tail, and on the genitals. Occasionally specks can be so dense they can merge together.

- Goldish gloss of hair: Not all champagne horses have this trait, and at the same time not all horses with glossy hair are champagne. Nevertheless, this is considered a characteristic feature of champagne colors.

- Dapples: Carriers of the Champagne gene sometimes have so-called "reverse" dapples—that is, not light against a dark background, as observed in the majority of dappled horses, but dark on a light background. However, not all champagne horses have such dapples, and reverse dapples are not unique to them. The International Champagne Horse Registry (ICHR—

www.ichregistry.com) in the United States keeps records of horses having this color, regardless of their breed.

Classic Champagne

This is the least common champagne color—a derivative from black. *Classic champagne*, to a certain degree, is similar to grullo (Photo 66). This color varies from dark-ashy, chocolate, or brown to golden and bronze, dark and brass, or light gray-brown, with a darker (chocolate or dark-chestnut, but not black) mane and tail. The lower part of the legs can be darker than the horse's body. The ashy hair sometimes has a bluish shade. The hooves of classic champagne horses are pigmented; the eyes are amber, or less often green.

Foals are born dark brown and lighten. Similar to black horses, champagne horses can become sun-faded in the summer. Experts separate this from a *light classic champagne*, which is an animal with very light bronze, almost yellow color, and those with a light but noticeable grayish shade.

Amber Champagne

This is a combination of the Champagne gene and a bay base (Photo 67). Amber champagne completely corresponds to its name: the body color is amber or goldish red. The mane, tail, ear rims, and lower part of the legs are chocolate or light brown. Occasionally there is an admixture of white, silvery, or pale-yellow hair in the mane and tail. This color can be confused with buckskin or silver buckskin.

The most typical amber champagne horse has body hair the color of saturated amber, apricot, or orange, and the mane, tail, and lower part of legs are chocolate. At birth, foals can be almost indistinguishable from classic champagne—it is with age that they become lighter. The eyes of an adult amber champagne horse are usually amber though they can remain light green in some animals. Hooves are pigmented.

Sable Champagne

Sable champagne is the Champagne gene on a seal brown base; therefore, it sometimes does not differ much from classic champagne color. The most common body color of a sable champagne horse is chocolate (of any intensity) with an ashy to dark or bronze shade (Photo 68). The guard hair is dark brown or chocolate; the lower part of the legs and ear rims often the same. For sable champagne horses that look similar to classic champagne, reliable distinction between them is possible via DNA analysis.

Gold Champagne

Gold champagne is a color determined by the Champagne gene combined with the chestnut base (Photos 69 & 70). Gold champagne horses have a goldish red or apricot body color. The tail and mane are usually light red (lighter than the body) or ivory, which is the reason that this color can be confused with palomino.

Occasionally you can see a horse with a saturated orange body color and a mane and tail with either the same shade, or even darker hair. In that case the horse is registered as *dark gold* or *dusky gold*. The main difference from a non-champagne color is pink skin and dark specks, as well as other characteristic signs of champagne (see p. 32). The eyes are amber, or less frequently, light green, and the hooves light or slightly pigmented.

Gold champagne foals are born red, often a quite saturated shade. Gold champagne color is characteristic for the American Cream Draft, although it is sometimes mistakenly identified as palomino or cremello.

Cream Plus Champagne—And Other Colors Determined by Champagne

A previously used term for horses who have one Champagne allele and the Cream Dilution allele was "ivory." However, the term "ivory" does not reflect the genetic nature of the colors of this group, and it has been recommended by the ICHR to use compound names containing the names of the genes/alleles involved instead. As an example: the color resulting from the combination of amber champagne with Cream Dilution is called *amber cream*.

The genetic base of such colors can be any—chestnut, black, bay, or seal brown. The genotype usually consists of one or two Cream Dilution alleles (C^{cr}) and one or two Champagne alleles.

Horses in this group are born with light pink skin that becomes covered by dark specks with age. Eyes at birth can be light blue, and with age they can become light green or amber—all being characteristic signs of champagne colors. The dilution of pheomelanin caused by the Cream allele combined with dilution of both types of melanin by the Champagne gene can have a varying effect, thus complicating color identification. It is possible to define color most precisely by DNA analysis. Here I will consider only those combinations that have authentic representative carriers and for which there is real phenotypic data, but note that other combinations are also possible.

Amber cream horses have pale yellow—sometimes almost white—body color and a light brown mane and tail. The lower part of the legs is occasionally a little darker brown. *Gold cream* horses have very pale yellow or ivory color body hair (Photos 71 & 72). Compared to amber cream, gold cream is lighter. As a rule, the mane and tail are white or pale cream. The eyes are yellow or golden, but occasionally can remain blue for the rest of the horse's life. A *sable cream* horse is similar to amber cream, but the color of the body, mane, and tail has a subtle brown shade.

Classic cream champagne horses are light bluish smoky color, sometimes almost white with a yellowish shade (Photo 73). The mane and tail are light brown with an admixture of reddish hair. In 2009, the ICHR began registering *double cream champagne* color. Such horses look almost white, but in good light it is possible to notice a pale shade of ivory or light cappuccino, and a weak golden gloss in the sun. The skin is pink and dark specks can be absent completely. If they are present, there are few and they are difficult to find. The skin of this horse is lighter than the skin of a double cream dilute. The eyes are ivory and have blue streaks running up and down from the pupil. The iris can be framed with a yellowish ring on the outer edge.

There are additional colors determined by the Champagne gene combined with other dilution genes, besides Cream. *Champagne dun* horses have a strongly diluted color similar to dun with noticeable primitive markings in coffee or dark gold. Most often this combination is found in Quarter Horses. Classic dun and classic grullo horses (see p. 24) differ from champagne dun in the whitish-ashy body hair and light-chocolate guard hair. *Sable dun* color looks similar, but is lighter, while *gold dun* animals have body hair that is light cream or light amber with a mane and tail that are ivory or white. *Amber dun* is a beige body color with pale brown guard hair and lower legs. The eyes of champagne dun horses of any shade described here are most often light green.

Silver champagne horses combine the action of both dilution genes. The resulting *amber silver* horse has a light pinkish-amber or light ashy body color, and the lower parts of the legs are the same shade or are slightly darker. The mane and tail may contain whitish hair.

Quite often you can find combinations of champagne with spotting or an Appaloosa-like pattern.

The ICHR separates a group of colors called *triple dilutes*. Here belongs the *double cream champagne* color described above, as well as other combinations of three dilution genes. For example, *classic cream dun* is a black-based horse carrying one gene of each: Cream, Dun, and Champagne. There are also other combinations, but their external differences are insignificant, and therefore, it is necessary to determine such colors by DNA analysis.

Inheritance Determined by the Champagne Gene

The Champagne mutation is a dominant allele in the gene SLC36A1 (solute carrier family 36, member 1) located in the fourteenth chromosome. The mutant allele dilutes both eumelanin and pheomelanin. Eumelanin under the influence of the mutant allele results in chocolate or yellowish-brown color, and pheomelanin results in in light orange or golden yellow. This Champagne allele has the symbol "Ch," and the "wild" recessive allele is designated "ch." There is a DNA test for the Champagne gene. The influence of the Champagne gene on color is described in Table 6.

Table 6.

Primary Color	Ch
Black	Classic Champagne
Bay	Amber Champagne
Seal Brown	Sable Champagne
Chestnut	Gold Champagne
Smoky Black	Classic Cream Champagne
Buckskin	Amber Cream Champagne
Palomino	Gold Cream Champagne
Grullo	Classic Grullo Champagne
Bay Dun	Amber Dun Champagne
Silver Black	Classic Silver Champagne
Silver Bay	Amber Silver Champagne
Silver Brown	Sable Silver Champagne

COLORS DETERMINED BY THE PEARL GENE

The effect of the Pearl gene resembles that of Champagne; however, it is recessive. It is likely an allele of the Cream gene, designated here as "C^{pr}," and if the horse has one Pearl allele, it can, at most, have one Cream Dilution allele. There is a DNA test for Pearl. On the MATP gene there are three known alleles, which interact among themselves as follows: $C^{cr} > C > C^{pr}$.

Pearl occurs in a very limited number of breeds, including the Quarter Horse, Paint Horse, Andalusians, Lusitanos, Peruvian Paso, and Irish Cob. Excepting the last one, all these breeds have Iberian origins. Barbara Kostelnik, who created a website devoted to the rarest dilution genes (www.hippo-logistics.com), assumes that pearl can be also present in the gene pool of Mustangs, Florida Crackers, and Creole Horses, as they also go back to horses of the Spanish conquistadors.

For names of the colors determined by the Pearl gene there are two nomenclatures in the United States. One is reflected in the third edition of the book by Sponenberg (2009) and based on the names of champagne colors (see pp. 33–34).

The second is used on the website(s) created by Kostelnik (2010). In a homozygous state in a chestnut-based horse, the Pearl gene results in an apricot color, called either *chestnut pearl* (Kostelnik) or *gold pearl* (Sponenberg). A light apricot color hair is characteristic for this combination. The skin is pink with rare dark specks, and the hoofs are light. At birth the eyes are blue. With age the hair can become slightly lighter, the skin can turn dark pink or lilac-pink, and the number of specks may increase. Although this genetic combination is rare, this color is the most widespread among horses homozygous for pearl (Photos 74–76).

Black pearl can have cocoa body hair and a chocolate mane, tail, and lower legs (Photo 77). The skin is pink with dark specks.

Kostelnik also speaks of a mare named Zorita Surprise imported to Norway from the Netherlands while she was still in her dam's womb. The dam was seal brown and the sire unknown. The mare was mated with a homozygous gray sire and produced a foal, which (at the time of writing) looks bay with primitive markings (these could be just juvenile markings). The foal is expected to eventually turn gray. Based on genetic analysis, Zorita Surprise has gray color on the basis of bay and pearl (*bay pearl based gray*, according to Kostelnik, or *amber pearl* according to Sponenberg). The body has a pale yellowish color with light brown guard hair, and the skin is pink with limited dark specks.

In October 2010 I was fortunate to see a horse with the Pearl gene. The stallion Oro Mafiozo, an Lusitano-Andalusian cross brought to Russia from Spain, is a color that is difficult to describe. His body is very light brown, almost mustard or bronze color, with a mauve shade, depending on light. He has lilac-tinged, brown countershading that runs down his shoulders, shoulder blades, and neck. His forehead and the bridge of his nose are also dark, which is characteristic for countershading. The lower legs are bronze-brown, the guard hair is light chocolate with admixture of lighter, as well as darker, hair, and the hair tips are reddish. The ears are light lilac or bronze with a noticeable pale chocolate border. The skin is lilac-pink and any dark specks are generally concentrated on the eyelids with only a few of them on the lips and genitals. Shades change depending on illumination. Indoors the horse has a lilac shade and outdoors he is bronze. The eyelashes are light brown; the hooves pigmented. The eyes are clear, the iris has a light oak color, and the sclera is pink. Unfortunately, we don't have exactly enough words to describe all the shades of this unique horse! The analysis of DNA of the stallion was performed at the University of California, Davis, which indicated Oro Mafiozo is a *seal brown pearl* (Photos 78–82). It should be noted that at the time of writing there isn't a lab currently providing the specific test for seal brown coat color.

Another pearl stallion, an Andalusian in Greece at the time of writing, is apparently homozygous Pearl but shows a color that is *between* black pearl and seal brown pearl. This stallion has no signs of countershading on his bronze-golden body with reddish toned guard hair and lower legs. While I can exclude the chestnut pearl color, without DNA analysis it is not possible to define his color more precisely.

Horses carrying one Pearl allele and one Cream allele differ very strongly in dilution. In a 2007 article I called this color *pseudo-cream* in agreement with the sometimes-used American terminology *pseudo-cremello*, *pseudo-perlino*, and *pseudo-smoky cream*. However, the English nomenclature has changed recently, and therefore I consider it necessary to slightly expand word choice, as well. I suggest using the term pseudo-cream as a generic term when DNA tests are *not* done. The names based on specific genotypes, which I list on the coming pages, should be used only in horses for which DNA analysis has been made.

Pseudo-cream horses are born with pink skin, blue eyes, and light color hair that becomes lighter with age. The eyes can later become dark blue or amber. Over time the skin also changes, developing dark specks. The color of such horses depends on their genetic makeup and varies from almost white called *palomino pearl* (Photo 83), to light beige with brown guard hair (*dun pearl*). *Smoky pearl* foals are born quite dark, ashy with a yellowish shade, but become lighter with brown guard hair and lower legs, which can also sometimes be golden yellow color (Photos 84–85). These colors are very rare.

NEW DILUTION GENES?

Kostelnik also describes two horses with color that cannot be explained by the dilution genes already known to science. The first one is a Paint Horse in Tennessee named Ropers Nova, also known as "Spade." His owner suspected he was champagne. According to DNA tests, the horse was heterozygous for "C^{cr}" while having the appearance of a homozygote, and he was tested for the Champagne and Pearl genes, and the results for both were negative. His diluted color did not find an explanation.

In addition, a stallion named Sunshine's DNA analysis said he should be a buckskin, but phenotypically he resembles a double cream. He is a pale yellow color with a weak golden gloss. His mane and tail are slightly darker, his skin is pink with rare brown, round specks, and his eyes are celestial blue. His sire is a smoky black Paint Horse, and his dam is a bay Quarter Horse. The skin of this stallion is sensitive to sunshine.

While there are similarities between these two stallions, Sunshine's guard hair has a yellower shade. His eyes also differ, with blue around the pupils while the main part of the iris has a pale yellow, slightly greenish color.

I can only suggest the unknown dilution factor at play here be called the "Spade factor," which I believe can be located on the MATP locus, like Cream and

Pearl. My assumption is based on the very strong similarity with Pearl, and also that it obviously interacts with Cream. However, it is impossible to exclude the possibility that the "Spade factor" is located in a different locus or even on another chromosome, and only imitates the action of mutant alleles of MATP.

FLAXEN CHESTNUT

Flaxen chestnut horses have a chestnut body color (shades from light red to dark brown), and a white mane and tail, sometimes with an insignificant admixture of red hair (Photos 86 & 87). To differentiate flaxen chestnut from silver (see p. 27), the distinctive features are:

- If present, the darkest hair in the mane and tail is brown or smoky brown, while silver horses can have dark ashy or even black hair. To determine the color of separate hairs, extract a sample and observe it against a background of white paper.

- The lower part of the legs is chestnut, sometimes whitish, while in silver horses this part of the legs is brown or ashy, often with marble markings.

Genetically, flaxen chestnut is a chestnut-based color, most likely inherited as a polygenic trait. At the end of 2009 American scientists began researching this color in Morgans, in which all these colors are present.

Observations show that light-colored guard hair is a hereditary phenomenon: American scientists found that crossing two flaxen chestnut horses will only produce flaxen chestnut offspring. Breeding two chestnut horses with darker guard hair can sometimes result in a foal with a snow-white mane and a tail. It seems that the mechanism of inheritance of this trait is much more complex than a simple case of "dominant/recessive."

Flaxen chestnut color is commonly found in Thoroughbreds, Arabians, Quarter Horses, and Russian and Soviet Heavy Drafts, to name just a few, and is characteristic for Haflingers and Belgians.

Colors Determined by Admixture of White Hair

Sponenberg divides such colors into two groups:

1 Colors with mixed white and pigmented hair—for example, *gray, roan, rabicano.*

2 Colors with white spots—such as *spotted, appaloosa-like spotting,* or *dominant white.*

GRAY

Since the time of Hippocrates the *gray* horse color was considered a base color, probably due to its relatively monotone appearance. However, genetic discoveries showed that this was incorrect. In essence, gray color is an early loss of pigment and can manifest itself in combination with any other color. Horses of gray color are never born gray: Foals and young stock begin with the color determined by their genetic makeup, but over time white hairs gradually appear in the coat in a progressive manner. Eventually the horse becomes gray, and finally, almost white in color. Foals that are carriers of the Gray gene and will eventually gray out have a very saturated color at a young age. For example, at birth true bay foals have light-colored legs; bay foals that will become gray are born with black legs.

The skin of gray horses is usually dark. After clipping, a gray horse doesn't appear lighter like horses of other colors, because the dark skin becomes more visible through the white hair. Some gray horses may have *vitiligo*, which is regional skin depigmentation. The skin of such individuals becomes covered by round and oval pink spots with irregular edges; these are noticeable on the lips, around the eyes, and in the groin area (Photos 88 & 89).

The graying process can begin at different ages. On average it starts one to three years after birth, but it can be later. The speed of graying is individual both for specific horses, and for different breeds in general. It is noted that horses of light colors (such as chestnut or palomino) turn gray faster than darker colors, and in a bay the redder hair becomes depigmented first.

Detailed inspection of a newborn foal with at least one gray parent makes it possible to tell with high probability whether the horse will turn gray. The most accurate signs are white hairs around the eyes, and it is also possible to find them in the mane and tail, and on the ears and muzzle. The process of graying always begins with the head, often around eyes. A light head is a distinctive feature of gray horses. The eyelashes also become white. Although there are variants of gray color, they appear during different stages of the graying process in almost all gray horses.

Dark gray color is present at the very beginning of the graying process. Usually this term is applied to genetically black horses (Photo 90). Sometimes the body hair can have a blue cast, which looks similar to grullo (see p. 24). The initial stage of graying in genetically bay or chestnut horses is not very noticeable, as white hair on a red or brown background does not provide as much contrast as on black. The mix of white and red hairs on the body results in a reddish shade (*rose*), especially noticeable from a distance (Photo 91). The mane, tail, and the lower part of the legs turn gray more slowly, staying dark longer.

The second stage of graying is gray with *dapples* (Photo 92). White dapples are scattered against a dark background and become gradually lighter. As a rule, this stage is observed in genetically black horses, although it can also be found in chestnut horses. Usually this stage begins from four to twelve years of age and has variable duration. Gray with dapples can be sometimes confused with a silver black (see p. 28); however, a gray horse has a lighter head, whereas in the silver black the head is darker or the same shade as the body, and the border between dark and light areas is smooth. Eventually the hair of the dapple gray lightens and dapples start disappearing.

The final stage of graying is *white gray* (Photos 93–95). The hair contains very little pigment or none at all and the body appears to be white. In fact, this color is sometimes mistakenly called "white."

The so-called *fleabitten gray* horse is whitish with small, colored specks or "freckles" on the coat (Photos 96 & 97). This stage of graying is less common, although often seen in the Arabian breed. Sometimes *blood marks* are seen in flea-bitten grays. These are markings or groups of hairs that are not gray but another color—often chestnut, giving the marking its name (Photos 98 & 99).

Sometimes horses in the initial stages of graying are mistaken for *roan*. The differences between these two colors are explained in more detail beginning on p. 43. Registration of gray foals as roan is a widespread issue in some breeds, and certain registries—for example, the Jockey Club (www.jockeyclub.com)—use the broader category "gray/roan."

In combination with diluted colors gray can cause unusual manifestations. For example, it is difficult to observe the graying stages in double cream horses. A special case is gray with any champagne colors. The foal is born darker than an ordinary champagne foal, and specks on the skin are darker and more abundant—they have a dark lilac or dark blue color, sometimes almost black. Also the fleabitten effect can gradually develop in parallel with graying. The color of the specks is often gold. Paradoxically, *gray champagne* horses don't turn white gray; their body hair remains a cream color noticeable at a certain distance.

Some gray horses have visible primitive markings, especially at an early age, and even in those breeds in which dun is not a factor. So far, there is not a scientific explanation for this phenomenon.

Gray occurs in many breeds. It is very frequent in the Arabian, Orlov Trotter, Lippizaner, Kladruber, and Andalusian. In some breeds, such as the Morgan and Akhal-Teke, this color is rare. In native breeds (for example, the Vyatka and Fjord) gray color is not present.

Many would offer that gray horses seem to roll in the dirt much more often than horses of other colors! Perhaps they sense their color is a vulnerability and try to mask it? Horses with gray color certainly have a reputation for being difficult to keep clean.

INHERITANCE OF GRAY COLOR

Gray color is determined by a dominant mutant allele "G" (gray) and recessive allele designated "g." This mutation is located in the STYX17 (syntaxin-17) gene on the twenty-fifth chromosome. The mutant allele codes for a cell membrane protein that is allegedly involved in the process of cellular division and strengthened formation of melanocytes before and early after birth, followed by their loss. This is the reason for the bright pigmentation at an early age with a subsequent termination of color production. The Swedish scientist Leif Andersson (2008) assumes that the mutated allele stimulates an excessive growth of melanocytes. This leads to a depletion of the stem cells forming melanocytes, resulting in the loss of pigment in the hair. At the same time there is expansion of melanocytes in the skin, which is responsible for its dark coloring.

A DNA test is available to determine if a horse is homozygous or heterozygous for the mutant allele. This allows us to determine whether a gray horse can or cannot produce non-gray offspring. Based on observations, homozygous horses tend to turn gray more quickly than heterozygotes. However, in the Percheron breed the majority of gray horses are homozygotes, developing gray color by the age of approximately nine years. It is possible that the speed of graying in this breed is influenced by additional genetic modifiers.

Based on observations of breeders of Percherons in Australia, heterozygous horses are more prone to formation of a fleabitten pattern than homozygous ones. This is consistent with observations in Arabian horses in which gray is common and thus there are also more homozygous animals. This said, the exact nature of fleabitten pattern and its formation is unknown.

Unfortunately, gray color is frequently associated with the development of melanomas (and also malignant melanosarcomas), which are tumors originating from melanocytes. The frequent appearance of melanomas in gray horses usually does not cause problems for the animal. However, they can sometimes develop into melanosarcomas, which can lead to death of the affected animal. Depending on the population and breed, by the age of 16 years or more the number of gray horses with melanomas can be between 30 and 80 percent. Most often melanomas develop under the tail, on the genitals, or near the ears, eyes or jugular vein. Many horses have melanomas on internal organs, but usually they do not cause discomfort. It is possible to treat melanomas surgically, but veterinarians do not always recommend it. As a rule, melanomas affect horses of light gray color and are much less common in fleabitten gray animals. Homozygous gray horses that are genetically black more frequently develop melanomas. Fortunately, it is possible to reduce the number of affected horses via selection.

In 2013, gray horses (generally in the Andalusian breed) were discovered that did not complete the graying process. Color change stops at the stage of dark gray or chestnut-gray color. It is possible that the reason is an unknown gene modifier interacting with the Gray gene.

ROAN

Characteristics and Types of Roan

In my home country of Russia, the *roan* color is very much misunderstood. There are two reasons: Firstly, it is rather rare in most breeds there, and secondly, the color has been neglected in Russian equine literature. Very often roan has been considered the same as other colors with similar phenotypes: There is confusion between roan, rabicano, sabino, and gray colors and patterns.

In some literature there is a more accurate designation: *true roan* or *classic roan* separates it from others. I advise care when using the term *roaning,* as it often implies simply an admixture of white hair, which is characteristic for roan as well as other colors. Roan color assumes the presence of a *permanent* (unlike gray color—see p. 40) and rather uniform admixture of white hair on *any* base color. The white hair is most obvious on the horse's trunk. Sometimes it is completely absent from the mane, tail, head, and lower part of the legs. The skin and hooves are pigmented. The contrast between white and colored hair is more noticeable on dark-based horses. Occasionally roan can be combined with gray—in these cases, it is hardly noticeable.

Roan has the following distinctive features:

- It is much less common than gray and represented in fewer breeds.

- Unlike gray, roan isn't a stage of graying—the horse keeps his pattern of white and colored hair throughout his entire life.

- The mane, tail, lower legs, and head have very little or no admixture of white hair, and therefore appear darker than the body color. Unlike gray, the body is the lightest part of a roan horse.

- Seasonally the hair can change. As a rule, the horse is lightest in the spring after shedding, then during the summer has a medium shade, and by winter sometimes becomes so dark that the animal can be mistaken for a non-roan.

- Some roan horses darken with age (gray horses only get whiter). Scientists have noted that the speed and intensity of age-dependent darkening is connected with specific bloodlines and families, and consequently can have a genetic basis. According to observations, mares are more prone to such darkening.

- Sometimes roan horses have *reverse (dark) dapples*, which appear independently from age or season.

- The hair on scars on a roan horse is mixed—both white and colored. In horses of other colors, the hair on scars is usually white.

On some roans you can see so-called *corn spots* or *corn marks*, which are small, colored specks without any white hair (Photo 100). Corn spots are especially characteristic for black roans. They are absent on foals and appear with age.

The shades of roan color depend on two factors: the ratios of white and colored hair, and the intensity of coloring of the pigmented hair. Because of this, roan colors are divided according to the base.

Black roan is roan against a black background (Photo 101). From a distance the horse looks dark gray or ashy with a bluish shade. The head, tail, mane, and lower part of the legs are always black, which helps to distinguish this horse from dark gray and grullo. Unlike grullo, a black roan also lacks primitive markings.

In *bay roan* horses the color of the head often corresponds to that of an ordinary bay, but the body shows considerable uniform admixture of white hair (Photo 102). The tail, mane, and lower part of the legs are usually black. Dark bay roans may have a lilac shade to their body hair.

Strawberry roans may look yellow or pink from a distance, especially when the pigmented hair has a light reddish shade (Photos 103–107). Often the head, legs, mane, and tail have a significant amount of white hair, although generally less extensively than on the body.

Besides the roan colors just mentioned, there are others that are found occasionally. A *seal brown roan* is typically more like a black roan than a bay roan (Photo 108). *Dun roan* is similar to light bay roan, only with a dorsal stripe and other primitive markings (Photo 109). *Palomino roans* look like graying palominos, but the head and the lower part of the legs are darker than the body. Other rare combinations—for example, roan with the Champagne gene—are known.

Roan foals are either born already roan, or show it after they first shed their baby coats. Roan color occurs in Quarter Horses, Peruvian Pasos, Paso Finos, American Miniature Horses, Mustangs, Welsh Ponies, Australian Ponies, Dartmoor Ponies, Newfoundland Ponies, Tennessee Walkers, and in the Russian, Soviet, Belgian, Ardennes, Italian, and Breton Heavy Drafts.

Inheritance of Roan

The roan color is defined by a dominant allele designated by "Rn," and the normal recessive allele is "rn." The "Rn" allele is a mutation in the KIT gene located on the third chromosome. A special DNA test for this exists. In 1979 scientists H.F. Hintz and L.D. Van Vleck hypothesized that roan in a homozygous state is lethal in the embryonic stage. However, in June 2009 the hypothesis was proven incorrect when a DNA test for the Roan allele was developed and many live homozygous individuals were documented in such breeds as the Quarter Horse, Paint Horse, Mustang, Paso Fino, Peruvian Paso, American Miniature Horse, Welsh Pony, and Belgian. As the "Rn" allele is dominant, at least one parent of a roan foal has to be roan.

The locus is a part of so-called second linkage group including the following genes: Extension (e), Roan (Rn), Tobiano (To), Esterase (Es), Vitamin D Binding Protein (Gc), and Albumin (Al). The linkage group was defined by the Swedish geneticists Anderson and Sandberg (1982), and the genes are positioned in the following order: Al – Gc – KIT – To – e – Es on the chromosome (see pp. 44 and 64 for more about KIT). They are linked close to each other and tend to be transferred together over generations. A linkage of genes distorts estimated probabilities of inheritance.

SPOTTED PATTERNS: CHARACTERISTICS AND TYPES

Spotted horses have large, irregular shapes of white on their bodies, set against a main color. Such white spots are often asymmetrical and can have a different form and size on each side of the same animal. Modern western scientists recognize six types of spotting, which varies phenotypically, as well as genotypically:

1   Tobiano
2   Sabino
3   Frame overo
4   Splashed white
5   Manchado
6   Macchiato

In the recent past, scientists united *splashed white*, *sabino*, and *frame overo* under the general name *overo*, as a contrast to *tobiano*. Today the term "overo" is used generally in relation to the frame spotting. The genetic base color of a spotted horse can be easily determined in most cases by the color of pigmented areas.

Each type of spotting is characterized by location and form of the horse's white spots. It is more difficult in cases of maximally spotted horses, when the white hair can cover practically the entire body. Occasionally different types of spotting can be combined on the same animal and visually it can be difficult or impossible to separate one from another.

Tobiano

A *tobiano* horse is typically characterized by light hooves, white markings on the legs, and white spots on the body crossing the back between ears and tail (Photos 110–115). The edges of white areas are sharply outlined, and the spots have a vertical orientation. The head of a tobiano horse may display a total absence of white markings or a *star* or regular *blaze* (see p. 90). Most of the head is colored when the horse does not carry any other type of spotting pattern.

A minimally expressed (spotted) tobiano has limited white leg markings, usually not above the carpal joint. Sponenberg states that careful examination usually unveils a small white spot in the spine area, most often under the mane or at the base of tail (2008). The opposite scenario is the maximally expressed tobiano. Such horses can have a completely white body and neck with colored hair present only on the head. According to Sponenberg, this variety of tobiano with only a colored head is sometimes called the *Moroccan* pattern. In general, the white spotting in tobianos is rather symmetrical on both sides of the body, although there are always exceptions. The eyes of practically all tobianos are dark; very rarely do you find individuals that are blue-eyed or that have two different colored eyes (Photo 116).

A special feature of tobianos is what is known as *ink spots*—small, colored specks of hair in the white areas. The skin of tobianos is also spotted. It is pink in the areas of white spots, and pigmented in colored parts. Sometimes the edges of pigmented skin slightly extend in the white area, thus resulting in so-called *halos* where the edges of the white spots appear diffused.

Tobiano spotting is found in many breeds of the world, including Paint Horses, Mustangs, Shetland Ponies (and many other European pony breeds), as well as a number of Asian breeds. Tobiano is controlled by a dominant mutation located on the third chromosome. The mutant allele is the result of a large inversion (a "reversal" in the opposite direction) of DNA before the KIT gene. The dominant allele is designated "To"; the recessive allele is "to." There is a DNA test for tobiano.

Homozygous tobianos can generally be distinguished visually from heterozygotes by the presence of clustered ink spots, which are not characteristic for heterozygotes. The sizes of white spots are independent from homozygosity or heterozygosity and most likely are influenced by genetic modifiers. Spotted horses carrying only the tobiano gene are very rare. The majority of spotted horses carry combinations of tobiano with other spotting genes.

Sabino

Sabinos are, first of all, characterized by the presence of a white marking of some kind on the head. The sizes can vary from a tiny faint mark to a bald face. White markings of any size on the legs are also obligatory. Usually they are more significant on the hind legs than on the front legs.

Other white spots on the body are on the stomach closer to the front legs, near the girth line. The edges of spots can have defined or "roaned" borders—the latter meaning white hairs are mixed in with the color. Sometimes a mix of white and colored hair occupies a considerable part of the body, appearing to extend from the stomach area (Photos 117–125).

Minimally expressed sabinos look like solid-colored horses with large white markings on the head, while the more average example has pigmented hair on the ears, neck, around the eyes, at the base of the tail, and on the chest, back, and hips.

Maximally expressed sabinos have white body color with only a small area of pigmented hair on the ears, which is sometimes called *medicine hat* in the United States, but experts working with different breeds may consider such horses to be *tovero*, not sabino only (see p. 54). This pattern is rare and occurs in breeds such as the Tennessee Walker, Paint Horse, Quarter Horse, Arabian, Clydesdale, and Welsh Pony.

Another variant of maximally expressed sabino has a weak resemblance to fleabitten gray (see p. 41) represented by small, pigmented specks, which can form clusters. An experienced observer can distinguish this type of sabino based on the fact that, unlike fleabitten gray, the specks are distributed unevenly and are concentrated on the head, around the eyes, and along the topline, running down onto the hips, shoulders, and from the top of the back to the sides. Some sabino spotting is called *roaning* (hence my word of caution regarding this term's use—see p. 43). Colored and white hair is almost evenly distributed over the entire body of the horse, and when white spots are present, they are very small. The horse is almost indistinguishable from classic roan, and depending on the base color, has either a bluish-ashy, reddish, or pinkish-reddish color. However, unlike true roan color, roaning in the sabino has practically no contrast between the color of the head and lower part of the legs, as compared to the rest of the body. You may find a small white spot on the stomach near the elbows, and white markings on the head are much larger than in roans. This variation is characteristic for Clydesdale, Criollo, and Paint Horses.

In sabinos, the skin under white hair is pink and under the colored areas, pigmented. Some sabinos have blue (wall or china) eyes, especially when the skin is pink around the eye sockets. Two-colored (brown-blue) eyes can occur when the border of a white head marking extends to one eye socket.

One of the rarest manifestations of sabino is *gulastra plume,* which is represented by a white tail on a fully colored horse. An example would be a bay horse with a white tail. However, scientists still do not know whether gulastra plume has relation to sabino or is controlled by other genes.

Sabino spotting is widespread and found in many breeds. In the Thoroughbred, Akhal-Teke, Arabian, American Saddlebred, Tennessee Walker, Criollo, Hackney Pony, Mustang, Quarter Horse, Morgan, and Welsh Pony, sabino spotting is only weakly expressed via the usual white markings you might see on a horse's head and legs, and such horses are often not considered "spotted." Strongly expressed sabino characteristics are present in the Shire, Clydesdale, and Gelderlander breeds. There are only a few breeds in which sabino is completely absent: These include the Standardbred, Rocky Mountain Horse, Kabardian, and Russian Trotter.

It is interesting to note that the sabino and roan colors are found in completely different breeds of heavy draft horses. True roan color is not present in the Shire, Clydesdale, and Vladimir Heavy Draft, while sabino—and in general, large white markings—are not characteristic for Russian, Soviet, Lithuanian, Belgian, Ardennes, Breton, and Italian Heavy Draft breeds. An exception is the Australian Heavy Draft, which originated from the Clydesdale, Shire, and Belgian breeds. In this breed, any color (including roan) is admissible, but the size of white markings on the head is limited, and white spots on the body are not allowed. Expressed sabino also is not typical for the Icelandic Horse, in which roan color is present. Small white markings are characteristic for roan Quarter Horses.

All this indicates that, genetically, roan color may somehow not be compatible with sabino. The inheritance of sabino spotting is quite complicated and breeding records do not reveal any clear mode of transmission. Scientists identified a mutation that is responsible for one manifestation of sabino: the allele is called Sabino-1 (Sb1). It is a mutation in the KIT gene and is incompletely penetrant (not phenotypically expressed in all members with the gene). Homozygous individuals are white with a medicine hat. Heterozygous individuals have large white spots with irregular edges on their bodies and roaning is typically present. Two or more legs have white markings, and there is also a large spot on the head. The presence of the Sabino-1 allele is confirmed by DNA test in the Tennessee Walker, American Miniature Horse, Azteca Horse, Paint Horse, Missouri Foxtrotter, Shetland Pony, Mustang, Gypsy Vanner, as well as some other breeds. It is completely absent in the Arabian, Thoroughbred, Standardbred, Shire, and Clydesdale breeds.

One cannot exclude the possibility that while "Sb1" alleles are responsible for some sabino spotting patterns, there may also be KIT gene mutations. Sponenberg believes that sabino can include manifestations of genetically and visually diverse types of spotting, and what we presently call "sabino" is actually a group of *several* types of spotting, which earlier were all summarized under the term "overo."

Large white spots are most often observed in red and palomino horses. Perhaps the reason is a special interaction between the genes controlling sabino, and the "e" allele. In such breeds as the Quarter Horse and Welsh Pony, horses with minimal white hair often give birth to spotted offspring. As a rule, these foals have red color and are born from bay or black parents. Most likely, the reason for the correlation between the main color and the size of white spots reflects the degree of expressiveness of sabino.

Frame Overo

The name of this spotting pattern precisely reflects the average appearance of the horse: white spots on the sides of the body are surrounded by a frame of pigmented hair (Photos 126 & 127). *Frame overo* is considered by some to be the most difficult spotted pattern to visually identify. Usually such horses do not have white markings on their legs, while white markings of any size can be on the head, ranging from a star to a large white blaze, which is quite often asymmetrical, sometimes expanding to the lower jaw. White spots are typically on the sides of the body and neck, and rarely cross the spine. In general such white spots have horizontal orientation and rather clear, sharp edges, but may be sometimes accompanied by a little roaning and uneven borders. The skin under white spots is pink and under the colored areas is pigmented. Often one or both eyes are blue, even if the surrounding hair is pigmented.

Horses with minimal expression of frame overo may not have any white spots on the body. Characteristic for these animals is a big white mark on the head and a lack of marks on the legs. In cases with maximal expression of frame overo, the horse may have an almost completely white head, white sides, and colored legs.

Frame overo is seen most often in breeds of North America, including the Paint Horse, Quarter Horse, Morgan, Mustangs, American Miniature Horse, and Tennessee Walker. Occasionally it is found in horses in South America. Recently, such color appeared in some Thoroughbreds.

Frame overo is determined by a dominant allele caused by a mutation in the EDNRB gene (endothelin receptor B) located on the seventeenth chromosome. The symbol is "OV" (Ov) abbreviated from "overo." So far it is unknown what influences the extent of spotting. According to researches, some carriers of the Frame Overo gene are deaf. These horses also have large, white markings on the head and legs, varying amount of white on the neck and body, and the majority has two blue eyes. A study by Magdesian, et al, found that carriers of the Frame Overo allele account for 91 percent of diagnosed or suspected deaf horses (2009).

In a homozygous state the Frame Overo allele is lethal, causing the *Overo Lethal White Syndrome (OLWS)*. Homozygous foals are born completely white, occasionally with insignificant dark marks, usually on the head, and with blue eyes. They die within two days after birth because of complete intestinal obstruction due to a lack of innervation in the colon. In order to avoid this, carriers of this mutation should be bred only to non-carriers. In the United States and Europe a DNA test is available to identify carriers of the mutation. This is especially necessary because the carriers of the Frame Overo allele often do not have external manifestations.

Splashed White

The *Splashed White* spotting pattern is characterized by white legs, large white markings on the head, and in certain cases, a white spot on stomach (Photo 128). Sometimes the distribution of the white color looks like the horse plunged into white paint, covering his legs, stomach, and head. The white mark size on the head varies and can encompass the entire head, lower jaw, and even the throatlatch area. The markings of the front legs can be more extensive than on hind legs. The edges of white spots are sharply defined. Eyes are usually blue; less often brown.

A minimally expressed phenotype may consist only of white stockings and a wide blaze on the head. The skin under the white hair on these horses is not pigmented, and the eyes can be blue or two-colored (note that in the latter case, blue color is usually present in the lower part of the iris). Such horses aren't registered as spotted. More moderately expressed spotting involves white on the stomach, in addition to the markings on the head and legs. The tail can be two-colored, with a white tip (in contrast with tobiano—see p. 46). These versions of splashed white can be mistaken for a minimally expressed sabino (see p. 47). On a sabino, however, the white hair is more apparent around the girth line, while in splashed white it is near the hind legs or evenly distributed along the entire stomach. Note also that the color of blue eyes in splashed white horses has a grayish shade when compared to blue eyes in sabinos or frame overos.

Strongly expressed splashed white consists of a very large spot on the stomach, which may rise up on the sides, sometimes reaching the spine. Occasionally the horse can be almost completely white, with a medicine hat on the ears (see p. 47).

The list of breeds where splashed white appears is very limited. It includes Quarter Horse, Paint Horse, Morgan, American Miniature Horse, American Saddlebred, Icelandic Horse, Finnish Horse, Kathiawari, Trakehner, Irish Cob, and Welsh and Shetland Ponies. Recently, the number of horses with this color pattern has risen due to the increased interest of breeders and owners.

Scientists have localized and identified several mutations that are responsible for Splashed White:

- Allele SW1 (Splashed White-1) in the gene MITF (microphthalmia-associated transcription factor) located in the sixteenth chromosome is found in Quarter Horses, Paint Horses, Morgans, American Miniature Horses, Trakehners, Icelandic Horses, and Shetland Ponies. The carriers of this allele in Quarter Horses, Paint Horses, and Trakehners can be traced back to a Thoroughbred stallion named Blair Athol, born in 1861. Probably the allele is much older because it is present in an isolated breed, such as the Icelandic. It indicates that this mutation has existed for several hundreds of years. Mature horses homozygous for SW1 have been recorded, allowing the conclusion that this allele is *not* lethal in a homozygous state.

- Allele SW2, in PAX3 (paired box gene 3), and even more rare SW3 in MITF, are present only in certain lines of Quarter and Paint Horses. SW2 is located on the sixth chromosome, and according to scientists, the mutation arose about 24 years ago. The allele SW3 resulted from an MITF gene mutation. Scientists believe through studies involving mice that alleles of SW2 and SW3 can be lethal in a homozygous state, and DNA tests for them help to plan which breedings should be avoided.

- SW4, an additional mutation of PAX3 gene, causing splashed white, was found in the Appaloosa breed in 2013.

Carriers of SW3 have large marks on the head and legs, and a moderate but noticeable white spot on the belly. During research involving 20 horses with strongly expressed splashed white spotting, it was found that these horses carry SW1 *and* SW2. One horse homozygous for SW1 and heterozygous for SW2 was completely white, with whitish eyes and deafness. Individuals homozygous for SW1 have big white markings on the head, almost entirely white legs, and a spot on stomach. Such white spots can sometimes extend over the entire rear part of the body. One Paint Horse homozygous for SW1 and with a mutation in the KIT gene (p.H40Q) was almost completely white, with a medicine hat of color and an extended spot on the crest of the neck with the corresponding section of the mane also being white. One horse with SW1/SW3 genotype was completely white. According to observations, splashed white genes combined with genes responsible for sabino and tobiano also influence the extent of manifestations of splashed white coloration.

Deafness is an issue in some splashed white horses, but at the same time, there are also many with normal hearing. According to some breeders, horses with large head markings involving the eyes are most susceptible to deafness. For many horse owners, the diagnosis of deafness is a surprise, as these horses generally have a quiet temperament and don't show unusual behavior. The ears of deaf splashed white horses move similarly to animals with normal hearing in response to sounds. Although the connection between splashed white and deafness is not clear, scientists recommend to breeders to cross such horses to individuals of a different color to, perhaps, increase the chances of a foal with normal hearing. There isn't any information on deafness in spotted Finnish Horses, so it is impossible to tell with confidence that SW genes always influence hearing.

Manchado

The type of spotted color called *manchado* was discovered quite recently and is very rare. It is observed in Argentina in such breeds as Thoroughbred, Arabian, Criollo, and Hackney; I was lucky to observe it once in an Orlov Trotter. The majority of manchado horses have large white spots with sharply defined edges, and scattered colored spots of different sizes (Photos 129 & 130). Such spots have a remote resemblance to the appaloosa pattern (see p. 55). However, unlike the appaloosa pattern, the spots of manchado are located in the top part of the neck, including the mane, and this is the *minimal* manifestation of this color pattern. The colored spots do not have a round or oval form, but are polygonal and asymmetric.

In a maximally expressed manchado, the white region extends on the neck and body, usually without involving the head and legs. White leg marks are not typical. They can be present on a particular horse, but in that case they are caused by other genetic factors, which are not connected with manchado.

The genetic basis of this spotting pattern has not been investigated yet. Because of the rarity of this color, it is very difficult to study the mechanism of its inheritance. However, as Sponenberg notes, it is very unusual that manchado has such a limited area of distribution. He also notes that on pictures from the beginning of the nineteenth century, Hackney horses do not have an appaloosa pattern, but rather manchado. This leads to the question as to whether this color appeared for the first time then, but subsequently, for some reason, remained hidden through many generations, and again began to appear only in the last few decades. Most likely manchado has a recessive inheritance.

Macchiato

During the research of the mechanisms of inheritance of splashed white, a new type of spotting was discovered called *macchiato*. This name was chosen because of color similarity with the Italian milk-based coffee drink.

Currently there is only one horse known with this color—a Frieberger (Franches-Montagnes) gelding born in 2008 (Photo 131). Both of his parents were bay with minimal white markings. His base color is also bay, but he has extensive white markings, including on the head and lower jaw, on the front legs (with irregular white stripes extending upward), on the belly (a white spot, parts of which include roaning), and on the hind legs (which also have the white stripes with roaned edges, extending up to the hips). The tail contains a considerable admixture of white hair, and a similar pattern is present at the edges of the mane. The eyes are blue, and the sclera is depigmented.

In general the horse is very similar to a sabino (see Photos 119 & 120). The pigmented parts of the body are diluted to a light brown color. The cause of this color is a mutation in the MITF gene. The mutant allele has been named $MITF^{N310S}$. The horse is a heterozygote and neither of his parents are carriers; therefore, it must be a new mutation. Unfortunately, macchiato appears to be connected with impaired health of the carrier.

OTHER COLORS RELATED TO SPOTTING

Calico Tobiano

Strictly speaking *calico tobiano* is *not* a form of spotting as it does not cause formation of white areas on a horse. However, Sponenberg describes this color under spottings, and after consideration, I have also placed the color in this group.

In buckskin and palomino tobianos, there can be "dabs" of red, brown, or dark yellow color in the pigmented areas of the horse's body, instead of or in addition to the expected base color. The size of such colored areas is variable, and when small, they may not be noticed. As a result of the addition of pigment, the horse becomes three-colored (white, "sand," and red or brown) with a vague resemblance to a calico cat (Photos 132 & 133).

This color is extremely rare, but it has been noted in Paint Horses, Tennessee Walkers, Paso Finos, and also in a population of Choctaw Mustangs. Based on observations, the calico tobiano color is said by Sponenberg to be controlled by the dominant allele "Cal-C" of a putative locus named *Calico* (2009). This allele appears to have a phenotypic effect only in tobiano horses carrying the Cream Dilution allele "C^{cr}." Probably, the manifestation of this color requires simultaneous action of genes from three different loci (MATP, Tobiano, and Calico), and so investigating the mechanism of inheritance is difficult. It appears that calico tobiano is *not* sex-linked (unlike calico color in cats).

Crypt Overo

As mentioned, spotted colors, regardless of the fact that most of them are determined by dominant genes, can appear in offspring born to non-spotted parents. This has been observed frequently in incidents of frame overo, sabino, and splashed white. Breeders of Paint Horses and Quarter Horses call spotted foals from non-spotted parents *cropouts*.

In breeds in which, historically, white spotting exceeding certain size was discouraged and/or eliminated (for example, Rocky Mountain Horses and Welsh Ponies), there still can be carriers of spotting genes, which are simply not expressed. If a spotted foal is born to non-spotted parents, it is necessary to look closely at the parents. In most cases they will have quite large white markings on the head. Thus, it is possible to say that the distinction between a spotted and non-spotted horse is conditional—from a genetic point of view. Thanks to the DNA tests for Tobiano, Sabino-1, and Frame Overo alleles, it is possible to identify carriers, even when the horses do not exhibit external signs of spotting.

Tovero

Cases when spotted horses have manifestations of only one type of spotting are quite rare. Usually spotted horses—like tobiano, for example—also display minimal manifestations of sabino in the form of white head markings. In these cases, it is accepted to determine spotting type by the most prevalent markings. However, it can happen that the pattern of *both* types is shown rather strongly: White spots characteristic for each type are superimposed and the horse's body is mostly white. Horses with mixed spotting type, such as tobiano together with sabino, frame overo, and/or splashed white (sometimes it is more than two types at the same time), are called *tovero*, which is derived from joining the words "tobiano" and "overo" (Photos 134–136) This term is used in the official studbook of Paint Horses.

As mentioned, horses with a strongly expressed tovero pattern can be almost completely white, except for maybe a medicine hat on the ears (see p. 47). (The majority of white horses with pigment on the ears are homozygous for Sabino-1— see p. 48.) There are also horses with pigmented areas around the eyes, on the chest, in the groin, and at the base of the tail. Sometimes medicine hat horses can have small "specks" of color on their foreheads, and others have so-called *badger faces*, which are the opposite of large, white marks. Instead, the badger face has the base color of the horse, and in principle is the "leftover" of a pigmented area, surrounded by a large white spot (Photo 137).

The borders of tovero white spots can be either delineated or "washed out" due to roaning. The eyes can be any color, often blue or multicolored.

Spotted horses are interesting because of the unpredictability and individual-ized arrangements of white spots. They have become very popular in the United States and Europe in recent years.

Tovero is common in the Irish Cob, Paint Horse, Quarter Horse, Mustang, American Miniature Horse, and Shetland Pony.

APPALOOSA-SPOTTED

There are many breeds of spotted horses throughout the world. We are now dis-cussing a kind of spotting that differs from those we just covered in size, shape, distribution, and accompanying characteristics. The general definition of *appa-loosa color* can be described as a pattern where a horse either displays small col-ored specks or spots scattered on a white body, or small white specks or spots scattered on a colored body. This definition can apply to the majority of (but not all) types of appaloosa-spotting patterns. I should note here that because of the international recognition of the Appaloosa breed (www.appaloosa.com), spotted patterns such as those we are about to discuss are now often simply referred to as "appaloosa" in general, meaning the *color*, not the breed. Some researchers call this type of spotting *Leopard complex* or *tiger spotting* to differentiate from the pinto and roan color patterns we've already discussed. In the text that follows, I will differentiate the breed from the color by capitalizing the breed (Appaloosa).

Types of Appaloosa-Spotted Patterns

Appaloosa-spotted horses, regardless of the type of color and pattern, may possess the following features:

- *Mottled skin*: On pink skin there can be small black specks or on pigmented skin, small pink specks (Photo 138). They can be oval or (less frequently) round, often grouped in large clusters. This is especially noticeable on the sites of the body where hair is sparse, short, or absent, such as the lips, eyelids, under the tail, and on the genitals. In other areas of the body, specks on the skin usually correspond to the spots visible on the hair.

- *White sclera*: On an appaloosa-spotted horse, the *sclera* (area of the eye encir-cling the iris) is white and visible, and most visible near the corner of the eye located closer to the forehead (Photo 139). In comparison to other horses, the eye opening can appear longer horizontally due to this trait.

- *Striped hooves*: Stripes on the hooves are very sharply defined and have a rect-angular shape (Photo 140). In comparison, stripes on the silver horse's hooves have less defined edges and are triangular (see p. 27). The color of the hoof and the arrangement of stripes on it do not depend on the hair and skin color. Not all hooves of an appaloosa-colored horse have to be striped—you might see markings on just one. It should be noted that sometimes striped hooves can be found in red or palomino horses, but these markings tend to not be as distinct.

An appaloosa-spotted horse may have all the features I've mentioned or one or two in any combination. They can also be observed on occasion in horses of other colors and patterns, although usually such individuals do not have more than one of the features at the same time. Strictly speaking, there aren't traits that can be said to be completely unique to appaloosa-spotted horses.

Appaloosa-spotted patterns vary greatly, and vary greatly in name and description from source to source. This means it isn't always possible to differentiate them accurately. Nevertheless, there are main pattern types to understand:

- Solid
- Blanket
- Leopard
- Few-spot leopard
- Snowflake (frost)
- Speckled
- Varnish roan

There are additional designations for various transitional types, depending on the part of the world in which you live and the language you speak, and I will mention as many of them as possible.

The minimal expression of appaloosa is a horse of any color *without* spotting who nevertheless may display mottled skin, striped hooves, and/or white sclera. This infrequent pattern is known as *solid*.

Blanket is the most common form of appaloosa pattern. These horses have an area of white hair that "blankets" the croup on which smaller, colored spots and specks are scattered (Photos 141 & 142). The blanket can be any size—from a small patch on the top of the croup to an extensive white area, covering the entire croup, back, belly, and even the top part of the horse's legs and neck. In the United States the latter manifestation is often called *large blanket*. The head on these horses remains colored. The borders of the blanket can be either sharply delineated or *roany*, with a mix of white and colored hair. *White blanket* is similar; however, it contains very few or no colored spots. When present, I have observed the spots tend to concentrate on the edges. The white blanket can cover not only the croup, but also the hind legs, belly, back, withers, and (rarely) the neck and the top of the front legs. It is some-

Color: Gold champagne: This color is very similar to palomino (see Photo 21) and differs from it mainly by the appearance of dark pink skin on the nostrils. This horse also has a pronounced glossy coat that is characteristic of champagne colors.

Expressed alleles: ee** Ch*

Breed: American Quarter Horse (Zippos Millenium Bug, owned by Heidi Trimber)

PHOTOGRAPHER: COURTESY OF CAROLYN SHEPARD

PHOTO 69

Detail: The head of a gold champagne horse—you can see the mottled skin on the lips and nose.

Expressed alleles: ee** Ch*

Breed: American Paint Horse (Sampson's Gold, owned by Kiri Rourke)

PHOTOGRAPHER: CAROLYN SHEPARD

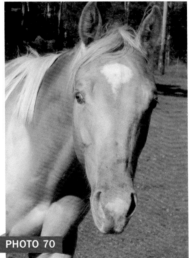

PHOTO 70

Color: Golden cream champagne is another double dilute color on a red base.

Expressed alleles: ee** C^{cr} Ch*

Breed: American Quarter Horse (Peppy Bar Cougar, owned by Roy Martin)

PHOTOGRAPHER: CAROLYN SHEPARD

PHOTO 71

PHOTO 72

Detail: The head of a golden cream champagne horse. The eyes are bright blue, even in adulthood. Note spotty skin on the nostrils and lips.

Breed: Arabian-American Quarter Horse cross (Blue Dakota Pecosblue)

PHOTOGRAPHER: CAROLYN SHEPARD

PHOTO 73

Color: Classic cream champagne—the horse is genetically black. His mane, tail, and lower legs are darker than the rest of the body. The skin on the nose is dark pink with light purple spots.

Expressed alleles: E* aa C^{cr} Ch*

Breed: American Quarter Horse (Vanzi Te N Te Glo, owned by Savana and Karla Keene)

PHOTOGRAPHER: TARA NOVOTNY

PHOTO 74

Color: A chestnut pearl horse: genetically chestnut, with dark pink skin on the nose, lips, and around the eyes consistent with homozygous pearl gene.

Expressed alleles: ee** C^{pr}C^{pr}

Breed: Andalusian (Yeguado Paco Marti)

PHOTOGRAPHER: PACO MARTI

Color: Chestnut pearl.

Expressed alleles: ee** $C^{pr}C^{pr}$

Breed: Andalusian (Yeguado Paco Marti)

PHOTOGRAPHER: PACO MARTI

PHOTO 75

Color: Another chestnut pearl, this one with a subtle grayish shade to the body hair. Note the difference in shade between this and other examples of this color.

Expressed alleles: ee** $C^{pr}C^{pr}$

Breed: Andalusian (Yeguada Paco Marti)

PHOTOGRAPHER: PACO MARTI

PHOTO 76

Color: Black pearl or classic pearl. This color is very similar to classic champagne (see Photo 66), but with fewer specks on the skin than champagne. Note that the mane, tail, and lower legs are darker than the rest of the body. The horse is genetically black—not bay, as you might suppose by the color.

Expressed alleles: E* aa $C^{pr}C^{pr}$

Breed: Lusitano (Isabelo stallion from Yeguada Paco Marti)

PHOTOGRAPHER: SANDRA LÓPEZ PÉREZ

PHOTO 77

PHOTO 78

Color: Seal brown pearl

Expressed alleles: EE A^tA^t C^{pr}C^{pr} chch (confirmed by DNA test)

Breed: Lusitano-Andalusian cross (Oro Mafiozo)

PHOTOGRAPHER: VERA KURSKAYA

PHOTO 79

Detail: The head of the same seal brown pearl horse. The skin on the nose is dark pink, light chocolate colored rim on ears.

Breed: Lusitano-Andalusian cross

PHOTOGRAPHER: VERA KURSKAYA

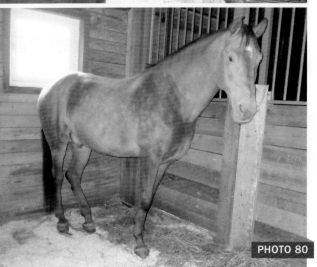

PHOTO 80

Color: The same seal brown pearl horse in the summer. It is particularly evident that the horse has his own pigment distribution over the body. His coat gives the overall impression of bay with pronounced countershading.

Expressed alleles: EE A^tA^t C^{pr}C^{pr} chch (confirmed by DNA test)

Breed: Lusitano-Andalusian cross

PHOTOGRAPHER: NATALIA EROSHKINA

Detail: The eye of the same horse. Upon close inspection you can see a light brown section in the lower part of the iris. The eyelids dark pink with dark specks.

Breed: Lusitano-Andalusian cross

PHOTOGRAPHER: VERA KURSKAYA

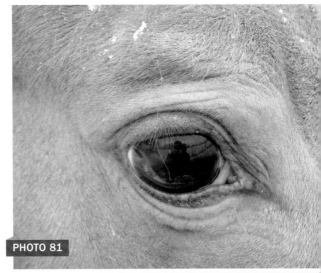

PHOTO 81

Detail: The muzzle of the seal brown pearl horse. The skin is dark pink with noticeable dark specks.

Breed: Lusitano-Andalusian cross

PHOTOGRAPHER: VERA KURSKAYA

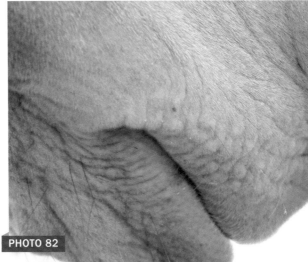

PHOTO 82

Color: Palomino pearl looks like a palomino (see Photo 21) but has dark pink skin with occasional specks and the eyes are golden.

Expressed alleles: ee** $C^{cr}\ C^{pr}$

Breed: Andalusian (Guindeleza, owned by Suzan Sommer, Sommer Ranch Andalusians, www.sommerranch.com)

PHOTOGRAPHER: SUZAN SOMMER

PHOTO 83

PHOTO 84

Color: Smoky black pearl has dark pink skin with almost invisible specks on the nose, lips, and around the eyes. Despite the fact that the horse is genetically black, the mane and tail have pronounced goldish-yellow color.

Expressed alleles: E^* aa C^{cr} C^{pr}

Breed: PRE Andalusian (Oso de Oro, owned by Suzan Sommer, Sommer Ranch Andalusians, www.sommerranch.com)

PHOTOGRAPHER: SUZAN SOMMER

PHOTO 85

Color: The same smoky black pearl horse as a foal—note how dark his body coat was.

Breed: PRE Andalusian (Oso de Oro, owned by Suzan Sommer, Sommer Ranch Andalusians, www.sommerranch.com)

PHOTOGRAPHER: SUZAN SOMMER

PHOTO 86

Color: Flaxen chestnut with a star turning into a stripe. The mane is flaxen to light red, but the tail has the same color as the body

Expressed alleles: ee**

Breed: Egyptian Arabian (Samsara, owned by Poets Manor Arabians, www.poetsmanorarabians.com)

PHOTOGRAPHER: RICHARD TEETERS

Color: Flaxen chestnut with a star turning into a stripe and white below the hocks on the hind legs.

Expressed alleles: ee**

Breed: Egyptian Arabian (Provocateur, owned by Poets Manor Arabians, www.poetsmanorarabians.com)

PHOTOGRAPHER: RICHARD TEETERS

PHOTO 87

Detail: Vitiligo on the muzzle and nose of a light gray horse.

PHOTOGRAPHER: VERA KURSKAYA

PHOTO 88

Detail: Weak vitiligo around the eye of a horse. The iris is brown and sclera pigmented. Light is reflected from the tapetum.

PHOTOGRAPHER: MARINA KHOMUTOVSKAYA

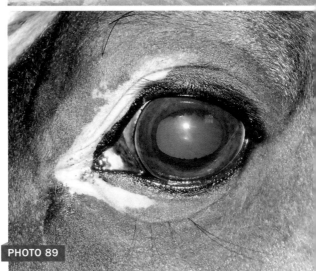

PHOTO 89

PHOTO 90

Color: A dark gray yearling with a star. This horse is genetically black (black at birth)—note the darker mane, tail, and lower part of the legs.

Expressed alleles: E* aa G*

Breed: Orlov Trotter

PHOTOGRAPHER: VERA KURSKAYA

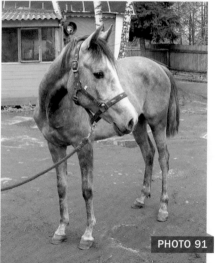

PHOTO 91

Color: A rose gray with a blaze. This horse is genetically bay, with reddish hair on the body and a dark tail, mane, and lower legs.

Expressed alleles: E* A* G*

Breed: Arabian

PHOTOGRAPHER: ANASTASIA ORLOVA

PHOTO 92

Color: Dappled gray.

Expressed alleles: E* aa(?) G*

Breed: Orlov Trotter

PHOTOGRAPHER: VERA KURSKAYA

Color: A white gray horse that is genetically bay and past the rose gray stage of graying. There remains a lot of pigmented hair in the mane and on the legs.

Expressed alleles: E* A* G*

Breed: Akhal-Teke

PHOTOGRAPHER: VERA KURSKAYA

PHOTO 93

Color: A white gray with dapples on the hindquarters and pigmented skin visible through the short hair around the eyes and muzzle.

Expressed alleles: G*

Breed: Orlov Trotter

PHOTOGRAPHER: SVETLANA DOLMATOVA

PHOTO 94

Color: A white gray, slightly fleabitten.

Expressed alleles: G*

Breed: Shetland Pony

PHOTOGRAPHER: VERA KURSKAYA

PHOTO 95

Color: A fleabitten gray with barely noticeable dapples on the hindquarters.

Expressed alleles: G*

Breed: Arabian

PHOTOGRAPHER: VERA KURSKAYA

PHOTO 96

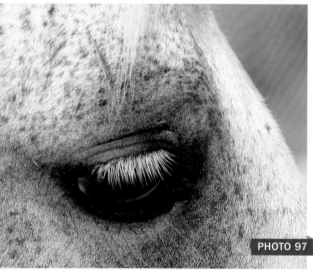

Detail: The head and eye of a fleabitten gray horse: White eyelashes, brown sclera.

PHOTOGRAPHER: VERA KURSKAYA

PHOTO 97

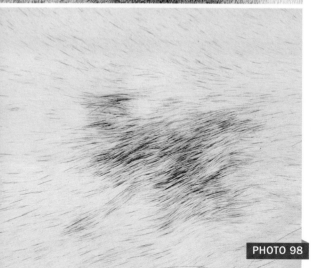

Detail: A blood mark is a cluster of red or black "fleabite" markings. This close-up image shows how such a marking breaks up into individual hairs.

PHOTOGRAPHER: VERA KURSKAYA

PHOTO 98

Color: A dappled gray with a wide blaze and a blood mark above the left eye. This is a rare type of blood mark that is not a "remnant" of the base color.

Expressed alleles: G*

PHOTOGRAPHER: OLGA YEREMEEVA

PHOTO 99

Detail: Corn spots on the body of a strawberry roan horse. According to the horse's owner, the spots were the result of an injection in that area.

PHOTOGRAPHER: VERA KURSKAYA

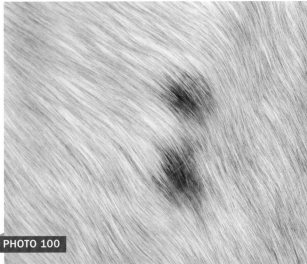

PHOTO 100

Color: A black roan with relatively little white hair.

Expressed alleles: E* aa Rn*

Breed: Unknown

PHOTOGRAPHER: VERA KURSKAYA

PHOTO 101

PHOTO 102

Color: A bay roan with white hair mostly on the back and the top of the croup. The head and lower legs are solid.

Expressed alleles: E* A* Rn*

Breed: Karachai-Russian Don cross

PHOTOGRAPHER: VERA KURSKAYA

PHOTO 103

Color: A strawberry roan with noticeable patches on the body containing little or no white hair.

Expressed alleles: ee** Rn*

Breed: Soviet Heavy Draft cross

PHOTOGRAPHER: VERA KURSKAYA

PHOTO 104

Color: A strawberry roan.

Expressed alleles: ee** Rn*

Breed: Unknown

PHOTOGRAPHER: VERA KURSKAYA

Detail: The coat of a strawberry roan horse in winter.

PHOTOGRAPHER: VERA KURSKAYA

PHOTO 105

Detail: The head of a strawberry roan horse with a star extending into a blaze. This blaze fades in summer.

PHOTOGRAPHER: VERA KURSKAYA

PHOTO 106

Color: Dark strawberry roan—judging by the very dark head and lilac shade of the body, this horse is roan on liver chestnut with a slightly lightened mane and tail.

Expressed alleles: ee** Rn*

Breed: Unknown

PHOTOGRAPHER: MARINA SLEPENKO

PHOTO 107

PHOTO 108

Color: This seal brown roan is a rare case where the contrast between the horse's head and lower legs and the body is almost indistinguishable. However, the mane and tail are significantly darker.

Expressed alleles: E* A^{t}* Rn*

Breed: Karachai

PHOTOGRAPHER: VERA KURSKAYA

PHOTO 109

Color: Likely a dun roan. While I cannot confirm the dorsal stripe on this horse, I believe he is dun roan rather than bay roan based on the characteristic brightening on the back side of the front legs (see p. 22 for more about this dun characteristic).

Expressed alleles: E* A* Dn^{+}(?)* Rn*

Breed: Hucul Pony

PHOTOGRAPHER: EKATHERINA BELIKOVA

PHOTO 110

Color: Black tobiano with a star and white socks on three legs. Spotting on this horse is minimal.

Expressed alleles: E* aa To*

Breed: Hanoverian cross

PHOTOGRAPHER: GREGORY SOLOVIEV

Color: Black tobiano with a characteristic white vertical spot, starting from the neck and white socks or stockings on the legs.

Expressed alleles: E* aa To*

Breed: Trakehner cross

PHOTOGRAPHER: VERA KURSKAYA

PHOTO 111

Color: Black tobiano.

Expressed alleles: E* aa To*

Breed: Shetland Pony

PHOTOGRAPHER: EKATHERINA BELIKOVA

PHOTO 112

Color: Bay tobiano with spotting that appears only on the dock in the form of a five-pointed star, extending into tail, which is partly white. White stockings and socks on the legs.

Expressed alleles: E* A* To*

Breed: Trakehner cross

PHOTOGRAPHER: VERA KURSKAYA

PHOTO 113

PHOTO 114

Color: Bay tobiano with average spotting and vertical contours on the neck and rump. The legs show the combined action of tobiano and sabino genes.

Expressed alleles: E* A* To*, Sabino genes

Breed: Trakehner

PHOTOGRAPHER: VLADISLAV RUTKOWSKI

PHOTO 115

Color: Chestnut tobiano foal.

Expressed alleles: ee** To*

Breed: American Paint Horse

PHOTOGRAPHER: COURTESY OF APHA/PAINT HORSE JOURNAL (APHA.COM)

PHOTO 116

Detail: This bay tobiano has one blue eye and one brown eye, which is rare for a tobiano. Note the dark eyelashes.

Breed: Unknown

PHOTOGRAPHER: VERA KURSKAYA

times so extensive that the head and legs are the only remaining pigmented areas by which it is possible to determine the main color. As a rule, foals with a blanket or white blanket are born with the pattern already noticeable, and the blanket may increase only a little in size with age.

The leopard pattern may be the most recognizable of appaloosa-spotting patterns (Photos 143–145). The horse appears to be completely white, covered with colored spots, varying greatly in size, which are the color of the horse's base color, and which are often extended in the direction of hair growth, creating the impression that they are spreading from the groin area. Sometimes, colored spots are concentrated in pigmented zones (in the groin, behind the elbows, on the neck and head), corresponding to the horse's base color. And sometimes, so-called *reverse markings* of the base color remain where common white markings usually are. This variant is called *near leopard* in the United States.

The *few-spot leopard* is characterized by an almost completely white body color with the remains of pigment mainly in the guard hair. There are very few spots, and sometimes they are completely absent. When present, they are concentrated on the elbows, in the groin, on the neck, and on the head, especially around the eyes. When there are relatively more specks on the head and the lower part of the legs but almost no spots in other places, the color is called *near few-spot leopard*. The skin on the body is quite often speckled, even under white hair.

A horse with *snowflake* or *frost* has a dark base with faint traces or streaks of white on the croup (it is, in fact, like a very small blanket) or along the spine (Photo 146). Sometimes there can be dark spots on both the white streaks and on the base-colored hair.

"True" *snowflakes* are the least common variant of appaloosa-spotting pattern. In these horses, there are white spots scattered on the dark-based body (the "opposite" of leopard), often concentrated on the croup and hips. With age, these spots can slightly increase in a size and quantity. On snowflakes the size and form of white spots are not less than 2 centimeters in diameter. Foals are usually born without "flakes," and it is often a transient pattern.

The most rare appaloosa-spotting pattern is the so-called *speckled* (Photo 147). I was lucky to come across it only once. Most breed registries do not recognize it. The speckled pattern is a result of snowflakes growing so large that there is more white hair on the horse than colored. The remaining colored hair forms small dots that can be easily distinguished from regular appaloosa-type spots. The speckled horse resembles a fleabitten gray (see p. 41) but can have varnish markings (see below) in addition to one or more of the three usual characteristics of appaloosa-spotted horses (see p. 55).

Roaning is genetically connected with appaloosa-spotted color, and despite its name, has no relation to the classic roan color (see p. 43). Sometimes referred to as *varnish roans,* these horses are born almost without white hair—some slight signs of roaning on the forehead and occasionally with a small blanket on the croup may be all that is apparent. With age—usually over a period of two to six years—an admixture of white hair develops on the body, often leaving behind the varnish markings I mentioned earlier on the head, along the mane, on the legs and elbows, and in the groin (Photos 148 & 149). In principle, roaning consists of a rather uneven mixture of colored and white hair. Specks and spots are always very small and sporadic in appearance. Sometimes they can be concentrated on the head.

However, sometimes horses have two types of appaloosa-spotting patterns at the same time (Photo 150)! For example, a combination of snowflake on the front part of the body and varnish roan on the back is common, and an interesting and beautiful combination pairs snowflake on the front with a blanket or white blanket on the croup.

The appaloosa-spotted color and patterning is remarkable in that, unlike other spotting types we've discussed, it is practically always symmetrical on both sides of the body. When the borders between dark and light parts of the body are located in the area of the rib cage, the dark and white hair can be grouped in the form of stripes that run parallel with the ribs (Photo 151). Spots on some horses can change over time: their color can become darker or lighter, and they can be roaned or have roaned edges. In England and the United States these are called *peacock spots* because of their similarity to the "eyes" on the tail feathers of a peacock (Photo 152). Black appaloosa horses can have dark olive spots, chestnut appaloosas can have golden, and on bay appaloosas they may be rusty brown. Bay appaloosas with expressed countershading can have both black and brown spots. They tend to be distributed on the body the same way as colored hair in countershading: the black are closer to the spine and brown or golden closer to the belly.

Very rarely on black or bay appaloosa-spotted horses you see what Kathman terms *bronzing* or *color-shifting* (2014). The hair that is supposed to be black has a brownish or bronze color, similar to a faded black horse (see p. 11). This is often noticeable on the legs, especially when the horse is bay-based. Kathman supposes it is a hereditable factor. I observed several appaloosa-spotted ponies in Russia and the Netherlands with bronzing, and all of them had relatives with the trait, so it seems likely to have a genetic basis.

In some horses, the hair in colored spots is slightly longer than surrounding white hair—you can identify these horses as spotted simply by touch! The skin is pigmented in areas with colored hair while surrounding skin is usually unpigmented and this dark skin becomes visible through white hair, often leading to the appearance of *halos* (see p. 46).

As mentioned previously, appaloosa-spotted color and patterning is not fully expressed at birth, and foals are usually born darker than they will look at an older age—sometimes without white body hair, although most often with some patterning visible. Blankets, for example, are expressed at birth. Both blanket and solid horses often roan out to varying degrees. The formation of color and patterning can be considered "final" when the horse is three to five years old (Photo 153).

Appaloosa-spotted horses can have white markings on the head (see chapter 3, p. 87), and you can find horses with so-called *lightning marks*—sharp white lines on the outer and inner sides of the legs (Photo 154).

Appaloosa-spotted horses may have a lack of hair in the mane and tail; at the same time, many have a "normal" amount of hair (see Photo 149). Sponenberg (2009) believes there is a genetic link between appaloosa-spotted color and thin mane and tail hair. He notes that black appaloosa-spotted horses, especially the leopard pattern, are more likely to have this hair feature than chestnut appaloosa-spotted horses. The condition of hair in these areas is also influenced by age, and possibly also "puberty," during which pigmented hair can become more fragile. P.W. Scott (2004) asserts that the reason for thin manes and tails in appaloosa-spotted horses is due to *follicular dysplasia* (a malformation of hair follicles) or *alopecia areata* (a form of patchy baldness).

It is interesting that in the article "Turkestan and Turkestani Breeds of Horses" published in 2006, the Russian scientist V. Firsov describes a special breed of the Kyrgyz horse as follows: "...different spots are located, mainly on the sacrum; mane and tail are thin and short, and on some horses the mane is almost missing....An interesting trait, which is passed on to offspring, is eyes with a rather small iris and large sclera. The eyes give an impression of an intense and vigorous look." Natives considered such horses capable of driving away evil spirits because of the look of their eyes. Such spotted horses protected herds and were used to treat patients who were believed to be ill due to the actions of evil spirits. The same features described by Firsov can be found in the Appaloosa and Knabstrupper breeds.

Appaloosa-spotting colors and patterns are found in a number of breeds, including the Appaloosa, Falabella, American Miniature Horse, Noriker, Knabstrupper, Colorado Ranger, British Spotted Pony, Australian Pony, Tiger Horse, Spanish Jennet Horse. Appaloosa color also appears in the Colonial Spanish breeds. There are some breeds in which appaloosa-spotted patterning is only occasionally seen, such as the Andalusian, Lusitano, Mustang, Altai Horse, Bashkir Horse, South German Coldblood, Gypsy Horse, and Karabair.

Inheritance of Appaloosa Color

Studying the inheritance of this color is extremely complex due to the fact that, unlike other colors and patterns, it consists of multiple phenotypic characteristics found in various combinations. Sponenberg (1990), Archer (2004), and Bellone (2010), specify three main components that contribute to the phenotype:

- Blanket
- Roaning
- Dark specks and spots

As all these characteristics can be present in different combinations, it is necessary to study the inheritance of each of these components separately. Therefore, as mentioned on p. 55, Western scientists use the term *Leopard complex* when talking about the inheritance of the appaloosa colors and patterns.

So far scientists can tell with confidence that all types of appaloosa-spotted color are defined by incompletely dominant mutant alleles of the gene determining Transient Receptor Potential Cation Channel (TRPM1). It is designated "Lp" (sometimes LP from Leopard, but I side with Sponenberg and will use Lp in this text) and located on the first chromosome. The symbol for the normal recessive allele is "lp." However, the mechanism of the effect of TRPM1 on the production of color remains unknown. A DNA test for alleles of the TRPM1 gene is available.

The extent of spotting depends on the genotype of a horse. Homozygous individuals have very few color specks or spots, while heterozygotes usually present higher numbers. Also, there is a correlation between genotype and the size of the white area on the horse: in heterozygous individuals sizes vary from several white spots to a leopard pattern, and in homozygotes it can range from a touch of frost to completely white body color of the few-spot type. Roaning can occur in both cases to a different degree. It should be noted there is also a connection with hoof patterns: in homozygotes, dark stripes are present on a light background, and in heterozygotes there are light stripes against a dark background.

In addition to the "Lp" gene, there is also a genetic modifier that impacts the size of a horse's blanket. It is called PATN-1 (from Pattern-1), presumably dominant, and located on the third chromosome in linkage with the MC1R gene. Therefore, a leopard horse has LplpPATN-1* genotype *, and few-spot leopard has LpLp-PATN-1*. (Asterisks designate the position in the genotype that can be occupied by any allele, dominant or recessive.) Horses with PATN-1, which at birth are 50 to 100 percent white, represent a pattern range from large blanket to leopard. In the majority of cases, approximately 80 percent of the horse's body is covered with white hair. In animals *not* carrying this allele, 65 percent or less of the body is covered with white hair.

Most likely there are additional genes contributing to the formation of the spotted pattern, and the degree of the expression of a white pattern (i.e. "blanket" and "roaning") has a polygenic type of inheritance. Sponenberg (2009) notes (and I can confirm) that chestnut-based horses have, in general, more white hair on their bodies, blacks have less, and bay horses fall somewhere between them. The largest amount of white hair in black- and bay-based horses is found in heterozygotes at the "E" gene. It has also been observed that chestnut-based horses show a tendency to have fewer color spots of smaller size. The largest spots are most frequently seen on black-based horses. (This is also true for few-spot leopard horses.) The spots found on homozygous "Lp" horses tend to be concentrated on the borders of a blanket.

It has been found that manifestations of appaloosa-spotted patterns depend on sex. Stallions and geldings have more white hair than mares, the average difference being from 12 percent to 18 percent (see Sponenberg, 2009). Mares have fewer dark spots than stallions. Such difference varies, depending on the specific population of horses.

Some horses with a large number of spots can have a pigmented head, and part of the body and legs also colored. Usually these horses are from leopard lines, having the PATN-1 allele. Sponenberg assumes that there are not only genetic modifiers increasing the extent of white hair, but also modifiers that have a similar effect on pigmented hair.

Appaloosa horses are prone to develop *Congenital Stationary Night Blindness (CSNB)*, a condition that prevents them from seeing in the dark. The first cases of night blindness in horses were described in the West in the 1970s, but the systematic research of this condition and its correlation with appaloosa color began in the United States only after the year 2000. Studies have now shown that this vision impairment or complete inability to see in the dark or dusk due to deficiency of nervous cells in the retina manifests in all LpLp homozygotes, but does not progress during the animal's life (Archer, Bellone, Sandmeyer, 2012). Similar hereditary defects also occur in humans. Research did not reveal anomalies in pigmentation or structure of the retina.

Analysis of genotype in affected horses is consistent with an incomplete penetrance of the Leopard allele. Functional impairments of vision in homozygous individuals is 100 percent, while no horse that is heterozygous for "Lp" will be night blind. Fortunately, in today's world, this is only a moderate disadvantage for affected animals. Healthy horses can see in the dark better than people, and many affected horses adapt to their eye condition, never showing strong indications of impaired vision at dusk or in the dark. However, the trait should be considered when breeding as some affected horses can demonstrate increased fearfulness at dusk, and it may be difficult to work with them, particularly in the fall and winter, when days and daylight are shorter.

A 2007 article by Sandmeyer, et al, found that in some horses homozygous for "Lp," the eyes may be small in size, unusually oriented, or give the impression that the horse is looking up at the sky all the time (*dorsomedial strabismus*). (Such abnormalities are rare in heterozygotes.) Sometimes a horse may also display *nystagmus* (the eyes make repetitive, uncontrolled movements).

Most horses suffering from night blindness are from the Appaloosa breed, but occasional cases have been observed in other breeds, including the Standardbred, Thoroughbred, and Paso Fino (see Brooks, 2002, and Nunnery, et al, 2005). Appaloosa horses also quite often suffer from *periodic uveitis*. This acquired inflammation of the vascular cover of the eyes can be caused by a trauma, an infection, or other disease, and over time it can lead to blindness. It is possible that a tendency to develop periodic uveitis is also connected with this color (see Fritz, et al, 2014).

DOMINANT WHITE

It is widely believed by most that "white" horses are actually gray (see p. 40); however, a true white color exists, though it is extremely rare.

In Russia we use a term equivalent to "white-born," and there is a similar term in German (*Weißegeboren*). The English term "white-foaled" might serve as a similar generic description for a white horse, which can have a diverse underlying genetic basis for similar phenotypes—that is, any horse born without (or nearly without) pigmented hair. This horse can be genetically a sabino, a homozygous frame overo (in a case of *Overo Lethal White Syndrome—OLWS*), a tovero, or *dominant white,* which I will discuss on the pages that follow.

Characteristics of Dominant White

In general, white color is connected with the concept of albinism, which is a congenital absence of pigment in an animal. One distinctive sign of a true albino is pink or red eye color caused by the absence of the pigment in iris, which allows the underlying blood-containing vasculature to become visible. Although albinos occur in many other species, there are no documented albino horses.

The dominant white color in horses is an example of *leucism*, which is a decrease of pigmentation in people and animals. A horse with dominant white color has white hair, pink skin, and dark (brown or hazelnut) eyes (Photos 155 & 156). Less often the eyes can be blue—their exact color can be determined only by a close inspection. When dominant white is caused by strongly expressed spotting, the eye color is almost always blue and can be accompanied by medicine hat.

Dominant white horses are born white, unlike white gray horses, which become lighter only with age (see p. 41). Another noticeable difference between dominant white and white gray is pink skin on the horse's nose—on grays it is practically always dark, except for those cases when there is a large white marking extending down and over the muzzle, when the horse displays vitiligo, or when a horse is also a double cream dilute.

Dominant white horses can sometimes have pigment residues in the skin and hair. In such cases, colored hairs grow most densely on the animal's back, gradually mixing up with white hair on the sides, and disappearing close to the underbelly. Phenotypically, such color is most similar to the color and pattern of a maximally expressed sabino (see p. 47).

From time to time there has been evidence of white horses that do not correspond to the criteria specified here. For example, one foal was born completely white, with pink skin and yellow eyes, but he was weak and soon died. Jeanette Gower (1999) calls similar cases "defective white" and considers them a result of other mutations that have not yet been studied but are *not* dominant white color. Some surviving "defective white" foals show various anomalies, such as deafness and infertility. Others can appear healthy, but produce offspring with defects—for example, contractures (shortening and hardening of muscles, tendons, or other tissue, often leading to deformity and rigidity of joints), incomplete or imperfect organogenesis (the process by which the ectoderm, endoderm, and mesoderm develop into the internal organs), and/or neurologic abnormalities. Mares, giving birth to such foals, can have a prolonged and difficult labor.

Dominant white color is very rare. It has been seen in Tennessee Walkers, Thoroughbreds, Arabians, Quarter Horses, Paint Horses, Standardbreds, Freibergers (Franches-Montagnes), Belgians, Icelandic Horses, Camarillo White Horses, South German Coldbloods, and Ban-ei Horses.

Inheritance of Dominant White

Dominant white color is caused by various dominant mutations in the KIT gene (see p. 48). These alleles are epistatic in relation to all other genes and alleles defining any color, thus turning it into white. The KIT gene is responsible for differentiation, migration, and the survival of melanocytes. According to genetic rules, a white horse has to have at least one white parent, but in practice exceptions occur as a result of spontaneous mutations. The following mutant alleles of the KIT gene responsible for dominant white color are currently known:

1   The *W1 allele* was found in the Freiberger (Franches-Montagnes) breed in descendants from a white mare named Cigale born in 1957. It is known that her parents did not differ from others of the breed in terms of displaying unusually

large white markings. This allele is a *nonsense mutation* in exon 15 and consists of a replacement of one base from a cytosine to a guanine (c.2151C> G). It significantly affects the function of the gene. The foal in this case is usually born white, although many have pigment along the topline, which disappears over time.

2   The *W2 allele* is present in Thoroughbred horses, descendants of the stallion KY Colonel born in 1946. He was a chestnut with large white markings. His white daughter, named White Beauty, was born in 1963 and produced several white foals. In this allele a glycine at position 654 is replaced by an arginine (p.G654R).

3   The *W3 allele* is characteristic for Arabian horses and goes back to an almost-white stallion, R Khasper, born in 1996 to colored parents with large white markings. R Khasper had some pigmented hair in his mane and spots on his skin, and his eyes were dark. Horses carrying this allele also often have colored specks on the body, which lose pigmentation over time, although there are also exceptions. Some representatives of this line have blue eyes, but Nancy Castle (2009) considers that this trait is inherited separately from the color of hair. The allele is the result of a nonsense mutation in exon 4, involving a replacement of an adenine by thymidin (c.706A> T). Researchers believe that this allele is homozygous lethal.

4   The *W4 allele* is characteristic for the Camarillo White Horse breed (www. camarillowhitehorses.org), which originated from a stallion named Sultan born in 1912. The allele is the result of a *missense mutation* in exon 12—a cytosine is replaced by thymidine (c.1805C> T), resulting in an amino acid replacement from alanine to valine. Some observations indicate that this allele is also homozygous lethal.

5   The *W5 allele* is present in Thoroughbred horses, originating from the stallion Puchilingui, born in 1984, who had sabino-type spotting and roaning. The mutation is a *deletion* (loss) of one nucleotide in exon 15 (c.2193delG), which leads to a shift in the reading frame, replacement of amino acid threonine with glutamine (p.Thr732Gln), and a premature *stop codon*, resulting in the synthesis of a truncated protein. The action of this allele is very variable: six studied carriers were white, and four had a sabino-like spotting. All were heterozygotes for W5.

6   The *W6 allele* was found in one white Thoroughbred horse with residual pigmentation, born to colored parents. The mutation represents a single

nucleotide *substitution* in exon 5 (c.856G> A), leading to the replacement of glycine-286 by arginine. The range of action of this allele is not known yet.

7   The *W7 allele* is also found only in one, almost completely white Thorough-bred born to non-spotted parents. Her dam produced colored foals and does not carry the mutation. The white mare carrying this allele has pigment on the ears, along the topline, and on the neck and back. The DNA defect under-lying the W7 allele is a mutation within a part of KIT important for proper processing of the RNA necessary for production of the protein—so-called *splice site mutation*. It is a single nucleotide change (c.338G> C) at the boundary of intron 2 and leads to a change of the amino-acid sequence, resulting in a non-functional protein.

8   The *W8 allele* is found in one Icelandic Horse, displaying a spotted sabino pattern. This allele is also a *splice site mutation* in intron 15 (c.2222G> A). It is not present in the parents or half-siblings of this horse.

9   The *W9 allele* was found in one, completely white Holsteiner born from col-ored parents. It is a *missense mutation* in exon 12 (c.1789G> A), leading to a replacement of glycine-597 by arginine (p.Gly597Arg) in the KIT protein.

10   The *W10 allele* was found in 10 Quarter Horses that go back to the stallion GQ Santana, born in 2000. Five of these horses are completely white, and five have sabino-like color. The mutation is a *deletion* of four nucleotides in exon 7 (c.1126_1129delGAAC), leading to a shift of the reading frame, a premature stop codon, and synthesis of a truncated protein. The phenotypes of carriers vary, including poorly expressed white color with large markings limited to the head and a small spot on the belly. Eyes are usually dark; seldom blue. As the stallion GQ Santana became a registered stud for Quarter Horses and Paint Horses, the DNA test for W10 is especially important for owners and breeders. It is believed that this mutation can be lethal in a homozygous state.

11   The *W11 allele* was found in three South German Coldbloods, originating from one white stallion considered the first carrier of this mutation. The allele is the result of a *splice site mutation* in intron 20 (c.2684G> A).

12   The *W12 allele* was found in a spotted Thoroughbred foal from parents with small white markings. This mutation represents a *deletion* of five nucleotides in exon 3 (c.559_563delTCTGC), leading to a shift of the reading frame and a premature stop codon. The foal died at five weeks of age. Autopsy showed a weak focal bacterial inflammation of the umbilical ring, ulcerations of the mucous membrane in the stomach, and a mild multifocal hepatitis. The death was caused by cardiovascular shock and ventricular arrhythmia. It is interest-

ing that some mutations of the KIT gene in people and mice are also accompanied by the development of stomach ulcers and similar heart problems. This means we cannot exclude the possibility that some mutants of KIT have a pleiotropic action.

13   The *W13 allele* is found in two white horses, resulting from crossing a Quarter Horse with a Peruvian Paso. According to the pedigree analysis, the mutation arose in the Quarter Horse parent. A *splice site mutation* in intron 17 (c.2472+5G> C) is present in both white horses.

14   The *W14 allele* was found in a completely white Thoroughbred and is due to a deletion of 54 nucleotides in exon 17.

15   The *W15 allele* was found in a spotted Arabian horse. It is a *missense mutation* in exon 10, leading to the replacement of cysteine-533 by arginine (c.1597T> C; p.C533R).

16   The *W16 allele* was found in three, almost completely white Oldenburgs. It is a *missense mutation* in exon 7, leading to the replacement of lysine-830 by isoleucine (c.2488A>T ; p.K830I).

17   The *W17 allele* was found in a white Ban-ei Horse with one dark and one blue eye. It is a *double mutation*, involving two nucleotides in exon 12 (2001A> T; 2020T> C), leading to amino-acid replacements of glutamic acid-667 by asparagine and leucine-674 by proline (p. [E667D; L674P]).

18   The *W18 allele* was found in a Swiss Warmblood with an extensive hair depigmentation.

19   The *W19 allele* was found in several half-Arabian horses with sabino-type of spotting.

20   The *W20 allele* is widespread, but the depigmentation due to its effect is weak.

We have information on a white stallion (born white) named Babylon that is a cross between the Orlov Trotter and Shetland Pony who at the time of writing is in Tolyatti, Russia. The horse has a few pigmented specks on the skin of the croup, which are visible through his white hair. The horse's eyes are dark or dark blue. It isn't known exactly what gene is the reason for his color, but it isn't excluded that it is a mutation in the KIT gene. We also know of a white pony, living in Tver, Russia. He was born completely white with pink skin and blue eyes. It is possible that this is also a *de novo* mutation (an alteration in a gene that is present for the first time as a result of a mutation in the egg or sperm or in the fertilized egg itself) in KIT. In 2012 a white Standardbred foal was born in the United States to dark bay parents. The foal had a very small, red medicine hat and admixture of red hair in the mane. It is remarkable that the dam only had a small white faint star (see p. 89) and the sire had no white markings. In the opinion of Samantha Brooks (Harvey, 2012), it can be explained by de novo KIT mutation, also indicated by the presence of the medicine hat.

At the present it is not clear why the KIT gene is so mutable—something that has been observed also in other animals. Other genes can be similarly affected, but mutations in KIT yield a very noticeable change of color. In 2011 the research of Bai et al was published, focusing on the genetics of "white" Mongolian horses living in Inner Mongolia. Scientists found that these horses *do not* have KIT gene mutations. Therefore, they cannot be classified alongside the dominant white alleles discussed on pp. 64–67. I doubt that these horses are truly white since the authors in the English introduction of the article describe them as "completely faded." Unfortunately, I have been unable to obtain photos of these "white" horses and so cannot comment further regarding their color.

In general crossings of two dominant white individuals should be avoided because, as mentioned earlier, the W alleles are considered possibly lethal in a homozygous state.

Dominant white is, in fact, a kind of spotted color close to sabino (see p. 47). The reason for this assumption is that sabino spotting is also controlled by the KIT gene. Furthermore, some pigment remains observed on some white horses, at birth and throughout their life. It is possible that the manifestation of white color is similar to the development of other spotted patterns. This can perhaps be due to a strong delay of the migration of melanocytes, which in spotted horses are "late" to arrive on some limited sites of the body. In white horses, this process involves almost the entire body.

Additional Color Phenomena

This category includes further discussion of traits I have already mentioned in this book, such as *countershading, pangaré, brindle, rabicano, giraffe markings,* and *false dun*. I also consider other color phenomena for which a genetic nature has not yet been proven or that are not stable in a specific animal. This includes *shades of colors, frosty,* and *"Catch A Bird."*

SHADES OF COLORS

Distinctions between *color shades* are most noticeable in colors with a significant amount of red hair—chestnut and bay. Thanks to shades, we distinguish *chestnut* from *light chestnut*, and *bay* from *red bay*, and so on, as we've already done throughout this book. This is due to the fact that pheomelanin provides the most variety in color, from dark red (almost black) to sand. Color shade variations can also be seen in black horses, but they are not so obvious to the observer because eumelanin gives a smaller range of color options (from black to light brown).

According to observations, color shades can be divided into three conditional groups (which you have read about already in this book): *dark, average or standard,* and *light*. Phenotypically, some colors can be mixed up because of similarity of shades. For example, *dark buckskin* (differing from average buckskin in the shade of pheomelanin-pigmented area—see p. 21) is not easy to distinguish from a *light bay*. Occasionally, the red shade shifts toward the brown end of the spectrum, resulting in a beautiful liver color of body hair, which especially stands out in the presence of dapples. This color completely justifies its English name *liver chestnut* (see p. 14).

In colloquial English there is rich and very figurative terminology sometimes used to designate shades of colors; however, "officially" these terms are seldom used in registration. The reason is that some shades change within a year or with age. It is important to understand distinctions in *intensity of color* of equine body hair as opposed to those that appear "darker" or "lighter" due to the presence of black or white hair. For example, when most describe a horse as dark bay or dark buckskin colors, the word "dark" indicates the presence and mixture of dark hair, rather than a darker shade of individual hair.

Some Western scientists offer the possibility that the difference between fading and non-fading black (see p. 11) is defined by the same genetic factors as shades of colors.

In Russia the richest shade terminology in practice is used for the registration of Russian Don and the Budyonny horses, in which the red color is common. The distribution of various shades varies. Most common are average bay, chestnut, palomino, and flaxen chestnut. In comparison, light bay, dark buckskin (as a shade), and very dark, almost black-bay are very rare. The genetic nature of differences in shades is not clear; however, most likely they have a polygenic nature of inheritance. According to Sponenberg (2003), the dark shade in the Freiberger breed is recessive in relation to the light shade. In general it is difficult to study inheritance of color shades, as the difference between shades of the same color is quite often subjective. For example, the horse that to one observer appears brown can look to another simply chestnut. In spite of the fact that shades can be divided conditionally into the three groups I've mentioned throughout this book (dark, average, and light), in practice, each group can have a wide range of variations. In addition, hair shade depends on the horse's nutrition and living conditions (for example, the horse that spends a lot of time at pasture is likely to have lighter hair due to sun exposure).

Dark shades are characteristic for bay and chestnut colors in the Morgan breed. An opposite example is the Belgian, especially those of American origin, for which light shades (light chestnut) are characteristic. According to Alekseev (2004), shade distinctions between the same colors in the Yakutian horses are expressed poorly, and in general, light colors are characteristic. Norwegian Fjords express a very light color caused by the combined action of genetic factors responsible for light shades, including the effects of Dun. According to the belief of some scientists, the Dun gene in a homozygous state gives lighter color than in heterozygotes. It isn't excluded that the expressed white *frost* (a staple of this breed—see p. 23) is also influenced by genes that are responsible for hair shades. Pay attention when light chestnut horses also have a light mane and tail, possibly due to the action of the same genes that affect the shade of body hair. I believe that some chestnut horses display guard hair that is lightened thanks to special genes that influence only the color of the mane and tail, and there are also light chestnut individuals with light guard hair as a result of the action of "shade" genes. Of course, it is also possible that there are light chestnut horses in which the action of both genetic complexes is combined.

According to the Polish scientists Stachurska, Brodacki, and Sochaczewska (2002), shades of colors can depend on two different alleles of one gene. These scientists noticed that dark-colored parents produce more dark foals than do light-colored parents. Perhaps the combination of alleles "e" and "a" defines light and dark shades.

Note: Everything I've just offered for discussion is based on the observations and opinions of horse owners and breeders, and as of writing, these phenomena were not yet explained scientifically.

COUNTERSHADING

Countershading is the presence of dark hair along the topline on the body of a horse. A weaker degree of expression is simply a dark stripe running along the horse's spine, which can be confused with the dorsal stripe specific to dun (see p. 22). The width of the countershading "stripe" can vary—usually from 2 to 8 inches. There also may be dark hair concentrated in specific areas, such as between the hind legs (Photos 157–159). An average expression of countershading consists of dark hair concentrated on the back and extending onto shoulders, croup, down the horse's sides, and on the neck and withers (Photo 160). The transition from a dark hair to lighter is often accompanied by dapples. One dramatic example is the countershading in a *golden buckskin*, where you see an unusual combination of black hair on the topline, with golden-yellow dapples below that, and followed by golden- and sandy-colored hair on the horse's sides and underbelly (Photos 161 & 162).

Strongly expressed countershading can cover almost the entire body of a horse, except the underbelly, on which it is also possible to find separate dark hairs (Photo 163). There can also be tan markings in the groin, on the underbelly, above the nostrils, on rear of the hips, and near the hocks and elbows. Less often the dark hair may be grouped in the form of a "dapple grid" that evenly covers the body. On a palomino (see p. 19), such a grid can change the color's appearance from sandy or light red to "dirty" or pale yellow. Quite often there is dark hair in the mane and tail. This kind of coloring is seen in some Morgans and Welsh Ponies, for example.

Countershading can be uneven. Sometimes, most of the dark hair is concentrated on the neck under the mane. Least often is countershading only present on the head, in the groin, around the eyes, and on the underbelly and elbows. Sometimes a dark vertical strip runs from the horse's forehead down the bridge of the nose (Photo 164). If present, it usually occupies the entire forehead and then becomes narrower on the nose. In the United States this marking is occasionally called a *mask* as it is similar to the one found in dun horses (see p. 23). The borders of the countershading mask are sharply delineated. It is most noticeable against light colors, such as buckskin and palomino. I have also observed that palomino and chestnut horses with strong countershading occasionally also have a dark rim on the ears.

The color of countershading depends on the overall color of a horse. In general, it is substantially darker than the base color of the body hair. In bay and buckskin horses, it is black; in chestnut and palomino, it is red or cinnamon; and in double cream horses, it is golden yellow or caramel. (Countershading is most often seen in bay and buckskin horses, and less often in chestnut, palomino, and double cream.) Some horses have countershading so strongly expressed that it is extremely difficult to visually determine their base color. This is seen in the Akhal-Teke breed: They have a uniform black color, practically on the entire body, but on the croup and behind the ears you can see uneven vertical stripes of red/tan color with rather clear boundaries. In Russia, these horses are registered as *dark buckskin*. Their red marks are located in places that are atypical for seal brown color—in seal brown horses, red/tan markings are characteristically near the eyes, on the muzzle, behind the elbows, in the groin, on the underbelly, and on the inside hind legs, but never behind ears and on the croup (see p. 22).

Dark bay with strongly expressed countershading has an unusual appearance. The dark bay hair is mixed with black, and the traditional characteristic of bay color—the red trunk—is not visible. Dark bay horses sometimes have dark brown areas on the head, sides, and underbelly, which can result in mistaken identification as faded black (see p. 11). For distinction, it is necessary to pay attention to the horse's head color: On a black horse, the head is much darker than the body, and the area around the eyes is also black.

Countershading against chestnut color usually manifests as a narrow stripe of brown color along the spine and admixture of the same hair in the mane and tail. It can have clearer delineation than most countershading, but with practice should be quite simple to distinguish from a dorsal stripe. Countershading against chestnut color can be also accompanied by a dark mask, as discussed on p. 23. It is also possible to see chestnut horses with such strongly expressed countershading that the horse is almost entirely dark brown, except for lighter areas on the lower legs, near the elbows, and on the underbelly. This color occurs in the Budyonny breed. On a chestnut horse with a flaxen mane and tail, it is possible to observe a bright contrast between the light, often white, guard hair and the dark hair distributed on the body. As mentioned, some dark hair can be also present in the mane and tail.

Sometimes countershading on palominos can be so strongly expressed that it covers the body completely. Phenotypically these horses are similar to dark flaxen chestnuts, dark bays, or smoky black horses. This is a color that is seen in the Quarter Horse and Morgan.

At birth horses with countershading have a light color—for example, dark palominos with strong countershading are born a sandy color, and dark buckskins with strong countershading are born a very light, pale yellow. Interestingly, countershading on a light bay horse is seldom expressed as strongly as it is on an average bay.

Inheritance of Countershading

It is difficult to investigate the mechanism of inheritance of countershading because, as mentioned, it isn't always easy to determine its manifestations against a horse's base color. In addition, external factors play a role, as I said earlier (nutrition, sun exposure, overall health), which also to a certain degree influence the base color. In any case, it is possible to tell with confidence that countershading is hereditary—this is supported by observations in such breeds as the Trakehner, Akhal-Teke, Russian Trotter, and Hanoverian (strong countershading is common in all of these). However, the exact mechanism of inheritance is, at the time of writing, still unknown. Most likely, it is polygenic, although not so long ago some scientists believed that it was caused by a dominant gene called "Sty" (from "sooty").

Henner, et al (2002), conducted research on Freiberger horses (n=1369) produced by five stallions and came to the conclusion that countershading has a recessive mode of inheritance. Sponenberg (2003) believes that studying the inheritance of countershading is complicated by dominant black color (see p. 11), which is more widespread in some breeds and confuses the identification of dark bay color. Politova and Reissmann (2003) write that among dark bay horses with strong countershading, there are significantly more individuals with the "EE" genotype than with "Ee." According to observations, chestnut color with countershading dominates standard chestnut more often than not.

PANGARÉ

Pangaré (sometimes called *mealy*) is characterized by the lightening of hair around the muzzle and the eyes, in the groin, near the elbows, on the insides of the legs, and frequently, on the underbelly. The areas with manifestations of pangaré are brightly colored, a shade that resembles ivory or even almost white. Pangaré is most often observed in bay horses; however, it is incorrect to believe that pangaré is limited to one color—other colors can be combined with it, as well. For example, chestnut horses with pangaré often also have a light mane and tail (Photo 165). (It should be noted, however, that it is not known whether this is an additional manifestation of pangaré or if it is perhaps connected to the genes responsible for the flaxen chestnut phenotype.) So far, black or grullo pangaré has not been observed.

I believe that pangaré should be specified in an animal's official documents as it is quite simple to detect by an observer, and it allows us to identify a horse more accurately.

Inheritance of Pangaré

In 1983, Sponenberg first talked about pangaré being caused by a dominant allele called "Pa" (from "pangaré") with the recessive allele designated by "Pa-np" (from "non-pangaré"). The "Pa" allele should be considered the "Wild" version of the gene because pangaré is found in practically all wild representatives of the horse family, including Przewalski horses and wild donkeys (Photo 166). Based on cave drawings, pangaré was also present in the wild ancestors of domestic horses. The majority of modern horses lost this marking over the course of evolution, and possibly also due to intentional selection against the trait by breeders.

The only breed in the world in which pangaré was *supported* by selection is the Exmoor Pony (Photo 167). Most horses in this breed have whitish pangaré; however, there are also animals with a light red color instead. Pangaré is found in other native breeds, such as Haflingers, and numerous draft breeds, including the Russian and Soviet Heavy Drafts and Belgians.

BRINDLE

The *brindle* pattern/color is frequently observed in cattle and dogs, but it is a rarity in horses. The brindling in mammals consists of vertical dark stripes against any color and does not involve the mane and tail, or the lower part of the legs. The

Color: A black sabino with a blaze on the head that extends onto the muzzle. The lower legs are white.

Expressed alleles: E* aa, Sabino genes

Breed: Shire

PHOTOGRAPHER: VERA KURSKAYA

PHOTO 117

Color: Black sabino with markings resembling both sabino and splashed white (see Photo 128): the "tooth"-shaped marking on the horse's side is a sabino trait; the bald face, a splashed white one. The horse has blue eyes with white eyelashes.

Expressed alleles: E* aa, Sabino genes, Sw1*(?)

Breed: Shetland Pony

PHOTOGRAPHER: VERA KURSKAYA

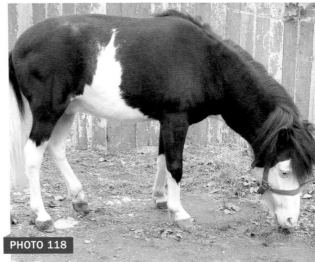

PHOTO 118

Color: Bay sabino with a white spot on the belly, expanding into a "tooth" on the horse's side, markings on the legs and head, and evident "roaning."

Expressed alleles: E* A*, Sabino genes

Breed: Unknown

PHOTOGRAPHER: VERA KURSKAYA

PHOTO 119

PHOTO 120

Color: Chestnut sabino with white markings on the legs and belly.

Expressed alleles: ee**, Sabino genes

Breed: Latvian cross

PHOTOGRAPHER: VLADISLAV RUTKOWSKI

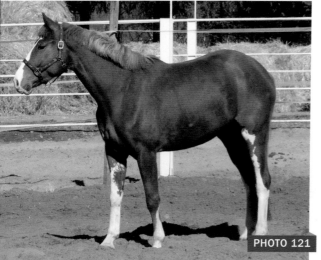

PHOTO 121

Detail: The same horse as in Photo 120 but viewed from the opposite site. Note the markings on the legs and blaze involving both lips.

PHOTOGRAPHER: VLADISLAV RUTKOWSKI

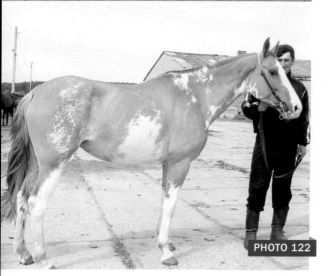

PHOTO 122

Color: A light chestnut sabino with a bald face, including the muzzle, and unevenly white legs. The white body spots have ragged, irregular edges.

Expressed alleles: ee**, Sabino genes

Breed: Argentinian Polo Pony

PHOTOGRAPHER: VERA KURSKAYA

Color: This dunskin sabino is a complex color and pattern combination. White markings come up in the shape of large "teeth," two per side, and two on the hind end, plus a large white mark on the head. The winter coat makes the base color quite pale, but you can faintly see the sandy body color, dark forelock, black-rimmed ears, and dorsal stripe.

Expressed alleles: $E^* A^* C^{cr} C Dn^+ *$, Sabino genes

Breed: Arabian-Pony cross

PHOTOGRAPHER: VERA KURSKAYA

PHOTO 123

Detail: The head and back of the dunskin sabino in Photo 123. Here you can really see the "tooth"-shaped spotting on the side, blurred black dorsal stripe, and a diffuse "wing" mark on the shoulder.

PHOTOGRAPHER: VERA KURSKAYA

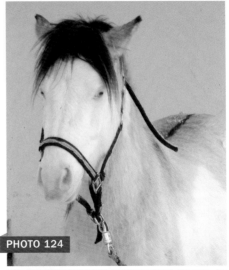

PHOTO 124

Detail: The legs of the same horse, showing that the lower front legs would be black if the color was not masked by large, white markings.

PHOTOGRAPHER: VERA KURSKAYA

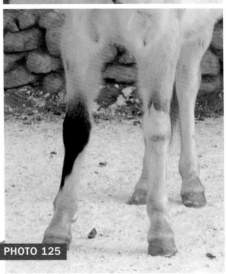

PHOTO 125

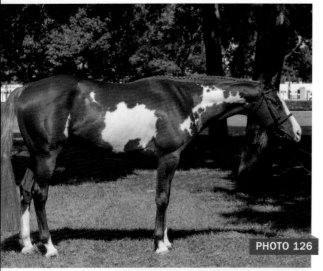

PHOTO 126

Color: Chestnut frame overo with white mark on head that extends over nose and white body spots with jagged edges and horizontal orientation.

Expressed alleles: ee** OvN

Breed: American Paint Horse

PHOTOGRAPHER: COURTESY OF THE APHA/
PAINT HORSE JOURNAL (APHA.COM)

PHOTO 127

Color: Chestnut frame overo with a white bald head marking skewed right, involving the right nostril, and an uneven white marking on the right front leg. The large white body spot has jagged edges on the left side. This is characteristic color distribution for a white frame overo pattern: white spot mid-barrel, bald face, and minimal white hair on the legs.

Expressed alleles: ee** OvN

Breed: American Paint Horse

PHOTOGRAPHER: ANNA MURATOVA

PHOTO 128

Color: Splashed white on chestnut. Unlike sabino (see Photo 118), white spots rise from the bottom up and relatively evenly. They have a smooth, rounded shape. White tails are often seen; a white mane is a rarity.

Expressed alleles: E* aa, SW1-3*(?)

Breed: American Paint Horse

PHOTOGRAPHER: COURTESY OF THE APHA/
PAINT HORSE JOURNAL (APHA.COM)

Color: Manchado spotting on a chestnut base. The spotting spreads from the middle of neck down and then onto the body, with colored hair grouped into characteristic "fragments."

Expressed alleles: ee**, Manchado genes

Breed: Argentinian Polo Pony (Vasco Piskui, Bred by Eduardo Heguy)

PHOTOGRAPHER: ALICE GIPPS

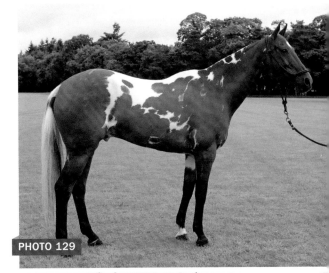

PHOTO 129

Color: Bay with a white spotting, resembling a poorly marked manchado. The markings on the horse's head are too small for a frame overo, and the configuration of white spots is also atypical. There is too little white on the legs and head for a sabino. Some of the white markings are located on the neck, close to the withers, which is typical for manchado.

Expressed alleles: E* A*, Manchado genes(?)

Breed: Orlov Trotter

PHOTOGRAPHER: VALERIYA ZANOSKA

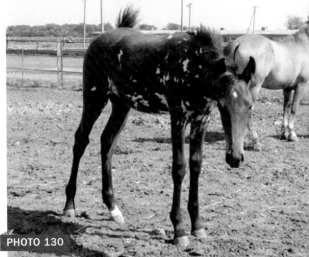

PHOTO 130

Color: Bay macchiato: the front legs are unevenly white up over the knees, the hind legs unevenly white up over the hocks all the way to the stifle, and the horse's colored hair is quite bright.

Expressed alleles: E* A* MITF^{N310S}/ MITF$^+$

Breed: Freiberger (Apache du Peupé, owned by Elevage du Peupé, www.elevagedupeupe.com)

PHOTOGRAPHER: ELEVAGE DU PEUPÉ

PHOTO 131

PHOTO 132

Color: Buckskin tobiano with dark spots on pigmented areas—this is probably an example of so-called calico tobiano.

Expressed alleles: E* A* C^{cr} C To* CalC*(?)

Breed: Paso Fino (Tres Colores de Ciente, owned by Terry Wallace)

PHOTOGRAPHER: TERRY WALLACE

PHOTO 133

Color: Buckskin tobiano with calico tobiano—again, notice the dark patches of hair in the pigmented areas, particular near the hip and at the girth line.

Expressed alleles: E* A* C^{cr} C To* CalC*(?)

Breed: Colonial Spanish Mustang (Turkey Track Jr., owned by Bryant Rickman of Rickman Spanish Mustangs and supported by The Friends of The Heritage Horse Foundation Herds. Find out more at TheSpiritofBlackjackMountain.com.)

PHOTOGRAPHER: FRANCINE LOCKE BRAY

PHOTO 134

Color: A dark bay tovero with an asymmetrical bald face, and unevenly white hind legs, extending to the hocks. This is a strongly expressed tovero (tobiano and sabino overo).

Expressed alleles: E* A* To*, Sabino genes

Breed: Argentinian Polo Pony

PHOTOGRAPHER: VERA KURSKAYA

Detail: Note the halo around the colored spot on the body of the tovero in Photo 134, with visible pigmented skin shining through the white hair on the borders.

PHOTOGRAPHER: VERA KURSKAYA

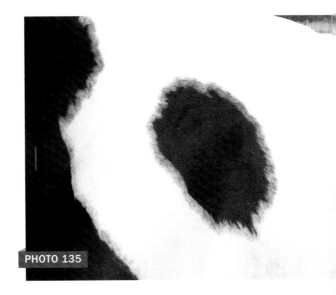

PHOTO 135

Color: Chestnut tovero, showing the interaction of spotting genes tobiano and sabino. Tobiano determines the preservation of pigment in specific locations, sabino is consistent with the white bald face, medicine hat, roaned edges of large spots, and small specks of color.

Expressed alleles: ee** To*, Sabino genes

Breed: Unknown

PHOTOGRAPHER: EKATHERINA BELIKOVA

PHOTO 136

Color: A black tovero with a badger face and medicine hat.

Expressed alleles: E* aa To*

Breed: American Paint Horse

PHOTOGRAPHER: SKIPPYTHEWONDER
(HTTP://CREATIVECOMMONS.ORG/LICENSES/BY/2.5)

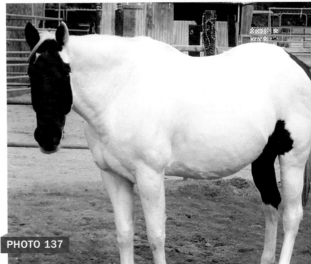

PHOTO 137

PHOTO 138

Detail: Mottled skin on the nose and lips of an appaloosa-spotted horse.

PHOTOGRAPHER: VERA KURSKAYA

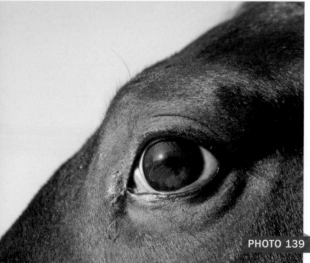

PHOTO 139

Detail: White sclera around the eye—often seen in appaloosa-spotted horses but otherwise a rarity. Note that the iris is slightly smaller than usual.

PHOTOGRAPHER: ELENA MOLCHANOVA

PHOTO 140

Detail: The hoof of an appaloosa-spotted horse showing sharply defined, light-colored stripes. The ratio of the dark and light horn is typical for horses heterozygous for the "Lp" gene.

PHOTOGRAPHER: VERA KURSKAYA

Color: A bay blanket Appaloosa.

Expressed alleles: EE A* Lplp patn1/patn1 (confirmed by DNA test)

Breed: Appaloosa (Taylor Brooke, owned by Lisa Estridge, Palisades Appaloosas, www.palisadesapps.com)

PHOTOGRAPHER: LISA ESTRIDGE

PHOTO 141

Detail: An aerial view of a black appaloosa-spotted horse with a half-roany blanket and spots on the croup, hips, back, and sides.

PHOTOGRAPHER: VERA KURSKAYA

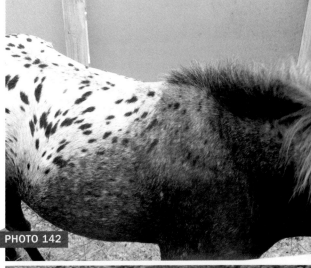

PHOTO 142

Color: A leopard Appaloosa with mismarks—the areas where the "Lp" gene is suppressed.

Expressed alleles: EE aa LpLp (confirmed by DNA test)

Breed: Appaloosa (Twilight Reemarkable, owned by Lisa Estridge, Palisades Appaloosas, www.palisadesapps.com)

PHOTOGRAPHER: LISA ESTRIDGE

PHOTO 143

PHOTO 144

Color: A bay leopard appaloosa-spotted horse. The "colored" head consists of clustered spots. Judging by the black colored spots on the horse's shoulder, there is a pronounced countershading, as well (see p. 70).

Expressed alleles: E* A* Lplp

Breed: Altai

PHOTOGRAPHER: VERA KURSKAYA

PHOTO 145

Color: A bay leopard appaloosa-spotted horse with very obvious mottling on the lips.

Expressed alleles: E* A* Lplp

Breed: Miniature Appaloosa

PHOTOGRAPHER: VERA KURSKAYA

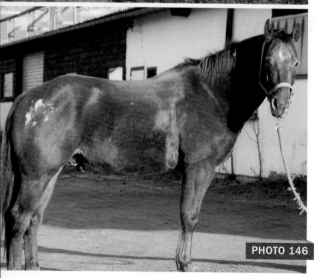

PHOTO 146

Color: A chestnut Appaloosa with white spots on the hind end. A controversial case because in principle the pattern could be called snowflake or frost, but the white spots are offset to the side, when frost is generally seen at the top of the croup. The horse has weakly expressed mottling on the nose and the genitals.

Expressed alleles: ee** Lp*

Breed: Appaloosa

PHOTOGRAPHER: ANNA MURATOVA

Color: Brown speckled appaloosa-spotted horse. This pattern is extremely rare. The horse also has varnish marks on the nose and ears.

Expressed alleles: E* A* Lp* PATN1/PATN1(?)

Breed: Netherlands Appaloosa Pony

PHOTOGRAPHER: IVAN FEDYAKIN

PHOTO 147

Color: Chestnut varnish roan Appaloosa, showing weakly expressed appaloosa color with a significant amount of pigmented hair on the body. The horse has mottling on the nose and white sclera around the eyes.

Expressed alleles: ee** Lp*

Breed: Appaloosa

PHOTOGRAPHER: ANNA MURATOVA

PHOTO 148

Color: Chestnut varnish roan Appaloosa with stronger roaning than the horse in Photo 148—there is much more white hair.

Expressed alleles: ee** Lp*

Breed: Appaloosa

PHOTOGRAPHER: ANNA MURATOVA

PHOTO 149

PHOTO 150

Color: This bay appaloosa-spotted horse appears to have two patterns: blanket and varnish roan. Note the white hair in the tail.

Expressed alleles: E* A* Lplp

Breed: Altai

PHOTOGRAPHER: VERA KURSKAYA

PHOTO 151

Color: A black appaloosa-spotted horse. You can see how the white and black hair form stripes parallel with ribs. This horse also shows another characteristic sometimes seen: a scanty tail.

Expressed alleles: E* aa Lplp

Breed: Bashkir Horse

PHOTOGRAPHER: VERA KURSKAYA

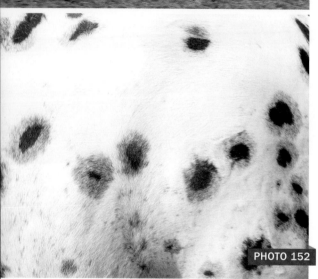

PHOTO 152

Detail: A close-up of leopard "peacock" spots on the rump, clearly showing their roaned edges and "eyes."

PHOTOGRAPHER: VERA KURSKAYA

Color: The foal on the right is a bay appaloosa-spotted horse with a large roany blanket and visible stripes on the sides that run parallel with ribs. Judging by the white hair on the foal's shoulders, neck, and head, he might lean more toward leopard, like the mare in the background.

Expressed alleles: Ee A* Lplp (foal); ee** Lplp (mare)

Breed: Bashkir Horse

PHOTOGRAPHER: VERA KURSKAYA

PHOTO 153

Detail: Lightning marks on the legs of a bay appaloosa horse. Combined with the right front hoof being striped with light bands on a dark background, you can determine that the horse is heterozygous for the Lp allele.

PHOTOGRAPHER: VERA KURSKAYA

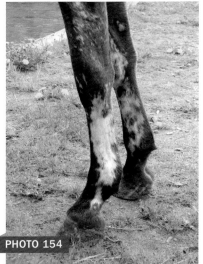

PHOTO 154

Color: Dominant white, and the skin, hooves, and coat lack pigment cells, giving the horse a pink-skinned white coat.

Expressed alleles:**** Ww(?)

Breed: Thoroughbred

PHOTO 155

Color: Dominant white, with some pigmentation areas combined in clusters.

Expressed alleles:**** Ww(?)

Breed: Thoroughbred (Painted Patchen bred by Patchen Wilkes Farm LLC)

PHOTOGRAPHER: KS VEITCH PHOTOGRAPHY

PHOTO 156

Detail: Weakly expressed countershading on a chestnut horse.

Breed: Budyonny

PHOTOGRAPHER: VERA KURSKAYA

PHOTO 157

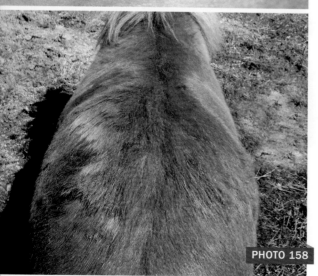

Color: Weak shaded stripe typical of a false dun (see p. 78) on a chestnut pony with a flaxen mane and tail. The visible dark band along the spine is too vague to be a dorsal stripe.

Expressed alleles: nd1(?)

Breed: Shetland Pony

PHOTOGRAPHER: EKATHERINA BELIKOVA

PHOTO 158

Detail: Faint darkening on the hind legs of the horse shown in Photo 158.

PHOTOGRAPHER: EKATHERINA BELIKOVA

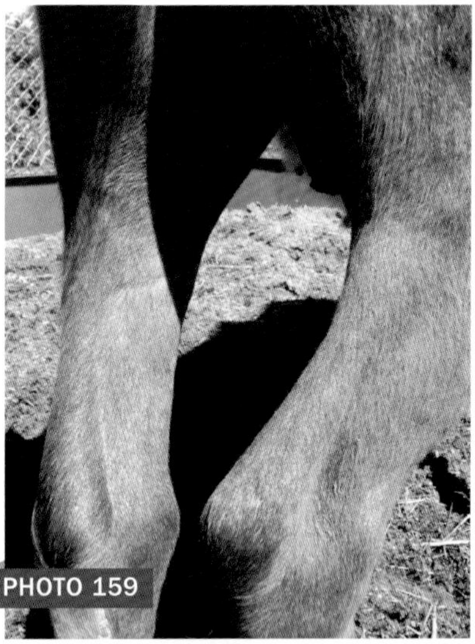

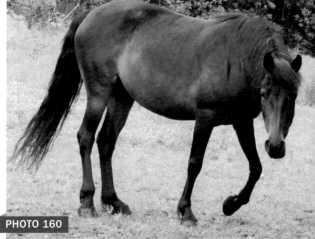

PHOTO 159

Color: Bay with average-to-strong countershading, extending onto the shoulders and hindquarters.

Expressed alleles: E* A*

Breed: Morgan (Luna, owned by Sharon Wilsie, Wilsie Way Horsemanship, www. wilsiewayhorsemanship.com)

PHOTOGRAPHER: RICH NEALLY

PHOTO 160

Color: Dark golden buckskin.

Expressed alleles: E* A* C^{cr} C

Breed: Morgan (PKR Primavera Brio, owned by John Hutcheson, Gab Creek Farm, www.gabcreekfarm.com)

PHOTOGRAPHER: LAURA BEHNING
(WWW.BROOKRIDGEMORGANS.COM)

PHOTO 161

PHOTO 162

Detail: The stunning head and neck of the golden buckskin in Photo 160. The countershading is very evident on the neck.

Breed: Morgan (PKR Primavera Brio, owned by John Hutcheson, Gab Creek Farm, www.gabcreekfarm.com)

PHOTOGRAPHER: LAURA BEHNING
(WWW.BROOKRIDGEMORGANS.COM)

PHOTO 163

Color: A flaxen liver chestnut with countershading. This is an extreme case of countershading on a chestnut base. Your first impression is of a silver color; however, the light reddish shade on the horse's nose and in the groin allows you to distinguish the color from silver.

Expressed alleles: ee**

Breed: Unknown

PHOTOGRAPHER: ANNA FALINA

PHOTO 164

Detail: The same horse from Photo 159: a dark bay with a mask.

Breed: Morgan (Luna, owned by Sharon Wilsie, Wilsie Way Horsemanship, www. wilsiewayhorsemanship.com)

PHOTOGRAPHER: RICH NEALLY

stripes are narrow, with uneven, diffuse edges. Sometimes they look like rows of small spots and specks, merging with each other. The shape of the stripes can curve, and individual stripes can sometimes even merge together. Usually brindle stripes are concentrated on the horse's croup, shoulders, and neck (Photos 168–170). Similar to some appaloosa-spotting patterns, brindle stripes have a different texture in comparison to the surrounding hair and can be detected by touch (see p. 78). Brindled horses, especially foals, sometimes look "moth-eaten" because of this. This can occur even in the absence of visible stripes on the animal.

Brindle is often found on dark bays, and according to recorded observation, it shows most distinctly in the presence of countershading. In fact, in the past it was also considered a rare variant of countershading. Some colors, such as dun, can be mistaken for brindle (the dorsal stripe, zebra stripes on the legs, and occasionally on the sides of the body and neck can confuse). There are horses on which dun markings are combined with brindle, in which case stripes will be present on the legs and trunk, as well. Gray horses at a certain stage of graying can display patterns in the form of brindle stripes—these, though, most likely have no relationship to real brindle, and completely disappear with age.

A pattern similar to brindle stripes can occur occasionally in appaloosa-spotted horses at the junction between a blanket and colored parts of the body (see Photo 151). However, in true brindle stripes, "blurring" is characteristic, as they are partially mixed with background hair, and practically always at least slightly curved, as mentioned earlier. Stripes in appaloosa-spotted horses tend to be rather accurately defined and follow the direction of the horse's ribs.

Brindle changes intensity, depending on the season and the horse's age. Foals are born with hardly noticeable dark stripes; they become more visible over time.

Brindle color has been recorded in Arabians, Thoroughbreds, Mustangs, Quarter Horses, Paint Horses, Tennessee Walkers, Criollo Horses, American Miniature Horses, Paso Finos, Norikers, Brazilian Sport Horse, Icelandic Horses, Standardbreds, American Bashkir Curlies, and German Warmblood breeds.

Inheritance of Brindle Pattern

So far there isn't consensus regarding the genetics of brindle coloring, or even whether or not there is a genetic piece at all. In some cases there is a question of chimerism (see p. 86). In other animal species—for example, cattle and dogs—brindle is heritable, but cases of true inheritance of this phenomenon are infrequent in horses. In 2013 a *nonsense mutation* (184C > T; p. Arg62 *) was discovered in the IKBKG gene (inhibitor of kappa light polypeptide gene enhancer in B-cells, kinase gamma) located on the X chromosome. In one studied horse family, this mutation led to the formation of partial baldness in the area of dark stripes. It is interesting to note that two mares from the studied family suffered repeated miscarriages. In 2016 an intronic variant close to an exon/intron boundary in intron 10 of the MBPTS2 gene (the membrane bound transcription factor peptidase, site 2) (c.1437+4T>C) was identified as being associated with brindle pattern in another horse family. One of the brindle horses lacked the entire exon 10 and parts of exon 11. It is possible that chimerism and IKBKG and MBPTS2 gene mutations are still not the only genetic reasons for horses to have brindle patterning, and some other mutations controlling brindle pattern exist (Murgiano, et al, 2016).

RABICANO

Rabicano is an admixture of white hair at the base of the horse's tail, in the groin, on the barrel, and less often, on the belly. In some parts of the world, this pattern is sometimes called *white ticking*. Characteristics usually include horizontal stripes at the base of the tail, vertical white strips on the horse's sides (parallel with the ribs), and white spots on the stomach located closer to the hind legs than the front (Photos 171–173). Rabicanos are often called *skunk tails* or *coon tails,* as the striped tail can resemble the tail markings of these animals.

Strongly expressed rabicano is rare—the admixture of white hair extends onto the croup, hips, and the trunk, approximately two-thirds of its length. It is distinguished from roan color (see p. 43) by the concentration of white hair at the base of the tail and/or in the groin. By careful examination it is possible to find small pink specks on the skin on some rabicano horses, especially on the genitals, which are not present in roan. These can be consistent with where white hair grows in small, unpigmented skin sites.

Rabicano is also sometimes thought to be sabino spotting (see p. 47). However, sabino spots involve the tail base only when there is a large amount of white hair on the horse's body, including the stomach, sides, and legs. Sabino is also always characterized by white marks on the muzzle and legs, which is not found in rabicano.

Most often rabicano is present in combination with chestnut color; on this base, it is expressed very strongly.

Rabicano is not visible in foals; it becomes noticeable with age, typically after five to six years, or even later (although there are also exceptions). The extent of white hair does not change with age, and as the manifestations are often insignificant, this pattern is usually not noted in breeding documents describing the animal.

In general this pattern is uncommon. It has been observed in Arabians, Thoroughbreds, Akhal-Tekes, and Warmbloods.

Inheritance of Rabicano

Perhaps the reader may ask why we discuss rabicano in this section of "other color phenomena," and not with other spotted colors and patterns. But spotted colors are patterns of white *spots*, which are not characteristic of rabicano.

This pattern has not been the subject of scientific studies yet. Some hold the opinion that, at least in some bloodlines, the color is controlled by a dominant allele "Ra" (the recessive allele is designated "ra"). There is also a hypothesis that the gene responsible for rabicano is linked to the gene responsible for sabino.

"CATCH A BIRD" PHENOMENON

I will now touch on one of the rarest color patterns seen in horses. It received the name "Catch A Bird" after the Thoroughbred stallion by that name. The stallion had white vertical stripes against dark bay color, running down from the spine on the neck, sides, and croup. Their arrangement and structure resembled brindle. The majority of the stripes are on the sides of the body, with fewer on the horse's shoulders and the base of the neck.

It was discovered that Catch A Bird was the carrier of a spontaneous roan mutation. He sired four foals, including a filly named Odd Colours, a typical bay roan color, but which was unknown in the Thoroughbred breed before her. Unfortunately, there are no records about whether the offspring of this stallion further reproduced. It has been established that Catch A Bird was a *chimera*—that is, he had at least two different sets of DNA, likely originating from the fusion of fertilized eggs—which explains the uneven manifestation of the roan color on his body (see further discussion of this on p. 86).

Another horse with white stripes is a Brazilian Warmblood stallion named Natal Clasi (Photos 174–176). His use for breeding was limited, and it is not known whether any of them inherited his stripes or a classic roan color.

In the third edition of Sponenberg's book *Equine Color Genetics* (2009) is a photo of a black horse with white stripes. The animal is almost entirely black on the left side and displays unevenly distributed stripes on the right side, as well as concentrated on the croup, the base of the tail, and the withers. From the croup the stripes run down almost to the right hock and from the withers onto the right front leg. The horse's right hip is black. Sponenberg writes that usually such stripes are the result of errors during embryogenesis and are not heritable. Only occasionally they are a spontaneous roan mutation and passed on to offspring.

GIRAFFE MARKINGS

Giraffe markings—also known as *lacing, cobweb,* and *marble* in various countries, not to be confused with other uses of these terms in this book—are a white pattern of thin, uneven, and sometime fragmentary lines on the back of a horse, occasionally extending onto the croup, base of the tail, and withers. Phenotypically, these marks are very similar to the pattern of white lines you see on the body of a giraffe. Giraffe markings are very rare. They generally appear on a horse older than one year and gradually increase in size until seven or eight years of age (Photos 177–179).

Gower (1999) notes that almost all owners of horses with giraffe markings tend to explain their emergence with external factors—that is, a poorly fitting saddle, a rigid or poorly cleaned or fit blanket, an allergy to insect repellents, pasture under coniferous trees, and so on. She mentions a Standardbred stallion named Aachen on whom such markings increased in size, even after completion of his running career, and therefore defy explanation related to possible injuries caused by the harness. In addition, some descendants of this stallion also had giraffe markings, which confirms their genetic nature.

These markings have been seen in a number of breeds, including the Quarter Horse, Peruvian Paso, Standardbred, Percheron, and American Miniature Horse. I have also observed two such horses—a black mare and a seal brown gelding, both from the Karachai breed (Photos 180–182). On both horses the markings covered the back, sides, and shoulders, and to a lesser extent, the croup. Some concentration of white hair was observed at the base of tail, and there were also small white specks above the eyes. Only a little is known about the ancestry of these two horses; we do know that the sire of the black mare had the same giraffe markings, but only a few of his offspring inherited this pattern.

Inheritance of Giraffe Markings

Sponenberg (2009) describes giraffe markings as a variant of *reticulated leukotrichia*, an uncommon form of dermatosis or skin disease. He writes that the hair first falls out and is then replaced by white hair. The scientist also reports that some horses are born with already visible giraffe markings.

At the end of 2013 it was hypothesized that giraffe markings are a variant of roan because roan is present in all breeds in which these markings have been observed. However, DNA laboratory analysis at the University of California at Davis was negative for the Roan gene. Having learned at the end of 2013 about the existence of gray horses with incomplete graying process, I worked with the owner of both Karachai horses mentioned on p. 76 to do DNA analysis for the Gray gene. The laboratory analyzed the samples several times, but claimed it was not possible to obtain accurate results and therefore necessary to send new samples. After we sent new samples and received the same answer yet again, we requested an explanation from the laboratory.

The lab responded as follows: "Unfortunately, we have been unable to obtain results for a portion of the Gray gene test, despite repeated attempts. I can confirm that both [horses] have at least one copy of the Gray gene, but can't resolve if they have two copies of gray."

Thus, both of the Karachai horses with giraffe markings were genetically gray. I therefore believe that the pattern—in these two horses, at least—is caused by previously unknown Gray gene mutations.

FROSTY

This concept is often referred to in documents and literature as any admixture of white hair, either minimal or on the entire body of a horse (but only if it is *not* roan color—see p. 43). In the United States, *frosty* is a generic term for all hair phenomena that cannot be explained by what is already known about colors. I feel that here, too, we must adhere to a genetic approach for the description of the color of a horse.

Some white hair is found in places where there are bones close to the skin, such as the horse's spine, shoulders, head. They can also appear in the mane and tail, and among Mustangs you can find individuals with white hair in the guard hair, which appear only with age.

I must note that a horse that is *really* frosty cannot possess the classic signs of roan, silver, sabino, or rabicano color. According to Sponenberg (2009), real frosty is not heritable *unless* it is a non-standard, most rare manifestation of roan color. As strongly expressed frost in the mane and tail and on the body is characteristic for breeds in which classic roan color appears, Sponenberg concludes that it is most likely a variant of the Roan gene. However, the genetic nature of this color is not defined, except what Sponenberg separately considers a similar phenomenon: *roaned.* It has an appearance of very small white specks, which are more or less evenly distributed on the horse's entire body or at particular sites. Some horses (but not all) with such white specks also have manifestations of sabino spotting. Sponenberg assumes that such specks are not related to roan color and are not heritable.

FALSE DUN

The phenomenon called *false dun* was discovered rather recently. False dun horses almost completely match the characteristics of real dun color (see p. 22), except for some important differences (Photos 183 & 184). Horses with one or more of the following traits should be considered false dun:

- Visible primitive markings that are absent on both parents.
- No sign of primitive markings but offspring that display them strongly.
- One or several primitive markings on a horse of a breed in which there isn't dun color.
- A gray horse that shows primitive markings before the graying process.
- Noticeable, uneven texture of hair in places where primitive markings would be on very dark base colors (against which primitive markings are not visible).

On the majority of false dun horses, a dorsal stripe is something between a "real" primitive stripe and weakly expressed countershading. This pseudo-stripe is quite narrow just like the real stripe, but has indistinct borders.

False dun horses are rare but have been found in the following breeds: Arabian, Morgan, Thoroughbred, Appaloosa, Andalusian, Lusitano, Russian Don, Budyonny, and Quarter Horse. Note that dun color is common in Quarter Horses.

Inheritance of False Dun

False dun is controlled by the allele nd1 of the Dun gene (see p. 26). Sometimes it is difficult to distinguish false dun from classic dun, but a genetic test for the nd1 allele is now available. Scientists say the mutation nd1 happened before domestication of the horse, and the mutation nd2 responsible for simple non-dun colors happened after domestication (Imsland, et al, 2015). The Russian scientist Tatyana Zubkova, to whom I and others give advisory support, confirmed false dun in Russian Don and Budyonny breeds.

METALLIC SHEEN

I consider *metallic sheen* (*hair gloss*) in horses a separate color phenomenon because it significantly changes the phenotype of the animal and is heritable. This color phenomenon produces a noticeable, permanent, metallic golden or silvery gloss to the body hair (Photos 185 & 186). I touched briefly on golden gloss in connection with the chestnut, bay, buckskin, and palomino colors, but there can be different kinds.

Practically any horse can have a brilliant hair coat when provided good nutrition and timely grooming, combined with being kept in a warm stable through the winter or living in a warm climate. The kind of gloss that comes with high quality care is especially visible on the hips and the neck; however, it can disappear if any of the factors I just mentioned change. Therefore, in this book I feel it is worth speaking about hair gloss *only* in the case when it is a permanent characteristic of the horse.

Permanent gloss that is very noticeable and vibrant is characteristic of the Akhal-Teke, Russian Don, Karabakh, Budyonny, Kustanai, and Tersk horses. It is occasionally seen in some Orlov Trotters. Silvery sheen against gray color is a trait of Tersk horses. All these breeds are related to each other. A more weakly expressed, but still noticeable, golden gloss is present in Vyatka horses and a few other native breeds of Russia. Metallic sheen of hair starts becoming visible after the foal first sheds his baby coat.

The first to research metallic sheen were Shimbo and Sponenberg (1998). In their opinion, the appearance of gloss depends on the structure of the involved hair.

In general, "normal" hair consists of three layers: the *core*, the *intermediate cortical layer*, and the external layer, called the *cuticle*. The core consists of keratin, and its structure can be compared to a sponge with empty spaces inside. The cortical layer is opaque and consists of spindle-shaped cells oriented along the axis of the hair and bonded together. It is responsible for the strength and elasticity of a hair. The cuticle, which is translucent, consists of scales formed by flat, keratinized cells, surrounding the hair core with continuous rings, or remaining on the surface in the form of adjoining or partially overlapping scales. The scales of glossy hair densely adjoin each other.

In most horses, the hair core is more or less uniform; however, in animals with metallic sheen, it has breaks and spaces that are not filled with keratin. In combination, these defects influence refraction of the light passing through a hair, thus resulting in the appearance of metallic gloss. The more breaks in the hair core, the stronger the gloss. In moderately glossy hair, the defects in the core occupy about 20 to 30 percent of its volume, and in hair with strong gloss, the defects represent 60 to 90 percent of the core. Hair with an intact core has only a weak gloss, mostly due to the light reflection from the scaly cuticle.

Metallic sheen is also influenced by the ratio of thickness of the core to overall hair thickness. Glossy hair has a relatively thicker core in contrast to low-gloss hair, which has a thicker scaly cuticle.

All this said, there are other opinions, regarding the cause of metallic sheen. Stegacheva (2011) who studied hair gloss in Akhal-Tekes claims that it doesn't depend on the presence or absence of empty spaces in the core, but rather the degree of density and adhesion of the scales in the external layer.

Metallic sheen can be found in combination with any color, although most often it is in chestnut, buckskin, bay, or palomino. It is observed in some champagne horses, but phenotypically this gloss differs from the gloss you see in other colors—it isn't as noticeable. As of writing this has not been researched by scientists yet, and so it is only possible to assume that it is a consequence of the processes happening in a hair under the influence of the Champagne gene.

A permanent and prominent gloss of the hair should be recorded in breeding documents. In practice it is possible to use such descriptions as *golden chestnut*, *golden brown*, *golden bay*, *golden buckskin*, and *golden palomino*. The gloss of black hair looks rather silvery. Based on my own observations and data provided by others, permanent metallic gloss on black color is seen very rarely. It it also worth noting that black color, in general, is very rare in the "glossy" breeds mentioned in this section.

Inheritance of Metallic Sheen

Judging by the prevalence of hair gloss in a limited number of breeds with a shared origin, it is logical to assume that permanent, vibrant gloss is inherited—for example, metallic sheen occurs in breeds that were crossed with Akhal-Teke in the past (Russian Don and Budyonny). Also, when Stegacheva investigated the distribution of glossy hair in the Akhal-Teke breed, she found that it is not as widespread as has been reported in popular literature. According to her research, metallic sheen is absent in 63 percent of Akhal-Teke horses.

Other Horse Color Factors and Considerations

CHANGE OF COLOR

The color of a horse is exposed to changes of a varying degree during the animal's lifetime. Sometimes you hear about surprising cases of *color change* in a horse, with one color specified in breed registration or veterinary documents, which some years later cannot be recognized. However, hair color has a genetic basis and *cannot* fundamentally change in the same individual. That said, the color phenotype and hair's appearance *can* change.

Age-Dependent Color Change

Age-dependent color change, especially from foal to adult, is a relevant issue for horse breeders. Many owners try to determine the color of a horse when the animal is very young, but it is actually important not to hurry with such definition. That said, even an approximate knowledge of the typical changes of color as an equine ages can help with initial registration of foals and also in disputable cases of animal identification.

Foals, as a rule, are born quite pale, sometimes with light eyes and almost pink skin. Throughout this book I have mentioned common variations in foal colors. For example:

- *Chestnut foals* sometimes need nearly a month for pigmentation of skin and iris to develop.
- *Bay foals* usually have so little black hair on the legs that their body is often perceived to be a single color.
- *Seal brown foals* are born similar to bay only with darker legs and don't develop their characteristic color until after shedding their baby coat.
- *Smoky black foals* are ashy, frequently with a yellowish or beige shade, and even regular *black foals* have an ashy and usually light color to the hair coat.

In general, pale body color in a foal is a natural protective mechanism, camouflaging them from predators. The mane, tail, stomach, and the lower part of the legs are especially pale.

Occasionally foals can have primitive markings—a dorsal stripe, zebra bars, "wings," and also distinct stripes running down the sides, parallel to the ribs (see p. 22)—even when they are not dun. This is very similar to the Tabby pattern in cats. This unusual occurrence is especially characteristic for foals that eventually become black, dun, or smoky black. The markings disappear after the baby coat is shed.

Young horses shed their baby coats around one year of age, which is followed by the manifestation of their "adult" color. Some colors are "completed" later—for example, as we've discussed, appaloosa, gray, and sabino spotting changes over time. In dominant black horses, color becomes rather stable in approximately two to three years.

Foals shed, beginning around the eyes, then the muzzle, neck, and finally the entire body. During this time more blood flows to the skin, causing the animal to become weaker and more sensitive to cold.

The hair of an adult horse is darker because it is more saturated with pigment. Exceptions are champagne colors (p. 32), and also gray (p. 40), in which a strengthened chromogenesis (pigment production) occurs in the foal and young horse, and then gradually weakens or stops.

The true color of a horse can only be determined "easily" in foals from breeds that have a narrow range of colors (no more than four—bay, chestnut, black, and gray). However, even in such cases there can be mistakes. The most distinct changes from foal to adult are in horses that are dun, champagne, cream, silver, pearl, and gray. As for white markings, they can be quite large at birth and usually decrease in size with age. Dapples are not characteristic for foals.

On the other end of the age spectrum, change will again be noted as the horse becomes more senior. The hair of aging horses can lose its gloss and color saturation, and some develop gray hair, especially on the forehead and in the groin. Unlike genetically determined early graying, which precedes the formation of gray color, *age graying* usually begins after 25 years, although in some cases it is already occurring around 15 years of age.

Environmentally Influenced Color Change

Hair color depends also on climatic and weather conditions. In temperate climatic zones with considerable seasonal temperature changes, horses tend to show noticeable changes of color through the seasons (although it should be noted that you can also find horses that remain almost unchanged over the course of the year).

In winter in certain climates, equine hair becomes longer, rougher, thicker, and rises over the skin surface. It becomes dull and loses its gloss. As for color, it can become lighter or darker, depending on the specific animal. Some roan horses strongly darken in the winter, with their real color only visually identifiable in summer months. In fact, roan, dun, and grullo (among other colors determined by dilution genes) undergo the most noticeable changes during the year. Sometimes the mane, tail, lower part of the legs, nostrils, and groin can "brighten" so much in a certain season that correct color identification becomes almost impossible. Taking into account seasonal fluctuations, the optimal time for determination of color is the beginning of summer, when the winter coat is shed but the horse has not yet been exposed to intense sun.

Swimming in seawater makes hair brighter, while sunshine, sweat, and sand fade it out. Also, an excessive use of shampoo can make the coat dull.

Nutritionally Influenced Color Change

Food rich in protein stimulates pigment formation. Horses with considerable amounts of pheomelanin (bay, chestnut, buckskin, palomino, dun) are especially sensitive to dietary changes. Linseed oil, alfalfa, clover, and legume hay make hair darker. Many young chestnut foals become quite dark after shedding their baby coats from the large supply of maternal milk and a good spring diet.

In general dull color in the horse is indicative of a health or diet problem. Various parasites or a lack of proper feed, for example, can cause anemia and general weakness, leading to a poor hair coat.

Hormonally Influenced Color Change

Color is also influenced by the hormonal balance of the horse. This is noticeable in, for example, the Appaloosa breed (www.appaloosa.com), where stallions and pregnant mares have a more intense color than non-pregnant mares. The hormonal status is, in turn, influenced by a number of factors, including the general state of health, use of medications, and diet. There is, to some degree, also dependence on the sex of the animal. Goubaux and Barrier (1901) note that the hair of stallions is darker and they display more shades and gloss than geldings and mares.

Dappling and White Specks

Dapples often appear on horses that are in good condition and well fed. They are darker than the main shade of body hair. The exceptions are in champagne, dun, and roan colors, in which so-called *reverse dapples* (light on a dark background) are observed. Dapples can accompany any color and are present in particular along with countershading (see p. 70).

Seasonal dapples can be visible after the spring shed, and then disappear within months. Dapple configurations copy the patterns of capillaries under the skin and are most likely caused by temperature differences between various skin sites. Hair over warmer sites with more capillaries has an increased saturation with pigment or retains pigment longer, as is the case with gray color at a certain stage of graying.

It is possible that a tendency to develop dapples is hereditary since many horses do not have them even under the best living conditions.

It is also necessary to mention several kinds of *white specks*, which can be puzzling for horse owners. Pilsworth and Knottenbelt (2005) describe such phenomena as *leukotrichia*—topical hair decoloration, which can be caused intentionally by cold branding or unintentionally by injury, from a poorly fitting saddle, for example (Photo 187).

Spotted leukotrichia is characterized by small white specks that appear suddenly on the horse, and which occasionally are followed by baldness in those areas. The number of such specks can grow, although they do not increase in size. The usual location is on the neck and chest of the horse. Most often they are observed in the Arabian, Thoroughbred, and Shire breeds.

Reticular leukotrichia, which I mentioned in the discussion of giraffe markings on p. 76, looks like an irregular pattern of white hair, usually concentrated on the horse's topline. The affected site may sometimes be painful. This has been most often observed in Quarter Horses, Thoroughbreds, and Standardbreds. The causes are unclear, perhaps due to medications or herpes virus.

Leukoderma is the thinning of hair because of a localized skin injury. A *focal leukoderma* is a decoloration of a hair because of an illness. Some horses suffering from laminitis, for example, develop spots in the shape of water drops that are lighter than surrounding hair. The reasons for these phenomena are unknown, and color changes are usually irreversible.

Many sources state that all horses grow white hair on scars. The appearance or lack of such changes in color depends on the extent of the skin damage. Deep or extensive damage usually results in the growth of white hair.

LAVENDER FOAL SYNDROME

The lethal *Lavender Foal Syndrome (LFS)* occurs in Arabian foals from Egyptian lines, but other cases outside of that have been observed. In Western literature it started being described only at the end of the twentieth century (Bowling, Ruvinski, 2000), although it has been seen for at least 50 years. Lavender Foal Syndrome is a hereditary disease, but color features in afflicted foals actually are *not* an invariant sign in all cases.

The unusual phenotype manifests in newborn foals as a bluish color similar to lavender roses. The color can also sometimes be pink with a grayish shade, and cases of a light silvery or ashy color, and also cases of almost "normal" color, are known. The eyes are grayish-brown or bluish. Because of the color variations, some scientists have offered a more exact name for this syndrome: *Coat Color Dilution Lethal (CCDL)*.

This syndrome is considered lethal because all foals are born with serious neurologic abnormalities. After birth they show uncoordinated movements, spasms, opisthotonus (backward arching of the head), fast and random motions of the eyeballs, and they cannot stand up, roll onto the back, or assume the half-sitting position. Sometimes these foals can have normal suckling reflex but also joint rigidity and cornea ulcerations. The biochemical parameters in the blood are normal, but treatments are unsuccessful, and eventually the foals have to be euthanized.

A histological analysis of the liver is consistent with disturbances of lipid metabolism, and necrosis of the spleen and exhaustion of lymphocytes is evident. Sometimes an accumulation of a large amount of melanin in the hair roots and in the core of the individual hair is observed, consistent with the unusual color of affected foals. It is remarkable that a necropsy does not reveal structural abnormalities of the nervous system, despite the obvious pathological symptoms.

In essence LFS is a convulsive state. Foals that are not euthanized within the first few days develop symptoms characteristic for neonatal sepsis (bacterial bloodstream infection). Arabians of Egyptian origin also tend to develop neonatal epilepsy so we cannot exclude a possible connection between these two diseases.

Inheritance of Lavender Foal Syndrome

LFS is inherited as an autosomal recessive trait. In 2010 a group of scientists at Cornell University in Ithaca, New York, under the leadership of Samantha Brooks, identified the cause of this syndrome as a mutation in myosin Va gene (MYO5A) on the first chromosome. It is a deletion of one nucleotide in exon 30, leading to a change of the reading frame and a stop codon. MYO5A gene, and also genes coding for Ras-associated protein RAB27a (RAB27A) and Melanophilin (MLPH), are responsible for the synthesis of the substances participating in the movement of melanosomes to the periphery of cells, from where they are transferred to keratinocytes. This research led to the development of a DNA test for the LFS mutation. Based on this test, about 10 percent of Arabian horses of Egyptian origin are carriers. The test allows breeders to select suitable matings and avoid the occurrence of this syndrome in offspring. This test is important for Arabian breeders, worldwide.

CHIMERISM AND MOSAICISM

At the beginning of this book I touched on mutations, which are the basis of the development of new traits. However, not all mutations occur at the stage of formation of a spermatozoon or an ovum. In the early stages of embryogenesis a mutation can occur in any of the cells of the embryo, and such mutations are called *somatic*. The earlier such a mutation occurs, the larger the part of a tissue or organ carrying it. Individuals with sites of mutant tissues are called *mosaics* and the condition is known as *mosaicism*—it means cells within the same organism have a different genetic makeup. In cases when two or more impregnated ova merge into one, the resulting organism is called a *chimera* and the phenomenon is known as *chimerism*—the single organism has cells from two different zygotes, and therefore two different sets of DNA. Both mosaicism and chimerism are very rare; however, many mutations can remain hidden, so not all cases are obvious to the observer. When the mutation occurs in a gene responsible for color, the effect *is* usually noticeable.

I mentioned the chimera Catch A Bird on p. 75. In addition, two cases of a chimerism in horses in the United States are well described in references. The mutation manifested in the Quarter Horse stallion Dunbars Gold (1996) and a mare named Sharp One (1999) as brindling against chestnut color (see p. 73 for my discussion of brindling). In a foal produced by these horses, DNA testing showed that neither could have been the parents. Dunbars Gold had to be tested three times before it was possible to define his DNA. The first two times the analysis was carried out on hair from the mane, each time showing a different genotype, as though the samples belonged to different animals. The third analysis was carried out with blood and also yielded strange results: the sex-linked markers were characteristic for a mare and not for stallion. In other words the Y-chromosome was not found in the blood cells. Having compared results of several blood and hair tests, scientists concluded that the stallion had cells of *both* male and female individuals, and it was established that the stallion was a chimera. He had a chimeric composition of skin and hair, but internally he was a male, including sexual organs.

Analyses of DNA from hair of the mare Sharp One did not reveal chimerism; however, such signs were found in blood. Unlike the stallion, this mare had both genotypes from females. Subsequently, hair samples from dark and light stripes on her body were tested, and they also contained different types of female DNA. Even more interesting were the results of comparison between both DNAs from Sharp One with DNA from two of her foals, born in 2003 and 2004, respectively. Each foal originated from a different chimeric part of the mother. Thus, the genitals of the mare were chimeric, created at the same time from diverse sites of the embryo. It is a very interesting and extremely rare case.

CHAPTER 3:
Markings

White Markings on the Head and Legs

White markings on the head and legs of a horse are very common, consisting of clearly expressed white spots or areas of varying size and shape. They have long allowed us to more easily distinguish one horse from another! The skin under white markings is usually pink. Sometimes the white hair extends beyond the borders of the pink skin, and the pigmented skin then appears as a grayish border at the edges.

As mentioned, the size of white markings on the head and legs vary, and there are correlations between them. For example, it is often the case that when a horse has a large white marking on the face (bald), he will also have high stockings (see p. 90). Usually markings are more significant on hind legs than on front legs. The "splashiest" (largest) markings occur in chestnut horses, and in bay and black individuals heterozygous for the red factor (Ee). An exception to this rule is breeds in which the size of markings is influenced by other factors, such as selection (see p. 59).

HEAD

The following types of white head markings can be found:

- Faint star (Photo 188).
- Star (Photos 189 & 190).
- Blaze (Photos 191–194).
- Stripe (Photos 195 & 196).
- Snip (Photo 197 and see Photo 196).
- Bald face (Photos 198 & 199).

Head markings are more commonly found on the forehead of the horse than on the nose. White markings between the nostrils often correlate with markings on the forehead. In addition, observations of white markings on the head allow us to state that there are three main centers of depigmentation: the center of the forehead (star, faint star), the bridge of the nose (blaze, bald face), and a point between the nostrils (snip).

A *star* is a white spot on the forehead, and a very small one is called a *faint star*. The shape of a star varies—it can be round, oval, diamond-shaped, triangular, bent. Occasionally you can find stars of very unusual shapes. It is necessary to specify the shape and exact location and arrangement in all documents related to a horse.

A *blaze* is a white stripe going from the forehead and running down the nose bridge. It can have differing widths and lengths, reach the middle of the muzzle or nostrils or not, deviate to the right or left, be straight or coiled, connect to a star, be continuous or be interrupted. It quite often reaches the edge of the upper lip. A very thin blaze is called a *stripe*. A *snip* is a white marking on the upper lip between nostrils.

A *bald face* is a large white mark, passing from the horse's forehead to the nostrils and frequently to the edge of upper lip. It expands from the forehead over a considerable part of the nose bridge. To define it, the following principle is sometimes used: if the white head marking is wider than the nasal bones, it is a bald face, but if it is narrower, it is a blaze.

LEGS

A number of white markings can be found on the horse's legs. It can be difficult to characterize these by popular name, which can differ in use, so for descriptive reasons (you often hear or read terms such as *sock* and *stocking* in informal conversation and equine-related literature), I will not "name" the various markings first, but rather explain the typical presentations commonly used in registration and veterinary documents for means of identification.

The leg is white:

- On the coronet above the hoof (Photo 200).
- On the pastern (see Photo 200).
- On the fetlock (Photo 201).
- Above the fetlock but below the knee or hock (Photo 202).
- To or above the knee or hock (Photo 203).

The upper boundary of such markings is often uneven. The white mark on the coronet above the hoof can be interrupted or represented by a dashed line of white specks. White markings on the legs can have "extensions" in the form of narrow, ascending stripes, which can be connected to or disconnected from other white markings. They can be not white at all, but roaned instead.

Sometimes pigmented spots "inside" white leg markings can be noted (it is my feeling these should be specified in physical descriptions of the horse). In certain cases they can help identify the horse's color—for example, if the spot is black on a horse with a red trunk and high white stockings (to or above the knee or hock) on all legs, the color of the horse is bay.

The hoof on the leg with a white marking can be partially or completely depigmented, depending on the location and arrangement of the marking. It should be noted, however, that a foal can be born with dark skin on the coronet on all four legs but with light hooves, and then after a while, start growing dark horn. This kind of age-dependent change of pigmentation is similar to the gradual accumulation of pigment in the hair of the maturing horse (see p. 82).

White markings are more frequently seen on the hind legs than on the front legs, and appear more often on the horse's left side than on his right side. Interestingly, it has also been observed that in the majority of breeds, male horses are likely to have more (in number) white markings than mares, and on average, their size is larger. (However, there are also exceptions—for example, the Akhal-Teke breed.)

INHERITANCE OF WHITE MARKINGS

The propagation of white markings in horses is the consequence of domestication. They occur frequently in domestic horses and practically in all breeds. There are a few breeds (Friesian, Menorquin, Cleveland Bay) in which breeders select *against* white markings. In some other breeds, white markings are admissible, but they cannot exceed a certain size (for example, in the Rocky Mountain Horse). White markings are not characteristic for native breeds (such as the Dartmoor and Exmoor Pony). Appearances of faint stars have been noted in separate cases in the Przewalski horses in Askania-Nova. An explanation could be inbreeding and/or admixture of domestic horses.

The attitudes of horse owners and breeders toward white markings within their preferred breeds differ. In Friesians, only a small faint star is allowed on the head, as in Norwegian Fjords (although in practice, such horses almost do not exist). Any Cleveland Bays with markings are excluded from breeding, and owners of Suffolk Punch and Percheron breeds also prefer horses without. Very few markings are present in the Standardbred, Russian Trotter, Kabardin, and Karachai breeds. At the same time, owners of Hackneys, Clydesdales, Shires, and Welsh Ponies prefer animals with large stockings, sometimes extending all the way to the stomach.

The distinction between white markings and weakly expressed sabino (see p. 47) or other types of spotting is difficult. The majority of registries in the United

States consider a horse spotted when white markings appear outside of imaginary lines drawn:

- Through the middle of the knee and hock, parallel to the ground.
- From the corner of the mouth to the outside corner of the eye to the base of the ears, down the opposite outside corner of the eye and corner of the mouth, and then under the chin.

It is my opinion that a horse can be considered *spotted* when he has a white spot of a certain size, shape, and location (large, asymmetrical, located on one side) on the stomach, as mentioned earlier in this book (see p. 47). Horses with extensive white markings on the head and legs should be simply considered *strongly marked*.

White markings from the point of view of genetics are at the same time both a *qualitative* and *quantitative* trait. When considering the mechanism of their inheritance, it is necessary to talk separately about their presence/absence, and about their quantity and size. Throughout the history of studying horse colors, there were three main views on the nature of white marks:

1   Partial albinism (Dyurst, Rouillier, 1936).
2   Spotting (Lovern, 1987).
3   A special phenomenon, not connected with either Option 1 or 2 (Schwark, 1985).

Leg and head markings have a polygenic type of inheritance. Most likely their size can be the result of a random event involving incomplete distribution of melanocytes in the body. It is consistent with observations in cloned horses, which differ in the size of their markings from the original animal, but their basic arrangements coincide. Woolf (1990), studying markings in Arabian horses, established that they are defined 68 percent controlled by genetics, and the remaining 32 percent depend on other factors. He also made the assumption that melanoblasts (the precursor cell of a melanocyte) differ in their migration, depending on alleles "E" or "e," and the allele "e" has another gene linked to it that is responsible for existence of white marks. This could explain the obvious connection between the size of white markings and red horses. Another possibility is that the "e" allele can have a pleiotropic effect and affect not only melanin type, but also melanocyte migration. There could also be an observable effect of some gene(s) located on the X-chromosome because of the observed differences between sexes. The asymmetry of markings can be caused by pre-natal factors.

The most widespread factor influencing white markings is the complex of the genes controlling sabino spotting. Carriers of Sabino genes that are not spotted usually have strongly expressed white markings. I will repeat that sabino spotting has a polygenic type of inheritance. Also, markings are caused by genes controlling other types of spotting, such as frame overo (bald face), tobiano (socks and stockings), and splashed white (blaze with a star, bald face, socks and stockings).

According to Chetverikova's research (2001), the quantity and degree of expression of white markings against specific colors are distributed as follows (listed from most significant to least):

1 Double cream
2 Palomino
3 Chestnut
4 Gray
5 Black
6 Buckskin
7 Bay, dark bay, dark buckskin

White markings are inherited from the sire with a coefficient of 0.64 percent, and 0.57 percent from the dam. Yanova (1999) studied the mechanism of inheritance of white markings in 1,168 Thoroughbred and Budyonny horses. She noticed that with an increase in the size of head markings the number of leg markings also increased. Horses with a bald face always had stockings. If there were not markings on the head, there typically weren't markings on the legs.

When breeding animals without markings in a closed group (among themselves), white markings appeared in 48 percent of the offspring, and 16 percent had markings on the head and legs. When crossing individuals who had markings on the head and legs in a closed group, 100 percent of their offspring also had them, but their localization was uneven. The offspring of parents either without markings at all or with limited ones did not have extensive markings. From these observations, Yanova draws the conclusion that the emergence of white markings and their size are influenced by gene modifiers, and markings on the legs and head are inherited differently.

According to Rieder, et al (2008), heritability of markings is high (> 0.5), and the inheritance is polygenic, based on research in Freiberger horses. Studies by Swiss, American, and Australian scientists carried out on Freiberger horses and published at the end of 2013 found that KIT and MITF genes are responsible for white marks. An accumulation of mutations in these genes in the same horse leads to an increase of white hair. The size of markings is also influenced by the recessive allele "e" of MC1R (Extension).

Non-Standard Markings

Besides the usual white markings on the head and legs, other white and/or colored markings can be found on other parts of the horse's body. They are conditionally called *non-standard* because they are less common and have a different basis.

ACQUIRED MARKINGS

So-called *acquired markings* are formed as a result of injuries from grazes, burns, frostbite, and other damage to the horse's body. One common cause is improperly fitting equipment, especially the saddle. White hair grows in affected areas after extended time or repeated trauma (see p. 84 where I discussed this earlier).

CHUBARI SPOTS

Chubari spots are oval or round, white or whitish spots, usually about the size of an egg. They occur in gray horses but should not be confused with dapples. Chubari spots are randomly scattered on the body of a horse and have sharply delineated borders. With the process of graying, the markings eventually become invisible, having merged with the "white" background.

Chubari spots are most often observed in Thoroughbred and Akhal-Teke horses. Although these markings have a genetic basis, their nature or potential connection with the Gray gene is not clear.

BIRDCATCHER MARKINGS AND BIRDCATCHER TICKING

Birdcatcher markings received the name commonly used to describe this phenomenon from the Thoroughbred stallion Irish Birdcatcher. They consist of round, white specks with sharp edges (sometimes called *flakes*) scattered irregularly on the horse's body (Photo 204). They can appear on a horse with age (foals do not have them) and can also disappear over time. Their number seldom increases, but sometimes they can increase in size.

Birdcatcher markings can either be located randomly or concentrated on any part of the body—the shoulder, side, topline. Flakes are often concentrated on the croup, especially on the top, and are surrounded quite often by weak roaning.

These marks are observed in particular breeding lines, and may have a hereditary nature. There are some who feel these markings are controlled by genes that are responsible for spotted sabino color. It has been observed that horses with these spots almost always have white markings on the head and legs (Photo 92).

Birdcatcher markings can be found in almost all breeds of horses; most often in Arabians and Thoroughbreds.

Western scientists also recently discovered *Birdcatcher ticking*. These white specks of very small size are concentrated in the groin, on the croup, hips, withers, along the topline, on the head and neck, and near the base of the tail. Sometimes the ticking is expressed so strongly that it may be mistaken for the roan color, especially in some heavy draft breeds.

Markings of Other Colors

BLOOD MARKINGS

Blood markings (see Photo 99) are represented by big red or brown (rarely black) spots and are found only in gray horses. Typically blood markings are found on the horse's shoulders, but sometimes on other parts of the body, as well. Blood markings can appear as a cluster of spots that form a colored area that doesn't turn gray with age. Their size varies, from several tiny specks to a sizeable colored area that covers a shoulder, side of the head, or other section of the horse. The color of blood marks does not correspond to the horse's base color.

There used to be an opinion that blood marks are the consequence of an injury, but it is now established that it is a *congestion of pigment*. These marks are rare and occur mainly in Arabian horses.

DARK MARKINGS

Occasionally you can find large *dark marks* on a horse's body, which—according to Sponenberg (2009)—are similar to birthmarks on people. Their emergence is spontaneous. These spots are rare but all the same can be found on representatives from practically any breed of any color. This said, Sponenberg notes that they are most often seen in combination with bay color and located on a shoulder.

YELLOW SPOTS

Yanova (2003) mentions observation of separate *yellow spots*, also using a term that means "gray-haired-yellow." Unlike white markings, yellow spots are characterized by weak hair pigmentation. They are extremely rare, observed only on chestnut and bay horses, and further details related to their nature is, as of writing, unknown.

BIDER MARKINGS

In 2007, Japanese and Mongolian scientists found unusual markings on Przewalski horses and native domestic horses of Mongolian origin. These markings are called *bider* by the Mongolian nomads. They have the appearance of dark stains on the horse's shoulder blades, shoulder joints, or base of the neck.

Bider markings can be of any size and have any structure. The underlying skin is also darker than the rest of the body. They are symmetrical in placement, appearing on both sides of the horse's body.

Bider markings are very rare and observed in approximately 1 percent of Mongolian horses. According to the Japanese and Mongolian scientists from the study, the marks have not been seen in other breeds. I have heard from colleagues, however, that they have also been found in the Bashkir breed and it is said they have been observed in the Yakut horse. They are heritable: It is supposed there is a dominant allele Bi (from "bider") that is responsible for them.

CHAPTER 4:
Hair Features

General Features

HAIR THICKNESS, DENSITY, AND FEATHERS

In addition to the colors and markings described in the previous chapters, I am now going to discuss the hair of the equine itself in a bit more detail. Let me repeat what I explained back at the beginning of the book: the hair in horses can be divided into body, guard, and tactile. The *core* and *root* of a white hair is thicker than in a colored hair; however, the density is lower. In addition, the pink skin under a white hair is thinner compared to skin that is pigmented.

On most horses, the mane and tail are dense and quite long. They are especially dense in so-called *baroque breeds*, such as the Friesian, Andalusian, and Lusitano (Photos 205 & 206). Dense manes are also found in ponies, draft horses, and many native breeds (Photo 207).

A distinctive feature of some breeds is what is called *feathers*—long dense hair on the lower legs and fetlocks (Photo 208). Breeds with feathers include the Friesian, Shire, Clydesdale, Belgian, Russian Heavy Draft, Vladimir Heavy Draft, Gypsy Horse, Fell Pony, and Dales Pony. The genetic nature of feathers is not known as of the time of writing; however, according to some information, strongly expressed feathers dominate over weakly expressed.

WHORLS

Horses tend to feature various types of *whorls* (swirls) on their body coat (Photos 209 & 210). These are patches of hair that grow in the opposite direction of surrounding hair. In Russia and some other countries, distinctive whorls help identify an animal, especially in the case of a lack of white markings. The most common whorls are located on the forehead between the eyes. You can find horses that carry more than one.

The Polish scientists Gorecka, Golonka, Sloniewski, Jaworski, and Jezierski (2006) investigated the heritability of whorls on the head of the Polish Koniks divided into groups, depending on the features of arrangement (on eye level, above, below) and configuration of whorls. Results showed that this qualitative trait is inherited quite regularly. In 2007 Gorecka, Golonka, Chruszczewski, and Jezierski continued the research and found correlations between the shape and location of whorls and behavioral features, as well as individual character traits. It is interesting to compare this data with the thesis of Linda Tellington-Jones in her book *Getting in TTouch with Your Horse*, as she came to similar conclusions.

In 2008 the Irish scientists Murphy and Arkins found a relationship between the direction of hair in whorls with the preference of horses to pick up the canter from a certain leg. This was further supported by studies in left- and right-handed humans, which also showed a correlation of "handedness" with the direction of hair growth. The mechanism of development of these features in humans is unknown, but probably it could reflect embryogenetic communication between the development of the nervous system—including distinctions between cerebral hemispheres—and arrangement of hair follicles. It is possible that these traits are also interconnected in horses.

Curly Hair

Curly hair is an interesting feature that is very rare in horses. On curly individuals both the body hair and guard hair are involved (Photos 211 & 212). Curls can take on various forms: from hard ringlets to smooth waves. Winter hair curls more strongly than summer hair. It is characteristic that during a spring shed, *both* the body hair and guard hair are replaced.

Curly-haired horses are not common, but at the same time, you can find them all over the world—for example, in both Russia and Argentina. Native Americans in the United States considered curly-haired horses sacred and they were reserved for leaders and healers.

According to American scientists there are two types of curliness, which have different genetic mechanisms. There is *recessive* curliness controlled by the "Cr-Rc" gene located in a hypothetical Curly Recessive locus. This type of curliness is the most widespread among horses and has been found in the Percheron, Missouri Foxtrotter, Appaloosa, Quarter Horse, Paint Horse, Morgan, Paso Fino, Tennessee Walker, and Arabian breeds. The *dominant* type of curliness is controlled by the "Cr-Dc" gene located in the putative locus of Curly Dominant. Horses homozygous for this allele have more expressed curliness than heterozygotes. This allele is generally found in horses of Asian origin—for example in the Lokai—and also in many curly horses in the Western hemisphere. In the Lokai breed there is the so-called *Farkhor's line* that produces curly-headed horses. In any case, curly hair seems to have a rather complex mechanism of inheritance, which is not surprising. For example, it is known that curly hair in dogs is controlled by alleles at three separate genes.

The majority of curly horses in the Western hemisphere originated from Iberian horses. Data exists that states that the first curly horses appeared in the United States among animals owned by Sioux and Crow tribes. There is a breed called the American Bashkir Curly Horse (www.abcregistry.org), but it would seem their origin from Bashkir is a very disputable question, as the real Bashkir horses in Russia do not have curly hair any more often than other breeds. The registry credits a photo of a curly-coated Russian Bashkir from a 1938 issue of *Nature* magazine as the likely inspiration behind the name, while acknowledging there is evidence curly-haired horses had already been in North America since the early 1800s.

Some representatives of the Zabaikal breed have curly hair. Curly Zabaikal foals are less viable than their non-curly counterparts, and in the past, breeders considered curly hair a sign of degeneration and eliminated such foals. The issue, however, has not been eradicated from the breed yet. Perhaps, this indicates an incomplete penetrance of the gene responsible for the curling hair in the Zabaikal. It is possible that it is linked to a lethal gene or has a pleiotropic action.

There are manifestations even of the same type of curliness that vary. In horses with the dominant type, curls are expressed weakly and guard hair usually does not shed. Under certain conditions they can be mistaken for non-curly horses. Scott (2004) describes horses with recessive curliness. In the winter their hair has strongly curled ringlets and in the spring they become softer and have a wavy appearance. Sometimes they go through a phase of baldness when they shed, which occasionally also occurs with the guard hair. Although it has been believed that the curly hair grows from a spiral-bended follicle, Scott found that the follicles of such hair are straight. Probably, the hair starts twisting *after* growing out of the follicle.

In popular horse literature you often read that curly horses, especially representatives of the American Bashkir Curly breed, are hypoallergenic, and therefore, allergic horse fans should have no problem interacting with them. More recent research, however, has revealed that such claims may be exaggerated, as people can be allergic not only to horse hair, but also to skin dandruff, as both contain numerous potential allergens. Currently The International Curly Horse Organization (www.ichocurlyhorses.com) continues to pursue research in this area.

Hairlessness

Horses without hair are incredibly rare. Two relatively recent cases include a Palomino foal (born in 2005) and an Akhal-Teke foal (born in 2002). The first had a dark pink skin and the second had dark gray skin. Based on information from Akhal-Teke breeders, such foals have been observed in the past (one of the first cases was recorded in 1938), but there does not appear to be information available describing how many. In published literature it is possible to read about Naked Foal Syndrome (Hairless Foal Syndrome) in Akhal-Tekes. Allegedly, it is inherited as an autosomal recessive trait. The affected animals either do not survive for long or develop serious deformities. There is a DNA test for the NFS gene responsible for Naked Foal Syndrome.

Pigment Distribution Features

Studies of structural features of hair by Yanova (146) found that white hair is thicker on the head and legs and that hair strands have the following features, depending on color and location on the body of a horse:

Table 7.

Color	Structure of Hair on Body	Structure of Hair on Head
White gray	Thick, rigid strands Cortical layer transparent	Brittle, loose strands Cortical layer transparent
Dark gray	Rigid strands, sometimes discontinuous	Rigid strands, sometimes discontinuous
Graying on body	Central strands pale, brittle, often discontinuous, may have pigment residues on end	Central strands pale, brittle, often discontinuous, may have pigment residues on end
Trauma, cut	Strand thin, discontinuous, pigment residues on end	Strand thin, discontinuous, pigment residues on end
Additional markings	Dark or pale strand, with brittle central part	Dark or pale strand, with brittle central part
Markings on head		Rigid strands, can be pale or often with pale tip, brittle, dark base
Markings on legs	Transparent hair, may have yellow streaks in the hair bulb, sometimes strand destroyed or thin	

According to Yanova's assumption, reduced blood supply to the skin on the extremities can be the reason for white hair on legs (the colorless cortical layer and discontinuous strands are "defects" of a sort). Sometimes it is not white but completely transparent hair, through which skin, usually pink, appears. Such hair is observed mainly between the nostrils and on body spots.

It is Yanova's claim that when it comes to the inheritance of structural features of white hair, the maternal type of hair structure prevails on white marks on the head.

Color: A mealy chestnut, with a light mane and tail, and a very noticeable pangaré pattern on the nose and legs, merging with white markings.

Expressed alleles: ee** Pa^{+*}

Breed: unknown

PHOTOGRAPHER: VERA KURSKAYA

PHOTO 165

Color: A bay dun with pangaré and a noticeable dark mask and ear rims.

Expressed alleles: E* A* Dn^{+*}, Pa^{+}

Breed: Shetland Pony-Przewalski Horse cross

PHOTOGRAPHER: EKATHERINA BELIKOVA

PHOTO 166

Color: A bay dun with pangaré. Note the white areas around the eyes, nostrils, and on the right front leg

Expressed alleles: E* A* Dn^{+*}, Pa^{+}

Breed: Exmoor Pony (Ricky, owned by Vanessa Bee, founder of the International Horse Agility Club, www.thehorseagilityclub.com)

PHOTOGRAPHER: BOBY ATKINS (FROM THE HORSE AGILITY HANDBOOK AND USED BY PERMISSION.)

PHOTO 167

PHOTO 168

Color: Buckskin brindle. The stripes are rather subtle.

Expressed alleles: E* A* C^{cr}C, Brindle genes(?)

Breed: American Paint Horse (Stars Stripes of Kala, owned by Janelle Osborne, Justa Brindle Horse Farm, www.justabrindlehorse.com)

PHOTOGRAPHER: JANELLE OSBORNE

PHOTO 169

Color: Champagne brindle—probably gold champagne.

Expressed alleles: ee** Ch*, Brindle genes

Breed: American Paint Horse (One of A Kind Vanzi, owned by Janelle Osborne, Justa Brindle Horse Farm, www.justabrindlehorse.com)

PHOTOGRAPHER: JANELLE OSBORNE

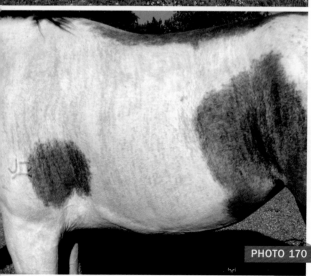

PHOTO 170

Color: Tovero brindle.

Expressed alleles: To*, Sabino genes(?), Brindle genes(?)

Breed: American Paint Horse (Justa Cleverly Punkd, owned by Janelle Osborne, Justa Brindle Horse Farm, www.justabrindlehorse.com)

PHOTOGRAPHER: JANELLE OSBORNE

Color: Black rabicano. This horse has pronounced whitening in the tail and on the ribs.

Expressed alleles: E* aa, Rabicano genes

Breed: Egyptian Arabian (The Night Mist, owned by Richard Teeters, Poets Manor Arabians, www. poetsmanorarabians.com)

PHOTOGRAPHER: RICHARD TEETERS

PHOTO 171

Detail: Rabicano markings on the side of a dark chestnut horse.

Breed: Arabian

PHOTOGRAPHER: VERA KURSKAYA

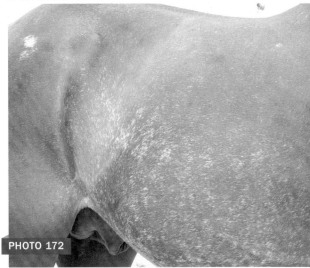

PHOTO 172

Color: A rare combination of roan with rabicano. This mare's foals apparently weakly manifest roan color.

Expressed alleles: ee** Rn*

Breed: Russian Don-Soviet Draft cross

PHOTOGRAPHER: NADYEZHDA SEREBRYAKOVA

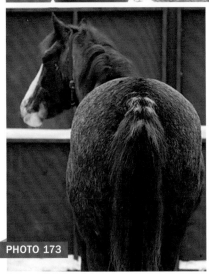

PHOTO 173

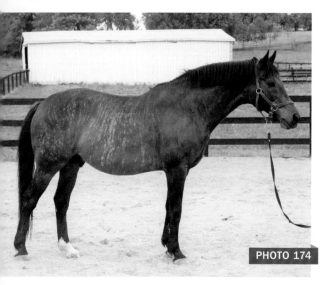

PHOTO 174

Color: The "Catch A Bird" phenomenon on dark bay (brown).

Expressed alleles: E* A*

Breed: Brazilian Warmblood (Natal Clasi, owned by Vivian Hill, Stonybrook Farm)

PHOTOGRAPHER: VIVIAN HILL

PHOTO 175

Color: The same horse as in Photo 174. The lighting highlights his color differently.

Expressed alleles: E* A*

Breed: Brazilian Warmblood (Natal Clasi, owned by Vivian Hill, Stonybrook Farm)

PHOTOGRAPHER: VIVIAN HILL

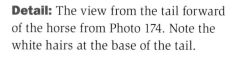

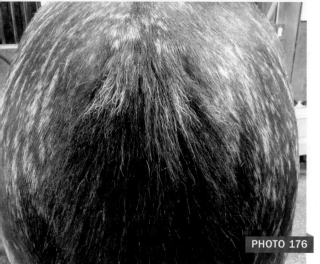

PHOTO 176

Detail: The view from the tail forward of the horse from Photo 174. Note the white hairs at the base of the tail.

PHOTOGRAPHER: VIVIAN HILL

Color: A black bay frame overo with giraffe marks or lacing. Frame overo is rather minimally expressed—on the head only. Note that the horse has graying above the eye—the same as the Karachai mare shown in Photo 180 that possesses at least on "G" allele.

Expressed alleles: EE Aa OvN (confirmed by DNA test)

Breed: American Miniature Horse (Pacific Lady Godiva, owned by Joanne Abramson, Pacific Pintos Miniature Horse Farm, pacificpintos.com)

PHOTOGRAPHER: JOANNE ABRAMSON

PHOTO 177

Detail: An aerial view of the same Miniature Horse from Photo 177, showing the extent of the giraffe markings.

PHOTOGRAPHER: JOANNE ABRAMSON

PHOTO 178

Detail: The same aerial view a year before Photo 178 was taken—note the progressive change in coloration over time.

PHOTOGRAPHER: JOANNE ABRAMSON

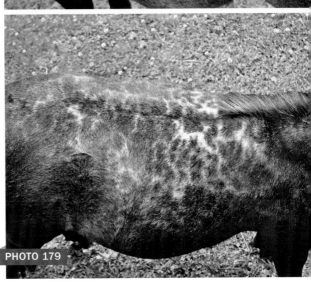

PHOTO 179

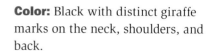

Color: Black with distinct giraffe marks on the neck, shoulders, and back.

Expressed alleles: Ee aa Gg or GG (DNA test failed to confirm the Gray gene of this horse several times)

Breed: Karachai Horse

PHOTOGRAPHER: VERA KURSKAYA

PHOTO 180

Detail: The head and neck of the horse the horse in Photo 180, showing both the graying effect and the giraffe markings.

PHOTOGRAPHER: VERA KURSKAYA

PHOTO 181

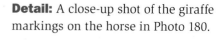

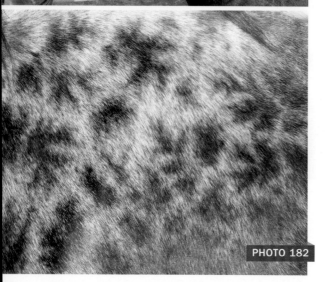

Detail: A close-up shot of the giraffe markings on the horse in Photo 180.

PHOTOGRAPHER: VERA KURSKAYA

PHOTO 182

Color: False dun on chestnut. The horse has a dorsal stripe, zebra bars on the legs, and the mane, tail, and lower parts of legs are darker than the barrel—the the same primitive markings red dun horses usually have.

Expressed alleles: ee nd1* (DNA test confirmed the absence of Dn$^+$ allele but was performed before the test for non-dun1 allele was available)

Breed: Russian Don

PHOTOGRAPHER: NATALYA GERASIMOVA

PHOTO 183

Detail: The dorsal stripe of the horse in Photo 183. It is not as well-pronounced as that of a dun horse but it is more defined than you would see with slight countershading. Unfortunately, such details are very difficult to visually indentify.

PHOTOGRAPHER: NATALYA GERASIMOVA

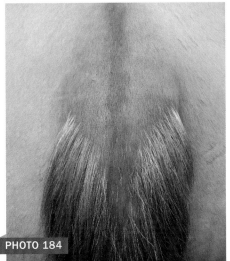

PHOTO 184

Color: Light golden palomino with metallic sheen typical for some breeds.

Expressed alleles: ee** C^{cr}C

Breed: Akhal-Teke (Kevlin, owned by Jack and Tish Saare of Pleasant Grove Akhal-Tekes, www.pleasantgroveakhaltekes.com)

PHOTOGRAPHER: SUSAN ARNOT

PHOTO 185

PHOTO 186

Color: Golden "Wild" buckskin. This horse is a good example of the special metallic sheen that is considered to be not a result of good grooming but an inherited trait.

Expressed alleles: E* A* C^{cr}C

Breed: Akhal-Teke (Asil Tumay, bred by Cascade Gold Akhal-Tekes, www. cgakhaltekes.com, owned by Shannon Mayfield)

PHOTOGRAPHER: KAREN WEGENHENKEL

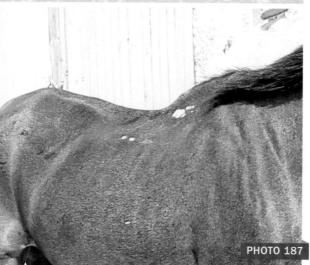

PHOTO 187

Detail: White spots, probably caused by an ill-fitting saddle.

PHOTOGRAPHER: VERA KURSKAYA

PHOTO 188

Detail: A faint star.

PHOTOGRAPHER: VERA KURSKAYA

Detail: A small star, high on the horse's forehead.

PHOTOGRAPHER: VERA KURSKAYA

PHOTO 189

Detail: A bold, well-placed star.

PHOTOGRAPHER: ANNA MURATOVA

PHOTO 190

Detail: A broad blaze.

PHOTOGRAPHER: GREGORY SOLOVIEV

PHOTO 191

PHOTO 192

Detail: A blaze that incorporates the nose and chin.

Breed: Amercian Quarter Horse (Sheza Big Chex Too, owned by Cheri Wallis of Wallis Performance Horses, www.wallisperformancehorses.com)

PHOTOGRAPHER: KAYLA STARNES
(WWW.KSTARNESPHOTOGRAPHY.COM)

PHOTO 193

Detail: A broad blaze that covers the lips on this gold champagne horse.

Breed: American Paint Horse (CC Sugar and Spice, owned by Carolyn Shepard)

PHOTOGRAPHER: CAROLYN SHEPARD

PHOTO 194

Detail: An unusually shaped blaze.

Breed: American Paint Horse (Roosters Dun It Smart, owned by Susan Gay, bred by Cheri Wallis of Wallis Performance Horses, www. wallisperformancehorses.com)

PHOTOGRAPHER: KAYLA STARNES
(WWW.KSTARNESPHOTOGRAPHY.COM)

Detail: A star and narrow stripe.

PHOTOGRAPHER: VERA KURSKAYA

PHOTO 195

Detail: A star, stripe, and snip between the nostrils.

Breed: Egyptian Arabian (Samsara, owned by Poets Manor Arabians, www.poetsmanorarabians.com)

PHOTOGRAPHER: RICHARD TEETERS

PHOTO 196

Detail: A small, pinkish snip.

PHOTOGRAPHER: VERA KURSKAYA

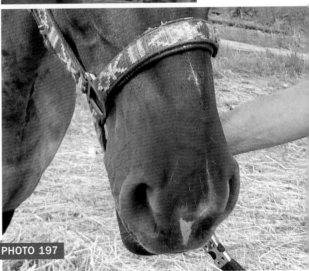

PHOTO 197

PHOTO 198

Detail: A bald face, partly involving the eye, with white eyelashes.

PHOTOGRAPHER: VERA KURSKAYA

PHOTO 199

Detail: An expansive bald face, extending far over the eye and incorporating most of the nose, lips, and chin.

PHOTOGRAPHER: COURTESY OF THE APHA/ PAINT HORSE JOURNAL (APHA.COM)

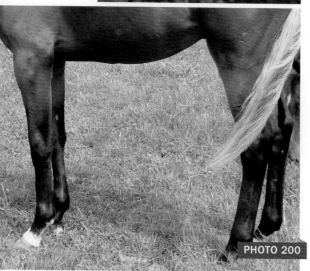

PHOTO 200

Detail: White on the coronet, above the hoof, and onto the pastern.

PHOTOGRAPHER: VERA KURSKAYA

Detail: White on the fetlock.

PHOTOGRAPHER: VERA KURSKAYA

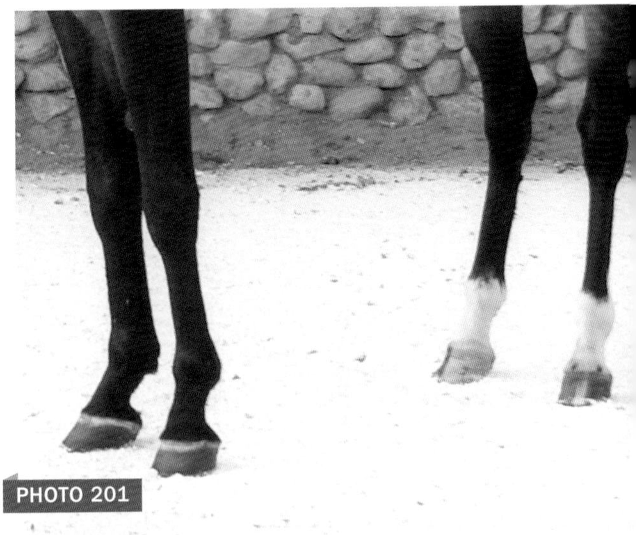

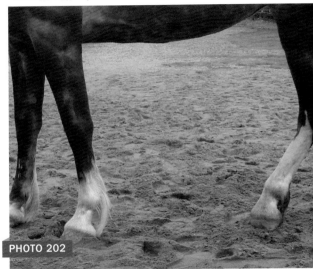

PHOTO 201

Detail: White above the fetlock but below the knee or hock.

PHOTOGRAPHER: VERA KURSKAYA

PHOTO 202

Detail: White to or above the knee or hock.

Breed: American Quarter Horse/ American Paint Horse (Dazzling Top Gun, owned by Cheri Wallis of Wallis Performance Horses, www. wallisperformancehorses.com)

PHOTOGRAPHER: KAYLA STARNES
(WWW.KSTARNESPHOTOGRAPHY.COM)

PHOTO 203

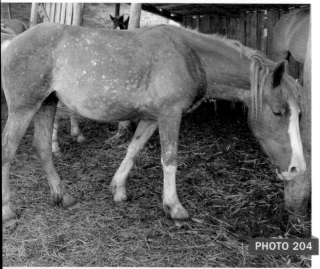

PHOTO 204

Color: Chestnut with a flaxen mane and tail, and a white face with the marking extending to the nostrils. Note the birdcatcher markings on what appears to be a sabino background.

Expressed alleles: ee**, Sabino genes

Breed: Unknown

PHOTOGRAPHER: JULIA KRASOUSKAYA

PHOTO 205

Detail: Thick, long manes are characteristic of Iberian breeds, such as the Lusitano.

PHOTOGRAPHER: YEGUADA PACO MARTI

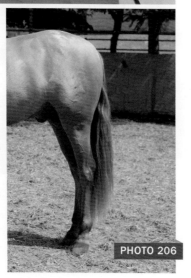

PHOTO 206

Detail: Dense tails, too, are typical of these breeds.

PHOTOGRAPHER: YEGUADA PACO MARTI

Detail: Many pony and native breeds also exhibit thick manes and tails.

PHOTOGRAPHER: VERA KURSKAYA

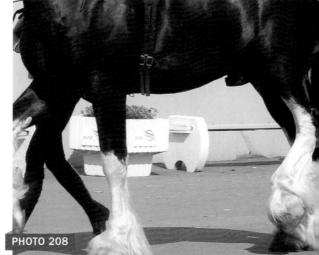

PHOTO 207

Detail: Striking white feathers on a Shire horse.

PHOTOGRAPHER: VERA KURSKAYA

PHOTO 208

Detail: A whorl on the crest of a Budyonny horse.

PHOTOGRAPHER: VERA KURSKAYA

PHOTO 209

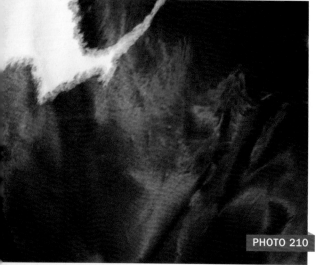

PHOTO 210

Detail: Note the various whorls on the chest of this American Paint Horse.

Breed: American Paint Horse (Roosters Dun It Smart, owned by Susan Gay, bred by Cheri Wallis of Wallis Performance Horses, www. wallisperformancehorses.com)

PHOTOGRAPHER: KAYLA STARNES (WWW.KSTARNESPHOTOGRAPHY.COM)

PHOTO 211

Color: Curly hair on a breed known for this trait.

Expressed alleles: C R^{c}*(?) or C D^{c}*(?)

Breed: American Bashkir Curly Horse

PHOTOGRAPHER: AMERICAN BASHKIR CURLY REGISTRY (WWW.ABCREGISTRY.ORG)

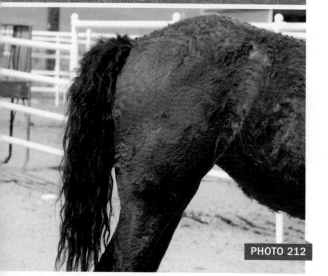

PHOTO 212

Detail: Note the extreme wave in the tail hair.

Breed: American Bashkir Curly Horse

PHOTOGRAPHER: AMERICAN BASHKIR CURLY REGISTRY (WWW.ABCREGISTRY.ORG)

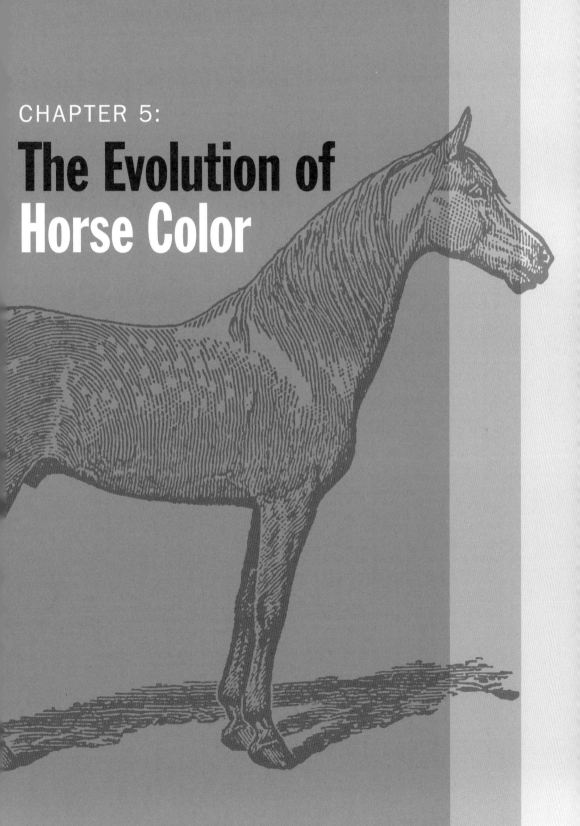

CHAPTER 5:
The Evolution of
Horse Color

A variety of the equine colors we see now are the result of domestication. Colors of modern domestic horses appeared gradually and expanded in different regions differently.

The coloring of a wild animal carries out an especially practical function: it serves for camouflaging. The domestic horse had a wild ancestor that, for certain, did *not* have a rich scale of colors. The transition to modern colors came from initial "Wild" coloring, and is both a result of spontaneous mutations and the selection of new markings. It is estimated that domestication of horses happened in the middle of the fourth millennium BC. Emergence of different colors and spotting patterns, and their purposeful propagation, is a part of domestication. A recent example could be the development of small white head markings in Przewalski horses bred in captivity (see p. 91).

In one of the articles Vitt (2003) writes about the English colonel Hamilton Smith who collected data at the beginning of the fourteenth century on various breeds of horses. Smith hypothesized that each breed of domestic horse went back to five primary "roots," which were initially different from each other in color: bay, white, spotted, black, and dun. He even named the distinctive characteristic of the dun color as "dark stripes on the body" (obviously, dorsal and zebra stripes). Witt reports that Darwin rejected Smith's version about a multiple-root origin of domestic horse breeds; however, through his own reasoning concluded the "probability of an origin of all existing races from one dun, more or less striped form." Developing the thoughts of Darwin and including current available data, Witt theorizes that at the time of domestication the horse had "Wild" coloring with a dark stripe along the back.

Tesio (1958) assumes his own classification of colors, according to which bay and chestnut are base colors. Further, he claims: "But in nature there are horses with a purely white coat. Such a horse is born white, and its skin is not black but pink. Therefore, before appearance of humans there were several populations of horses, which differed in three primary colors: bay with dark skin, chestnut with dark skin, and white with pink skin....We can be sure about one thing: there were only three natural colors—bay, chestnut, and white with pink skin."

It is possible that Tesio's reasoning was affected by the fact that he was engaged in the breeding of Thoroughbred horses, among which, especially at that time, the most common colors were bay and chestnut, and to a lesser extent black and gray. Further, Tesio continues to debate that humans bred a white mare to a bay or chestnut stallion and received a spotted foal. According to Tesio, humans then continued further breeding work with repeated crossing of spotted horses with non-spotted, causing a gradual reduction of the size of white spots on the body. Then breeders determined that some stallions with small white markings were quite powerful and could be used to improve the breeding stock, and thus maintained such white markings by selection.

Studying the evolution of colors is challenging. It is very difficult (or impossible) to obtain from the past written or visual resources possessing authentic data on what colors were found in horses living many centuries ago. The exact meaning of the diverse terminology used to describe the horse in various parts of the world is difficult to correlate with real colors, and artworks are often very conditional and subjective, and do not focus on strictly copying reality.

The recent development of DNA extraction methods from fossil remains of horses has finally provided an unbiased approach to obtaining objective information. This method allows researchers to claim quite accurate results, as the genetic code is the universal "language" that determines features and characteristics of living organisms. At the beginning of the twenty-first century, scientists Ludwig, Pruvost, Reissmann, Hoks, Hofreiter, et al (2009), carried out studies of DNA extracted from fossil remains of horses found in several different locations in Eurasia. DNA was successfully prepared from 89 samples and tests were performed for six main genes, which are responsible for colors in horses: Extension, Agouti, Cream, Tobiano, Sabino-1, and Silver.

All the most ancient samples—ages between 9,500 and 20,000 years—showed a uniform picture of genotypes consistent with bay color. Here it is necessary to point out that the color phenotype of these horses could not have been simply "bay." Wild horses had "Wild" coloring—what we call today the dun color. However, at the time this research was conducted, the test for the Dun gene was not yet developed, and thus the analysis of this locus could not be performed. This means this group of scientists could not answer one of the main questions many of those who study equine colors ask: When did the color of horses stop looking "Wild"?

In the samples from Spain from the sixth millennium BC, the recessive allele "a" of Agouti was detected. It was also found in samples from Romania and Ukraine dated later. However, here would be appropriate to talk about the genotype of black dun (grullo—see p. 24) and not simply assume a black horse. We have to remember that this was the color of the Tarpan, a wild horse in Europe. There is a theory that claims the fixing of the grullo color in wild horses was connected with the end of the Ice Age, when warming and the development of a more humid climate led to an expansion of forests. The grullo color would have served really well as protective coloration for horses living under tree shadows, whereas the bay dun color was suitable for living on the steppe.

The variety in equine genotypes sharply increased since the end of the Copper Age, and especially during the Bronze Age. According to the study, it has been estimated that the recessive allele of the gene Extension (e) and the mutant allele of Sabino-1 (Sb1) were already present about 3,000 years BC. Therefore, there were horses with large white markings, including the chestnut sabino.

In the eighth century BC the dominant allele of Silver (Z) appeared. It was found in a sample from Tuva in Russia. This rare gene mutation is characteristic for the Icelandic Horse breed, which for almost a millennium lived in full isolation, and therefore scientists are inclined to consider the British Isles and adjacent territories as a place of origin of the Silver mutation. However, we cannot exclude the possibility that this mutation occurred several times independently in different parts of the world. The colors of the horses found during this research as carrying this mutation were likely silver dun, silver black dun, and red dun.

In the seventh century BC the co-dominant mutation Cream Dilution appeared. This would have resulted in the buckskin color (possibly also dunskin), palomino (possibly also dunalino), and smoky black (possibly also smoky grullo). In one excavation site in Tuva, samples were found and dated seventh century BC with genotype results consistent with a chestnut-spotted, Tobiano-like color, as well as buckskin tobiano. Thus, the mutant "To" allele already existed at that time. It is also logical to assume that, at that time, horses of all other colors that could result from the combinations of these mutations lived in the same region.

At the end of 2011, research performed by a group of Western scientists carried out on the remains of 31 fossil horses found in Europe and Siberia was published. The analysis included mutations in genes EDNRB, KIT, MATP, MC1R, ASIP, PMEL17, and TRPM1. According to the results, 18 horses were bay (possibly dun), seven black (possibly grullo), and six appaloosa-spotted. Four of the appaloosa-spotted horses could be traced to the Pleistocene Epoch (spanning about 1.8 million years ago to 11,700 years ago), and two to the Bronze Age (about 4,000 years ago), and all of them were found in the territory of Western and Eastern Europe. The corresponding mutation of TRPM1 was absent in all Siberian horses.

Thus, it has been successfully established that appaloosa-spotted horses existed in Europe even before domestication. This is a very important discovery as it allows us to look at the evolution of horse color in a new way. Before this finding, some experts believed that appaloosa-spotted horses first appeared in Northern China, since the very first images seen depicting such color are from the Han Dynasty era (206 BC to 220 AD). Appaloosa spotting was one of the most popular colors during the Baroque Period and found in the ancestors of modern Lippizzan, Kladruber, and Friesian horses. This is the color that has been maintained in the Noriker and Knabstrupper breeds. It is unlikely that these breeds are related to the Chinese horses, however, because Western Europe is so far from China that transportation of horses in the ancient times over such distance was unlikely. At the same time, the newer study confirms the oldest evidence of the existence of appaloosa-spotted horses comes from Europe—paintings in the Pech Merle Cave (France) show white horses covered with dark round spots.

From everything I just shared, it is possible to conclude that the mutations of the TRPM1 gene that are responsible for the appaloosa-spotted color may have occurred independently from each other in Northern China and in Western Europe, and descendants of both populations live until present.

This research unfortunately did not survey other important color genes, including Roan and Dun. Based on the current prevalence of certain colors, we can assume that the origin of Roan is Northern Europe (it is characteristic for the European heavy draft breeds and also for the Icelandic Horse). Roan color is widespread in Quarter Horses—evidence that it was carried by the Iberian horses brought by the Spaniards to the New World. It is difficult to tell whether these Iberian horses are distant relatives of horses of Northern Europe; this is a subject for separate research.

The history of the Silver gene is puzzling. Because the mutation is associated with eye defects you would expect this condition to interfere with its persistence and wide distribution. However, for many centuries this mutation not only escaped natural negative selection, but also extended into rather a large territory. It is possible that it is not as adverse for horses as one would expect.

The emergence of the Frame mutation is interesting. It is not a characteristic color for Europe, and frame overos started appearing in the Old World only during the last decade. The color is widespread in the New World, however. The mutation was introduced to Australia only in the early 1970s through imported Paint Horses. It is difficult to say much about the genes.

Also, not everything is known about the history of the Champagne gene. According to the International Champagne Horse Registry (www.ichregistry.com), the first horse recognized as a carrier of the Champagne gene was a Tennessee Walker named Golden Lady, born in the state of Tennessee around 1910. The attention of researchers was captured for the first time by a classic champagne mare named Champagne Lady Diane (1969), also a Tennessee Walker. Currently there are several lines of Quarter Horses, originating in Texas, with known carriers of the Champagne mutation. There are additional lines in the Missouri Foxtrotter. According to American experts, the Champagne allele arose relatively long ago. Because of the fairly wide distribution of this mutation in 13 breeds in the United

States, it is estimated that this mutation has been in existence for not less than a century.

It is known that in 1905 in Iowa the mare Old Granny was born with gold champagne color. This was the founder of the American Cream Draft Horse (www.acdha.com). Researchers refer to her as "a result of a genetic accident." The Palomino Horse Breed Association (www.palominohba.com) registers not only Palomino Horses, but also any horses similar to them, including those with speckled skin and hazelnut eyes, which are characteristics of gold champagne horses.

It is interesting that all first-known carriers of the Champagne mutation were mares. Probably, the mutation occurred at the beginning of the nineteenth century, but it is impossible to trace its history.

Pearl is a new dilution mutation first described by Shepard in the article "The Barlink Factor. Possible New Dilution Gene in Paint Horses" (2006). She wrote: "In the study of what 'is' champagne, one also needs to address what 'is not' champagne. Several horses have been presented to me over the past several months as 'possible champagnes' who are not. All of these horses are related to the Paint stallion, Barlink Macho Man, a chestnut splashed white/frame overo. The Barlink factor dilution gene is not Champagne, but can mimic it. I believe this gene has not yet been described in the literature. It appears to work as an incomplete dominant, similar to the Cream gene, and also enhances the Cream gene, as does Champagne."

Using genetic tests it was found that Pearl in the American Paint Horses could be traced back to the mare My Tontime, the grandmother of Barlink Macho Man. For some time the gene was called the Barlink Factor after this stallion. Most likely the Pearl mutation occurred a long time ago somewhere on the Iberian Peninsula because it is found not only in breeds of the New World, but also in some European breeds, such as the Andalusian, Lusitano, and Gypsy Horse, which originated in Ireland. It is a matter of fact that some Iberian horse breeds—the Garrano, for example—are closely related to the breeds of the British Isles because the Celts inhabited both the British Isles and the Iberian Peninsula in ancient times.

When studying the history of colors it is possible to also take advantage of folklore, although there are admittedly potential problems when doing so. For example, the true meanings of terms can be displaced. This occurred with the word "sabino," which initially was meant to describe strawberry roan color, and now is used as a term for a particular type of spotting. In addition, in archives of ancient and medieval literature, horse color designations are generally not explained, and modern scientists have to be guided either by the context, or by the meaning of the same words in relation to other objects or by etymology. In general, studying the etymology of the names of horse colors faces a number of its own problems. Systems dealing with color terminology in different languages have undergone changes and developed gradually, in general from a smaller to a larger number of terms and designations. This means that in the past the same word could have been inclusive of several different colors.

CHAPTER 6:

Influence of Color
on Performance, Fertility, and Character

Numerous regional aphorisms and proverbs exist expressing certain beliefs that the color of a horse determines his character and other qualities. On the other hand, the majority of authors of books about horses emphasize that color of course does not influence working capacity and other characteristics of the animal. In reality, scientists have carried out a number of studies concerning the influence of color on a horse's physical capability and behavior. I will summarize some of them here.

Regional Beliefs

Similar sayings around the world claim that a white ring around the eye of the horse reflects an evil, unstable temper. Inhabitants of the Gobi Desert prefer brown and generally dark horses, while in other regions of Mongolia, they prefer bay, chestnut, buckskin, and black. Why is this? Is there any truth to such beliefs?

In my native land of Russia, it is said that if a horse has one white leg, he is worth 10 rubles. If two legs are white, 20 rubles, and if three, 30 rubles. But, when *all* four legs are white, the horse is only worth 4 rubles. It is thought that the white hoof is weaker than a pigmented one, and therefore, a horse with four weakened feet is undesirable and not valuable. But at the same time, white markings on the legs make horses look elegant and attractive, and the proverb reflects a compromise between elegance and practicality: three white legs are still beautiful and safe enough, but four can indicate problems. This is similar to the well-known English saying, "One white hoof, buy a horse. Two white feet, try a horse. Three white feet look well about him. Four white feet, do without him."

We also often hear in Russia that roan color is associated with laziness. This color is characteristic for heavy drafts, which are typically phlegmatic—so perhaps this saying reflects real observations. But according to cowboy wisdom, a roan horse brings good luck, has strong hooves, and is hardy in work on the ranch. Claims that the temperament of a horse depends on his color can be traced back in history.

For example, in the Middle Ages (and also modern times in Europe) there was widespread acceptance that color was connected to the four primary elements: fire, water, air, and earth. It was claimed that the temperament of a horse depended on his color—so, for example, chestnut horses were the most ardent ("fiery") and more difficult to accustom to work because they were difficult to train. Black, on the other hand, was considered the calmest, with bay and gray taking an average place between. Countering this, Gurevich (2008) refers to his experience of service in a cavalry where he had opportunity to observe regiments riding horses of different colors. Regardless of color, each regiment had both very hot and very phlegmatic horses.

The opinion is widespread that horses with pale pigmentation are weak. In Bulatovym's notes from the same article, this point is not only made about horses of light colors, but also about horses with excessively strong pigmentation. It should be noted, however, that the author emphasizes that there is not sufficient data for confirmation.

Prince Urusov (2000) writes that a majority of horse experts consider that a chestnut horse has a choleric temperament, bay—sanguine, black—melancholic, and gray—phlegmatic. Urusov, however, does not share this opinion, and recognizes that some observations contradict these generalizations. That said, he does claim that horses of dark colors are more hardy and capable of hard work than horses of light colors. He advises readers to beware "of the dusty chestnut horses with lighter extremities and white hoofs." Horses "pale with uncertain color, and light extremities," according to Urusov, seldom happen to be efficient. Horses of dark bay color are hardy, quiet, and reliable while light bay can have "unpleasant temperament." Chestnut "quite often demand a firm hand" and light gray horses are "sheepish." He also states that delicate body build often accompanies light colors, especially a combination of "white hair with black and red." (Does he mean spotted bay? Bay roan?) According to the author, an explanation for that is the fact that horses from ancient breeds often have just one color, and modern lighter breeds differ in a variety of colors.

Is There Research to Support Such Beliefs?

BEHAVIOR

In general, the history of human observer's connecting the qualities of an animal, especially psychological, to color, occurs because the vast majority of people are visual learners. Therefore, in their minds, the visual image of an animal (in particular its color) is interwoven with that animal's behavior and strongly fixed.

In her study, Yanova (2003) claims that Thoroughbred horses with unusual markings are good jumpers, but her research does not provide enough information about grouping horses according to their markings. Therefore, it is impossible to assume any correlation between these parameters of a horse.

Konovalov and Kiyko (2009) studied correlation of color in Orlov Trotters with playful behavior. They noted that the prime reason some deny an influence of color on playfulness lies in insufficient research of this aspect by scientists. Their research results allowed them to draw the following conclusions: Overproduction of eumelanin (black) under the conditions of a maximal muscular activity (galloping, for example) can suppress neuromuscular functions. Unlike black, chestnut color is connected with more difficult pigment synthesis. At the same time complicated regulatory processes affecting melanin-catecholamine exchange are involved. At high muscular work, this leads to problems with homeostasis, which reduces playfulness in the horse. Bay color owing to the codominant regulation of synthesis of a pigment increases the regulatory flexibility of melanin-catecholamine exchange. According to Konovalov and Kiyko, gray color is associated with metabolic plasticity, thus reducing various metabolic complications in horses.

Podkorytov, Zaborskih P., and Zaborskih Y.Y. (2007) investigated Altai horses, making the observation that dun, gray, and roan horses of this breed show less proclivity to being "tamed." In the case with dun horses, perhaps we can assume that this color, conditionally speaking, is the "wildest" of all horse colors—that is, it is the color of wild representatives of the horse family.

REPRODUCTION

In 1985 Filippov studied the effects of color selection on reproductive ability in Thoroughbred horses and revealed a certain correlation. According to Filippov's observations, when mating horses of the same color (for example, chestnut with chestnut), the percent of live foals from bay versus chestnut pairs was higher, and thus when selecting breeding combinations, it is necessary to give preference to bay horses. The combination chestnut with chestnut should be avoided. In 1986 Filippov and Aleshina studied the same question, but this time using Orlov Trotters. Scientists revealed the following production of viable healthy foals, taking into account the colors of parents:

Table 8.

Color of Parents	Percent of Viable Foals
Black x Bay	80.3%
Black, bay, gray [Author's note: as appears in original table in the source of the data]	80%
Bay x Bay	80%
Chestnut x Chestnut	65.7%

Thus it is noted that the production of viable foals is higher at heterogeneous selection for color. Scientists also recommend limiting selections of uniform parental couples with chestnut-based colors.

In 2003, Knyazev, Fadeeva, Kukovitskiy, and Nikitin conducted research of the effects of color on the reproductive longevity of Orlov Trotter mares. The ratio of live, healthy foals to number of coverings of a mare of gray, bay, and black colors was studied. It was revealed that gray color appears to have a negative influence on pre- and perinatal viability of foals, and the scientists draw the conclusion that the color of mares influences perinatal viability. In general, fertility is increased in bay mares. In foals of homozygous gray mares, the mortality is higher. However, it must be noted that this research was conducted in 2003 and the test for the Gray gene wasn't developed until 2008. Therefore, the authors could not reliably determine which gray mares were homozygous.

Then, in 2003, Politova, Reissmann and Vagner studied the influence of a genotype in the Extension and Agouti loci on working capacity and fertility of horses of a Russian breed. In this breed the prevailing alleles are "E" and "a." The scientists noted that black mares showed poorer reproductive abilities than bay. They consider that perhaps this indicates a pleiotropic action of the Agouti gene product ASIP. The further research of horse color influence on mare fertility in the Russian Heavy Draft, Soviet Heavy Draft, and Netherlands Appaloosa Pony is one of the aims of my doctoral thesis.

ATTRACTION TO BITING INSECTS

Anderson, Belton, and Kleider (1988) studied the sensitivity of horses in British Columbia to stings of representative *Culicoides* (biting midges), carrying Eastern Equine Encephalomyelitis (EEE). The researchers showed that sensitivity to stings by these insects, and also the frequency of stings, did *not* depend on the color of a horse. But, according to research by Lutsuk and Ponomaryova (2009), horses of light gray color living on pasture suffer from more bites by ticks than horses that are bay or chestnut.

Then, in 2010, scientists from Hungary, Sweden, and Spain found that horses with white body hair (light gray, dominant white, or white sabino) are *less* subjected to stings of blood-sucking insects than horses of dark colors. Results of this research were published, and according to the authors, flies perceive (in one way or another) the light reflected from the hair of the horse as a guide to the potential victim. In 2012, further results were published citing experiments carried out with dummies of horses of different colors. The horse with zebra stripes was the least attractive to insects when compared with black or dark bay.

At this point I want to emphasize that currently we cannot say that there is or is not a connection between the colors of horses and their behavior or physical qualities. It is still very early in actual research examining such considerations, and more studies are needed. I must remind the reader that color genes known to scientists at the time of writing are located in 9 of 32 (diploid number is 64) chromosomes in a horse, and there is a possibility that at least some of them can be linked to genes influencing functions of the nervous system.

Bibliography

1. Adamkovskaya M. Rod loshadinyi (2005). *Konnyi Mir,* № 3. P. 46-49.

2. Adamkovskaya M. Smes' bul'doga s nosorogom, ili chto budet, yesli... (2006) *Konnyi Mir,* № 2. P. 42-45.

3. Akayevskiy A.I., Yudichev Y.F., Seleznyov S.B. *Anatomiya domashnih zhivotnyh.* Edited by Seleznyov S.B. 5th edition, revised. Moscow, 2005. 640 p.

4. Albaum E. Equine Colors: It's All in the Genes (2008). *The Resource,* October. P. 39-41.

5. Alekseev N.D. Sovremennoye opisaniye mastey yakutskih loshadey. Problemy razvitiya tabunnogo konevodstva v Yakutii: materialy respublikanskoy nauchno-prakticheskoy konferentsii, posvyashchennoy 100-letiyu so dnya rozhdeniya prof. M.F. Gabysheva. Novosibirsk, 2004. P. 71-77.

6. Alekseeva V. Povest' L.N. Tolstogo "Kholstomer" (2006). *Konnyi Mir,* № 6. P. 42-45.

7. Andersson L.S., Axelsson J., Dubielzig R.R., Lindgren G., Ekesten B. Multiple congenital ocular anomalies in Icelandic horses (2011). *BMC Veterinary Research,* May 26; 7:21.

8. Anderson G.S., Belton P., Kleider N. The Hypersensitivity of Horses to Culicoides Bites in British Columbia (1988). *The Canadian Veterinary Journal,* vol. 29, № 9. P. 718-723.

9. Andersson L.S., Juras L., Ramsey D.T., Eason-Butler J., Ewart S., Cothran G., Lindgren G. Equine Multiple Congenital Anomalies maps to f 4.9 megabase interval on horse chromosome 6 (2008). *BMC Genetics.* 9:88.

10. Andersson L.S., Lyberg K., Cothran G., Ramsey D.T., Juras L., Mikko S., Ekesten B., Ewart S., Lindgren G. Targeted analysis of four breeds narrows equine Multiple Congenital Ocular Anomalies locus to 208 kilobases (2011). *Mammalian Genome,* June, 22(5-6): 353-60.

11. Archer S. Leopardovyi kompleks (2006). *Konnyi Mir,* № 6. P. 38-41.

12. Archer S., Bellone R., Ph.D., Sandmeyer L., DVM (2012) Appaloosa Genetics Explained. Part III. How is Night Blindness Related to Appaloosa Coat Patterns. *Appaloosa Journal,* July 2012, p. 138-142.

13. Bai D.Y., Yang L.H., Unerhu U., Zhao Y.P., Zhao Q.N., Hasigaowa H., Dugarjaviin M. (2011). Yi Chuan, November; 33(11):1171-8.

14. Bakhilina N.B. *Istoriya tsvetooboznacheniy v russkom yazyke.* Moscow, 1975. 288 p.

15. Balakshin O.A. *Arabskaya loshad' Rossii. Arabskaya loshad'.* Moscow, 2003. P. 233-378.

16. Bartolomé E., Goyache F., Molina A., Cervantes I., Valera M., Gutiérrez J.P. Pedigree estimation of the (sub) population contribution to the total gene diversity: the horse coat color case. (2010). *Animal,* June; 4(6):867-75.

17. Baskina S. Put' domoy dlinoyu v vek (2002). *Konnyi Mir,* № 2. P. 42-44.

18. Bellone R.R. Pleiotropic effects of pigmentation genes in horses (2010). *Animal Genetics,* Volume 41 (Suppl. 2), 100-110.

19. Bellone R.R., Archer S., Wade C.M., Cuka-Lawson C., Haase B., Leeb T., Forsyth G., Sandmeyer L., Grahn B. Association analysis of candidate SNPs in TRPM1 with leopard complex spotting (LP) and congenital stationary night blindness (CSNB) in horses (2010). *Animal Genetics,* Volume 41, Issue Supplement s2, December. P. 207.

20. Bellone R.R., Brooks S.A., Sandmeyer L., Murphy B.A., Forsyth G., Archer S., Bailey E., Grahn B. Different Gene Expression of TRPM1, the Potential Cause of Congenital Stationary Night Blindness and Coat Spotting Patterns (LP) in the Appaloosa Horse (Equus caballus) (2008). *Genetics,* August, 179(4):1861-1870.

21. Belova Y. Skazaniye o konyah (2004). *Konnyi Mir,* № 2. P. 62-65.

22. Berdiyeva E. Fenomen izmeneniya okraski u loshadey (2005). *Praktik,* № 3-4.

23. Billington H.E., McEwan N.R. The relationship between parental coat color and prize-winning Palominos (2009). *Journal of Equine Science,* Vol. 20, № 4. P. 73-77.

24. Blaghitko Y.M. Kauriye i seriye, soloviye i ryzhiye... Novosibirsk, 1997. 190 p.

25. Bobarykin P.A. *Konevodstvo: Prakticheskoye rukovodstvo k izlecheniyu bolezney loshadi i k pozzniyu yeye po naruzhnomu osmotru.* 2nd edition. Moscow, 2012. 456 p.

26. Bobkova N. Relikt rossiyskoy glubinki (2003). *Konnyi Mir,* № 5. P. 34-37.

27. Bobkova N. Vyatskaya loshad' (2009). *Konnyi Mir,* № 10. P. 42-48.

28. Bobkova N. Vyatskaya loshad' (2009). *Konevodstvo i Konnyi Sport,* № 1. P. 6-11.

29. Borisov M.N. *Kushumskaya poroda loshadey.* Alma-Ata, 1983. 160 p.

30. Bowling A.T. Dominant Inheritance of Overo Spotting in Paint Horses (1994). *Journal of Heredity,* 85(3): 222-224.

31. Bowling A.T., Ruvinsky A. (2000). *The Genetics of the Horse,* Cabi Publishing. 535 p.

32. Brooks D.E., DVM, PhD (2002) Equine Ophthalmology, Vol. 48 AAEP Proceedings, p. 300-313.

33. Brooks S.A., Bailey E. Exon skipping in the KIT gene causes a sabino spotting pattern in horses (2005). *Mammalian Genome,* 16 (11). P. 893-902.

34. Brooks S.A., Gabreski N., Miller D., Brisbin A., Brown H.E., Streeter C., Mezey J., Cook D., Antczak D.F. Whole-Genome SNP Association in the Horse: Identification of a Deletion in Myosin Va Responsible for Lavender Foal Syndrome (2010). *PLoS Genetics,* Volume 6(4), April.

35. Brooks S.A., Lear T.L., Adelson D.L., Bailey E. A chromosome inversion near the KIT gene and the Tobiano spotting pattern in horses (2007). *Cytogenetic and Genome Research,* 119. P. 225-230.

36. Brooks S.A., Terry R.B., Bailey E. A PCR-RFLP for KIT associated with tobiano spotting pattern in horses (2002). *Animal Genetics,* № 4. P. 301-303.

37. Brunberg E., Andersson L., Cothran G., Sandberg K., Mikko S., Lindgren G. A missense mutation in PMEL17 is associated with the Silver coat color in horse (2006). *BMC Genetics*, 7:46.

38. Būtavičiūtė I. *Genų, atsakingų už spalvos paveldėjimą, tyrimas arklių genome*. Magistro darbas, Kaunas, 2007. 53 p.

39. Castle N. Equine KIT gene mutations. Dominant White and Sabino-1, May 15, 2009, available on: www.duncentralstation.com

40. Castle N. Flaxen Theory, available on: www.duncentralstation.com

41. Castle N. Primitive Marking Theory (2008), available on: www.duncentralstation.com

42. Caution Knowledge. By AHA's Equine Stress, Research and Education Committee (2007). *Modern Arabian Horse*, August-September. P. 100-105.

43. Chandley A.C., Short R.V., Allen W.R. Cytogenetic studies of three equine hybrids (1975). *Journal of Reproduction and Fertility*. Supplement, October (23). P. 356-370.

44. Chernyh P.Y. *Istoriko-etimologhicheskiy slovar' sovremennogo russkogo yazyka v 2 tomah. Vol. 1.* Moscow, 1999. 623 p.

45. Chetverikova T.V. Vzaimosvyaz' mezhdu belymi otmetinami, mastyu, eksteryerom, tipom i promerami v akhaltekinskoy porode loshadey. Konevodstvo na poroge XXI veka: tezisy dokladov konferentsii molodyh uchenyh i aspirantov. *Divovo*, 2001. P. 47-50.

46. Chetverikova T.V. K voprosu o nasledovanii belyh otmetin u loshadey. *Akhal-Teke Inform*, 2000.

47. Chetverikova T.V. Rasprostraneniye, nasledovaniye i svyaz' belyh otmetin s selektsioniruyemymi priznakami v akhaltekinskoy porode loshadey. Nauchiye osnovy sohraneniya I sovershenstvovaniya porod loshadey. Sbornik nauchnyh trudov. *Divovo*, 2002. P. 60-61.

48. Chirak A.M. Sokhraneniye genofonda narymskih loshadey. Nauka o konevodstve na rubezhe vekov. *Divovo*, 2005. P. 348-353.

49. Coh G. High resolution physical and comparative maps of horse. Chromosomes 14 (ECA14) and 21 (ECA21). A Thesis submitted to Texas A&M University in partial fulfillment of the requirements for the degree of Master of Science. May 2005. P. 180.

50. Cook D., Brooks S., Bellone R., Bailey E. Missense Mutation in Exon 2 of SLC36A1 Responsible for Champagne Dilution in Horses. *PLoS Genetics*, 4(9), September 2008.

51. Danilov A.S. Mifologhema «seriy kon'» v «Edde» i saghe (k voprosu o semantike tsvetooboznacheniy v drevneislandskom). Vestnik Moskovskogo Universiteta, Seriya 9 (philologhiya), № 5, 2008. P. 175-181.

52. Danilov A.S. Sinkretizm tsvetovyh i mifopoeticheskih priznakov v semantike tsvetooboznacheniy eddicheskoy poezii. Doctoral Thesis (philology). Moscow, 2009. 219 p.

53. Darzha V. Loshad' v traditsionnoy praktike tuvinstev-kochevnikov. Kyzyl, 2003. 184 p.

54. Dmitriyeva Y. Arghentinskiy polo-poni: igry vseryoz (2011). *Konnyi Mir*, № 4. P. 58-62.

55. Dmitriyeva Y. Byl u mistera Morgana kon'... (2006) *Konnyi Mir*, № 11. P. 34-39.

56. Dmitriyeva Y. Voronoy s kholmov (2008). *Konnyi Mir*, № 1. P. 48-54.

57. Dmitriyeva Y. Yego zovut Unico (2009). *Konnyi Mir*, № 1-2. P. 88-89.

58. Dmitriyeva Y. Yedinstvenniy i nepovtorimiy (2006). *Konnyi* Mir, № 3. P. 42-43.

59. Dmitriyeva Y. Kustanaytsy (2009). *Konnyi Mir*, № 3, 2009. P. 38-43.

60. Dmitriyeva Y. Legenda Fergany (2011). *Konnyi Mir*, № 6. P. 38-43.

61. Dmitriyeva Y. Malenkiy sportsmen (2009). *Konnyi Mir*, № 8. P. 50-55.

62. Dmitriyeva Y. Mashina vremeni: model' ghenticheskaya (2009). *Konnyi Mir*, № 6. P 50-53.

63. Dmitriyeva Y. Orlovskoye chudo (2010). *Konnyi Mir*, № 1. P. 44-50.

64. Dmitriyeva Y. Ochen' dikiy... ochen' redkiy... (2007) *Konnyi Mir*, № 7. P. 50-52.

65. Dmitriyeva Y. Potomki Tsilindra i Tsenitelya (2009). *Konnyi Mir*, № 4. P. 34-40.

66. Dmitriyeva Y. Skazka Chernogo lesa (2008). *Konnyi Mir*, № 8. P. 42-47.

67. Dobrynin V.P., Kalinin V.I., Stepanov N.N., Yakovlev A.A. *Konevodstvo*. Moscow, 1955. 400 p.

68. Dorofeeva A. Trakenenskiy konniy zavod (2002). *Konnyi Mir*, № 4. P. 46-51.

69. Dorofeeva A., Gorskaya N. Samiye russliye nemtsy (2003). *Konnyi Mir*, № 3. P. 50-56.

70. Dorofeeva N. Pod znakom beloy loshadi (2005). *Konnyi Mir*, № 5. P. 36-40.

71. Dreger D.L., Schmutz S.M. A new mutation in MC1R explains a coat color phenotype in 2 "old" breeds: Saluki and Afgan hound (2010). *Journal of Heredity*: 101(5): 644-9.

72. Dreger D.L., Schmutz S.M. A SINE insertion causes the black-and-tan and saddle tan phenotypes in domestic dogs (2011). *Journal of Heredity*: 102(Suppl1): S11-S18.

73. Dubovskaya Y.B. Zakonomernosti nasledovaniya pegoy masti u shetlendskih poni. Perspektivy konevodstva Rossii v XXI veke: tezisy nauchno-prakticheskoy konferentsii i koordinatsionnogo soveshchaniya, posvyashchennyh 70-letiyu VNIIK. *Divovo*, 2000, 41. P. 34-35.

74. Dubrovina Y.V., Lukash N.S. *Sezonniye izmeneniya pigmenta pokrovnogo volosa voronyh loshadey*. Moscow, 1985. 12 p.

75. Dürst U. *Eksteryer loshadi*. Moscow, 1936. 344 p.

76. Eizirik E., David. V.A., Buckley-Beason V., Roelke M.E., Schäffer A.A., Hannah S.S., Narfström K., O'Brien S.J., Menotti-Raymond M. Defining and Mapping Mammalian Coat Pattern Genes: Multiple Genomic Regions Implicated in Domestic Cat Stripes and Spots (2010). *Genetics*, January; 184(1): 167-275.

77. Eksteryer loshadi (i opredeleniye vozrasta rogatogo skota i sobak). Zapiski, sostavlenniye v 1902 N. Bulatovym. Edited by prof. I.M. Sadovskiy. Khar'kov, 1907. 206 p.

78. English-russian vocabulary of hippilogical terminology. *Konnyi Mir*, № 8, 2006.

79. Etimologhicheskiy slovar' Fasmera, available on: http://vasmer.narod.ru/

80. Faclairean. Modern English – Proto-Celtic, available on: www.gaelic.ru

81. Fadeeva N.S., Knyazev S.P., Kukovitskiy Y.A. Zavisimost' perinatalnoy zhiznesposobnosti zherebyat orlovskoy rysistoy ot vozrasta i masti ih materey. Zhivotnovodstvo Zapadnoy Sibiri i Zauralya: problemy i resheniya. Sbornik nauchnyh trudov, posvyashchenniy 100-letiyu osnovatelya kafedry razvedeniya i genetiki selskohozyaystvennyh zhivotnyh zooinzhenernogo fakulteta prof. A.Y. Malakhovskogo. Omsk, 2001. P. 186-188.

82. Fanelli H.H. Coat colour dilution lethal ('lavender foal syndrome'): a tetany syndrome of Arabian foals (2005). *Equine veterinary education*, № 5. P. 260-263.

83. Fayzullina Z.S. Etnokulturniye osobennosti tsvetooboznacheniya v sovremennom bashkirskom yazyke. Doctoral Thesis (philology). Ufa, 2005. 170 p.

84. Fedorova Y. Genetika tikirovannogo okrasa (2010). *Moy Drug Koshka*, № 5. P. 68-70.

85. Felix K., Ferrándiz R., Einarsson R., Dreborg S. Allergens of horse danger: Comparison among breeds and individual animals by immunoblotting (1996). *The Journal of Allergy and Clinical Immunology*, July, Volume 98, Issue 1. P. 169-171.

86. Filippov S.P. Vliyaniye podbora po masti na vosproizvoditelnuyu sposobnost' loshadey chistokrovnoy verhovoy porody. Intensifikatsiya konevodstva. Sbornik nauchnyh trudov. *Divovo*, 1985. P. 43-51.

87. Filippov S.P. Nasledovaniye voronoy, gnedoy, ryzhey, bulanoy, solovoy, myshastoy i savrasoy mastey u loshadey (1992). *Izvestiya Timiryazevskoy akademii*, № 1. P. 1-6.

86. Filippov S.P., Aleshina A.I. Vliyaniye podbora po
88 na vosproizvoditelnuyu sposobnost' loshadey orlovskoy rysistoy porody. Puti uskoreniya nauchno-tehnicheskogo progressa v konevodstve. Sbornik nauchnyh trudov. *Divovo*, 1986. P. 50-56.

89. Fritz K.L., Kaese H.J., Valberg S.J., Hendrickson J.A., Rendahl A.K., Bellone R.R., Dynes K.M., Wagner M.L., Lucio M.A., Cuomo F.M., Brinkmeyer-Langford C.L., Skow L.C., Mickelson J.R., Rutherford M.S., McCue M.E. (2014) Genetic risk factors for insidious equine recurrent uveitis in Appaloosa horses. *Animal Genetics*. Jun;45(3):392-9.

90. Fuster F., Beysterbos J. Zagadka ostrova Menorka (2009). *Konnyi Mir*, № 11. P. 42-49.

91. Gantz T. Gray isn't a color (2006). *Paint Horse Journal*, August. P. 60-64.

92. Gaydukova Y. Chistaya seraya krov' (2004). *Zolotoy Mustang*, № 1. P. 58-63.

93. Geurts R. *De haarkleur bij het paard*. Centrum voor Landbouwpublikaties en Landbouwdocumentatie. Wageningen, 1973. 99 p.

94. Gorbukov M.A. *Byelorusskaya poroda loshadey*. Brest, 1997. 72 p.

95. Grizone F. Nastavleniya po verkhovoy yezde ot Federico Grizone, neapolitanskogo dvoryanina, quoting from: *Alpha Kentavra*, № 3, 2006, P. 81-86.

96. Gorbukov M., German Y., German A. Byelorusskiy universal (2008). *Konnyi Mir*, № 11. P. 42-47.

97. Gorecka A., Golonka M., Chruszczewski M., Jezierski T. A note on behaviour and heart rate in horses differing in facial hair whorl (2007). *Applied Animal Behaviour Science*, June, Vol. 105, Issue 1-3. P. 244-248.

98. Gorecka A., Sloniewski K., Golonka M., Jaworski Z., Jezierski T. Heritability of hair whorl position on the forehead in Konik horses (2006). *Journal of Animal Breeding and Genetics*, December, Vol. 123, Issue 6. P. 396-398.

99. Goubaux A., Barrier G. *Eksteryer loshadi*. Oryol, 1901. 819 p.

100. Gower J. 1999. *Horse Color Explained: a Breeder's Perspective*, Trafalgar Square Publishing, North Pomfret, Vermont. 144 p.

101. Graig L., Vleck L.D. Van Evidence for inheritance of the red dun dilution in the horse (1985). The *Journal of Heredity*, № 2. P. 138-139.

102. Green B.K. 2001. *The Colour of Horses*. Mountain Press Publishing Company, Missoula, Montana. 128 p.

103. Gribnenko M. Zagadka belogo konya (2008). *Konnyi Mir*, № 10. P. 58-59.

104. Gronet D., Pikuła R. Dziedziczenie umaszczenia u koni (2001). *Przegląd Hodowlany*, № 8. S. 19-23.

105. Gurevich D.Y. *Spravochnik po konnomu sportu i konevodstvu*. Moscow, 2000. 325 p.

106. Gurevich D., Volkova Y. Do konchika hvosta (2006). *Konnyi Mir*, № 11. P. 58-62.

107. Haase B., Brooks S.A., Schlumbaum A., Azor P.J., Bailey E., Alaeddine F., Mevissen M., Burger D., Poncet P.-A., Reider S., Leeb T. Allelic heterogeneity at the Equine KIT locus in dominant white horses (2007). *PloS Genetics*, November, 3(11).

108. Haase B., Brooks S.A., Tozaki T., Burger D., Poncet P.-A., Reider S., Hasegawa T., Penedo C., Leeb T. Seven novel KIT mutations in horses with white coat colour phenotypes (2009). *Animal Genetics*, Volume 40, Issue 5, October. P. 623-629.

109. Haase B., Jude R., Brooks S.A., Leeb T. An equine chromosome 3 inversion is associated with the tobiano spotting pattern in German horse breeds (2008). *Animal Genetics*, June, Volume 39, Issue 3. P. 306-309.

110. Haase B., Obexer-Ruff G., Dolf G., Rieder S., Burger D., Poncet P.A., Gerber V., Howard J., Leeb T. Haematological parameters are normal in dominant white Franches-Montagnes horses carrying a KIT mutation (2010). *Veterinary Journal*, June; 184(3): 315-7.

111. Haase B., Rieder S., Tozaki T., Hasegawa T., Penedo M.C.T., Jude R., Leeb T. Five novel KIT mutations in horses with white coat colour phenotypes (2010). *Animal Genetics*, 42, P. 337–339.

112. Hamilton C. One in a Million (2006). *The American Quarter Horse Journal*, February. P. 52-55.

113. Harland M.M., Stewart A.J., Marshall A.E., Belknap E.B. Diagnosis of deafness in a horse by brainstem auditory evoked potential (2006). *Canadian Veterinary Journal*, February; 47(2):151-4.

114. Harvey E. "Rare white Standardbred colt born" (2012). UStrotting.com.

115. Hauswirth R., Haase B., Blatter M., Brooks S.A., Burger D., Drögemüller C., Gerber V., Henke D., Janda J., Jude R., Magdesian K.G., Matthews J.M., Poncet P.-A., Svansson V., Tozaki T., Wilkinson-White L., Penedo M.C.T., Rieder S., Leeb T. Mutations in MITF and PAX3 Cause "Splashed White" and Other White Spotting Phenotypes in Horses (2012). *PLoS Genetics*, April.

116. Hellström A.R., Watt B., Fard S.S., Tenza D., Mannström P., Narfström K., Ekesten B., Ito S., Wakamatsu K., Larrson J., Ulfendahl M., Kullander K., Raposo G., Kerje S., Hallböök F., Marks M.S., Andersson L. Inactivation of Pmel Alters Melanosome Shape But Has Only a Subtle Effect on Visible Pigmentation (2011). Issue of *PLoS Genetics*, September, available on: http://www.plosgenetics. org/article/info%3Adoi%2F10.1371%2Fjournal. pgen.1002285

117. Hemon R. *Breton Grammar*. Translated, adapted, and revised by M. Everson. Evertype, 3rd edition, 2011. 88 p.

118. Henner J., Poncet P.A., Aebi L., Hagger C., Stranzinger G., Rieder S. Pferdezucht: Genetische Tests für die Fellfarben Fuchs, Braun und Schwarz. Ergebnisse einer ersten Untersuchung in der Schweizer Freibergerpferderasse. Schweiz Arch Tierheilkd 144(8): 405-12.

119. Holl H., Brooks S., Bailey E. De novo mutation of KIT discovered as a result of a non-hereditary white coat-colour pattern (2010). *Animal Genetics*, Vol. 41 (Suppl. 2), P. 196-198.

120. Holmes F. The Mistery of Tovero (1997). *Paint Horse Journal*, December. P. 130-139.

121. Hustad C.M., Perry W.L., Siracusa L.D., Rasberry C., Cobb L., Cattanach B.M., Kovatch R., Copeland N.G., Jenkins N.A. Molecular Genetic Characterization of Six Recessive Viable Alleles of the Mouse Agouti Locus (1995). *Genetics*, Vol. 140. P. 255-265.

122. Ignatyeva Y.A. Sostoyaniye i razvitiye gheneticheskogo raznoobraziya v sovetskoy tyazhelovoznoy porode loshadey kak malochislennoy populyatsii. Doctoral thesis (agriculture). Ryazan', 1997. 17 p.

123. Imsland F, McGowan K, Rubin CJ, Henegar C, Sundström E, Berglund J, Schwochow D, Gustafson U, Imsland P, Lindblad-Toh K, Lindgren G, Mikko S, Millon L, Wade C, Schubert M, Orlando L, Penedo MC, Barsh GS, Andersson L. (2015). Regulatory mutations in TBX3 disrupt asymmetric hair pigmentation that underlies Dun camouflage color in horses. *Nature Genetics*. Dec 21. doi: 10.1038/ng.3475.

124. Inshakova G. Zemniye puti nebesnogo vsadnika (2004). *Konnyi Mir*, № 5. P. 40-42.

125. Inshakova G. Pir dlya ochey (2004). *Konnyi Mir*, № 6. P. 52-56.

126. Inshakova G. Po sledu skifskogo konya (2002). *Konnyi Mir*, № 2. P. 34-37.

127. Ishikawa Y., Mukoyama H., Matsuura T., Mukai T., Watanabe S. Establishments and biological characteristics of melanoma culture cell lines derived from aged grey horses (2000). *Journal of Equine Science*, 33. P. 75-82.

128. Kakoi H., Tozaki T., Nagata S., Gawahara H., Kijima-Suda I. Development of a method for simultaneously genotyping multiple horse coat colour loci and genetic investigation of basic colour variation in Thoroughbred and Misaki horses in Japan (2009). *Journal of Animal Breeding and Genetics*, Dec., 126(6):425-31.

129. Kaleta T., Bugucka-Ścieżyńska A. The racehorse reactivity in Służewiec Race course – quantitative analysis (2002). Annals of Warsaw Agricultural University. *Animal Science*, № 39. P. 41-46.

130. Kharchenko V.K. Slovar' tsveta: real'noye, potentsial'noye, avtorskoye: svyshe 4000 slov v 8000 kontekstah. Moscow, 2009. 532 p.

131. Khotov V.Kh. O geneticheskih stsepleniyah masti (1992). *Izvestiya Timiryazevskoy akademii*, № 1. P. 177-181.

132. Khrabrova L. V genah zapisano vse (2008). *Konnyi Mir*, № 2. P. 38-41.

133. Khrabrova L. Vse tayny vydast DNK (2006). *Konnyi Mir*, № 4. P. 36-38.

134. Khrabrova L. Novosti genetiki (2008). *Konnyi Mir*, № 11. P. 60-61.

135. Khrabrova L. Popast' v mast' (2004). *Konnyi Mir*, № 1. P. 44-48.

136. Khrabrova L., Yemelyanova V. Rodoslovniye bolezni (2006). *Konnyi Mir*, № 9. P. 46-49.

137. Kibort M. Loshadi donskoy stepey (2001). *Konnyi Mir*, № 4. P. 4-8.

138. Kibort M.I., Nikolayeva A.A. Budyonnovskaya poroda loshadey. Ryazan', 2000. 148 p.

139. Kibort M.I., Nikolayeva A.A. Donskaya poroda loshadey. Moscow, 2005. 287 p.

140. Kibort M., Nikolayeva A. Zoloto donskih stepey (2002). *Konnyi Mir*, № 4. P. 34-40.

141. Klar A.J.S. Human Handedness and Scalp Hair-Whorl Direction Develop from a Common Genetic Mechanism (2003). *Genetics*, September, 165. P. 269-276.

142. Klark L.A., Tsai K.L., Starr A.N., Nowend K.L., Murphy K.E. A missense mutation in the 20S proteasome β2 subunit of Great Danes having harlequin coat patterning (2011). *Genomics*, April, Volume 97, Issue 4. P. 244-248.

143. Kleiner S.D. Problemy etimologhii latinskih leksem, oboznachayushchih konskuyu mast'. Doctoral thesis (philology). Saint-Petersburg, 2011.

144. Kniga o loshadi. Edited by C.M. Budyonny. Vol. 1. Moscow, 1952. 608 p.

145. Knyazev S.P. Kartirovanoye ghenov loshadi (1988). *Konevodstvo i Konniy Sport*, № 8. P. 26-27.

146. Knyazev S.P. Tol'ko ot serogo konya mozhet rodit'sya seriy zherebyonok (2005). *Kon' Moy Voronoy*, № 4.

147. Knyazev S.P., Gutorova N.V. Struktura populyatsiy orlovskih rysakov po ghenotipam lokusov pigmentoobrazovaniya MC1R i Tyr i fenotipam masti (2003). *Selskohozyaystvennaya biologiya*, № 2. P. 73-78.

148. Knyazev S.P., Nikitin S.V. Assotsiatsiya masti i antighenov sistemy D grupp krovi loshadey (1999). *Genetika zhivotnyh*, № 4. P. 499-503.

149. Knyazev S.P., Fadeeva (Glushchak) N.S., Kukovitskiy Y.A., Nikitin S.V. Reproduktivnoye dolgoletiye kobyl orlovskoy rysistoy porody v svyazi s ih mastyu. *Doklady Rossiyskoy akademii selskohozyaystvennyh nauk*, № 4, 2003. P. 33-35.

150. Komáromy A.M., Rowlan J.S., La Croix N.C., Mangan B.G. Equine Multiple Congenital Ocular Anomalies (MCOA) syndrome in PMEL17 (Silver) mutant ponies: five cases (2011). *Veterinary Ophtalmology*, September; 14(5):313-20.

151. Konovalov V.S. Mekhanizm pleyotropnogo deystviya genov melaninovoy okraski u zhivotnyh. Doctoral thesis (biology), 1983. 32 p.

152. Konovalov V.S., Kiyko I.V. Assotsiativnaya svyaz' kolor-markerov masti orlovskogo rysaka s yego rezvostyu. Sovremenniye problemy evolyutsionnoy biologii: Mezhdunarodnaya nauchno-metodicheskaya konferentsiya, posvyashchennaya 200-letiyu so dnya rozhdeniya Ch. Darwina i 150-letiyu vyhoda v svet "Proishozhdeniya vidov", 12-14 fevralya 2009 Sbornik statey. Vol. 2. Bryansk, 2009. P. 262-265.

153. Konysheva V. Britanskaya palitra (2010). *Moy Drug Koshka*, № 1. P. 18-25.

154. Kosowska B. Dziedziczenie wybranych cech jakościowych u niektórych zwierząt gospodarskich i domowych (1993). *Przegląd hodowlany*, № 4. S. 1-6.

155. Kostikova N. Privetstvuyu tebya, Oldenburg! (2001) *Konnyi Mir*, № 2. P. 18-22.

156. Kovalevskaya V.B. Kon' i vsadnik: Istoriya odomashnivaniya loshadey v yevraziyskih stepyah, na Kavkaze i Blizhnem Vostoke. 2nd edition, revised. Moscow, 2010. 160 p.

157. Kovalyova V. Pegoye chudo Ameriki (2009). *Konnyi Mir*, № 5. P. 34-39.

158. Konevodstvo. Edited by M.I. Rogalevich. Moscow, 1957. 341 p.

159. Kocherghina V.A. Sanskritsko-russkiy slovar'. Edited by V.I. Kalyanov. S prilozheniyem «Grammaticheskogo ocherka sanskrita» A.A. Zaliznyak. 3rd edition. Moscow, 2005. 994 p.

160. Kozlova N.Y. Faktory, vliyayushchiye na rabotosposobnost' loshadey standardbrednoy porody. Aktualniye voprosy ekologii: Sbornik nauchnyh trudov. Moscow, 2000. P. 133-138.

161. Kral E. Kleuren genetica, available on: http://www.appaloosa-stamboek.com/kleureng.htm

162. Krasikova N.V. Svyaz' geneticheskih markerov s selektsioniruyemymi priznakami loshadey orlovskoy rysistoy porody. Doctoral thesis (biology). Novosibirsk, 2004. 146 p.

162. Kuznetsova M.M. Sovremennaya zootehnicheskaya kharakteristika narymskoy loshadi. Zootehnicheskiye i veterinarniye aspekty razvitiya zhivotnovodstva v sovremennyh usloviyah agrarnogo proizvodstva. Sb. nauch. tr. Mezhdunarodnoy prakticheskoy konferentsii 14-15 aprelya 2009. Michurinsk, 2009. P. 84-86.

163. Kuleshov P.N. Konevodstvo. Moscow, Leningrad, 1933. 349 p.

164. Kulpina V.G. Sistema tsvetooboznacheniy russkogo yazyka. Naimenovaniya tsveta v indoyevropeyskih yazykah: Sistemniy i istoricheskiy analiz. Moscow, 2007. P. 126-184.

165. Kuptsova N. Nemetskaya «klassika» (2011). *Konnyi Mir*, № 2. P. 52-57.

166. Kuptsova N., Dubrovskaya Y. Istinniy poni s nordicheskim kharakterom (2003). *Konnyi Mir*, № 4. P. 42-45.

167. Kurskaya V. Bryzghi champanskogo (2007). *My Horse*, № 5. P. 57-58.

168. Kurskaya V. Vse tsveta raduzhki (2010). *Konnyi Mir*, № 2. P. 50-51.

169. Kurskaya V. Zhemchuzhina v champanskom (2007). *Konnyi Mir*, № 10. P. 54-57.

170. Kurskaya V. Inohodtsy, part 1 (2009). *Konnyi Mir*, № 12. P. 48-52.

171. Kurskaya V. Masti loshadey (2010), available on: www.kskverona.ru

172. Kurskaya V.A. Nasledovaniye mastey: sovremennoye sostoyaniye izucheniya voprosa (2015). *Konevodstvo i Konnyi Sport*, № 4. P. 17-19.

173. Kurskaya V. Pyatnistiye iz peshchery (2012). *Konnyi Mir*, № 1. P. 60-61.

174. Kurskaya V. Remen' remnyu rozn', part 1 (2010). *Konnyi Mir*, № 3. P. 70-72.

175. Kurskaya V. Remen' remnyu rozn', part 2 (2010). *Konnyi Mir*, № 4. P. 52-54.

176. Lau A.N., Peng L., Goto H., Chemnick L., Ryder O.A., Makova K.D. Horse domestication and conservation genetics of Przewalski's horse inferred from sex chromosomal and autosomal sequences (2009). *Molecular Biology and Evolution*, January; 26(1):199-208.

177. Lauvergne J.J., Silvestrelli M., Langlios B., Renieri C., Poirel D., Antaldi G.G.V. A new scheme for describing horse coat colour (1991). *Livestock Production Science*, vol. 27. P. 219-229.

178. Lebedev M. Bratya po krovi: osly, muly, loshaki i zebroidy (2007). *Zolotoy Mustang*, № 6. P. 86-91.

179. Lehmann Von E. von Zur sogenannten Apfelung im Haarkleid des Pferdes (1989). *Journal of Animal Breeding and Genetics / Zeitschrift für Tierzüchtung und Züchtungsbiologie*, Vol. 106 (3), June. P. 237-239.

180. Lewczuk D. Zmiany pokroju koni wielkopolskich dawnego typu mazurskiego na przykładzie SK Plękity (1993). *Przegląd Hodowlany*, № 9. S. 23-24.

181. Lietuvių-rusų kalbų žodynas: apie 65 000 žodžių / Antanas Lyberis. – Ketvirtoji laida. – Vilnius: Mokslo ir enciklopedijų leidybos inst. 2005. 951 p.

182. Lightbody T. Foal with Overo lethal white syndrome born to a registered Quarter horse mare (2002). *The Canadian Veterinary Journal. La Revue vétérinaire canadienne*, September, Vol. 43, № 9. P. 715-717.

183. Lighter J.K. Post-Flood mutation of the KIT gene and the rise of white coloration patterns (2010). *Journal of Creation*, 24(3). P. 67-72.

184. Livanova T.K. Loshadi. Moscow, 2001. 256 p.

185. Livanova T.K., Livanova M.A. Vsyo o loshadi. Moscow, 2002. 384 p.

186. Locke M.M., Penedo M.C.T., Bricker S.J., Millon L.V., Murray J.D. Linkage of the grey coat colour locus to microsatellites on horse chromosome 25 (2002). *Animal Genetics*, № 5. P. 329-337.

187. Locke M.M., Ruth L.S., Millon L.V., Penedo M.C.T., Murray J.D. The cream dilution gene, responsible for the palomino and buckskin coat colours, maps to horse chromosome 21 (2001). *Animal Genetics*, № 6. P. 340-343.

188. Ludwig A., Pruvost M., Reissmann M., Benecke N., Brockmann G.A., Castaños P., Cieslak M., Lippold S., Llorente L., Malaspinas A.S., Slatkin M., Hofreiter M. Coat color variation at the beginning of horse domestication (2009). *Science*, April; 324(5926):485.

189. Lukash N.S., Dubrovina Y.V. Pigmentatsiya pokrovnogo volosa loshadey v zavisimosti ot razlichnyh faktorov. Vyvedeniye i mikroevolutsiya porod loshadey v usloviyah intensifikatsii selskohoziaystvennogo proizvodstva. *Divovo*, 1988. P. 43-44.

190. Lukash N.S., Moiseeva L.M. Nasledovaniye mastey u loshadey chistokrovnoy arabskoy porody. Moscow, 1984, 10 p.

191. Lutsuk S.N., Ponomaryova M.Y. Immunologicheskiye podhody pri bor'be s kleshchami i svyazannymi s nimi zabolevaniyami u loshadey (2009). *Rossiyskiy Parazitologicheskiy Zhurnal*, № 1. P. 62-67.

192. Lynghaug F. *Horses of Distinction. Stars of the Pleasure Breeds*. Hallelujah Publications. 80 p.

193. Magdesian K.G., Williams D.C., Aleman M., Lecouter R.A., Madigan J.E. Evaluation of deafness in American Paint Horses by phenotype, brainstem auditory-evoked responses, and endothelin receptor B genotype (2009). *Journal of the American Veterinary Medical Association*, November 15; 235(10):1204-11.

194. Mariat D., Taourit S., Guérin G. A mutation in the MATP gene causes the cream coat colour in horses (2003). *Genetics Selection Evolution*, 35(1). P. 119-133.

195. Marklund S., Moller M., Sandberg K., Andersson L. Close association between sequence polymorphism in the KIT gene and the roan coat color in horses (1999). *Mammalian Genome*, 10. P. 283-288.

196. Masuda M., Tsunoda J., Nomura H., Kimura N., Altangerel G., Namkhai B., Dolj U., Yokohama M. New Primitive Marking (Bider) in Mongolian Native Horse and Equus przewalskii (2007). *Journal of Equine Science*, Vol. 18, № 4. P. 145-151.

197. Mazurina V.V. Nasledovaniye mastey u loshadey chistokrovnoy arabskoy porody. Puti uskoreniya nauchno-tehnicheskogo progressa v konevodstve. Sbornik nuachnyh trudov. *Divovo*, 1986. P. 56-61.

198. Mayzina A.N. Semanticheskoye pole tsvetooboznacheniy altayskogo yazyka v sopostavlenii s mongolskimi yazykami. Doctoral thesis (philology). Novosibirsk, 2006. 25 p.

199. Mikhailova T.A. Sistema tsvetooboznacheniy v goydelskih yazykah. Naimenovaniya tsveta v indoyevropeyskiy yazykah: Sistemniy i istoricheskiy analiz. Edited by A.P. Vasilevich. Moscow, 2007. P. 229-242.

200. Milko O., Sorokina I. Mal, da udal (2004). *Konnyi Mir*, № 1. P. 38-42.

201. Milko O.S., Trofimov A.B. Fenotipicheskoye raznoobraziye i osobennosti nasledovaniya mastey vo vladimirskoy porode loshadey. Zootehnicheskiye i veterinarniye aspekty razvitiya zhivotnovodstva v sovremennyh usloviyah agrarnogo proizvodstva: Sb. nauch. tr. Mezhdunarodnoy prakticheskoy konferentsii 14-15 aprelya 2009. Michurinsk, 2009. P. 86-89.

202. Minkevich T.V. Myshastiki (pri chem zdes' myshi?) (2007). *Koni Vyatskiye*, № 2. P. 46-48.

203. Moates T. Horses of a different stripe (2006). *Equus*, November. P. 21-23.

204. Mongush A.N. Sostoyaniye i puti razvitiya konevodstva v respublike Tyva. Povysheniye effektivnosti selskohozyaystvennogo proizvodstva na opustynennyh zemlyah aridnoy zony. Rossiyskaya akademiya selskohozyaystvennyh nauk, Sibirskoye otdeleniye, GNU NII agrarnyh problem Khakasii, GNU Tuvinskiy NII selskogo khozyaystva, Mongolskaya akademiya selskohozyaystvennyh nauk, Otdeleniye NII rasteniyevodstva i zemledeliya v UVS-aymake. Edited by V.K. Sevostyanov, R.B. Chysym, D. Ulziy. Abakan, 2006. P. 111-117.

205. Mongush B.M., Mongush A.N. Sovremennoye opisaniye mastey tuvinskih loshadey. Problemy razvitiya APK Sayano-Altaya: materialy mezhregionalnoy nauchno-prakticheskoy konferentsii. Part II. Composed by Ulturgasheva O.G. Abakan, 2008. P. 97-99.

206. Morozova I. Mir v miniatyure (2009). *Konnyi Mir*, № 7. P. 38-44.

207. Moskovkina N.N., Sotskaya M.N. Genetika i nasledstvenniye bolezni sobak i koshek. Moscow, 2004. 448 p.

208. Motoriko M.G. Kustanayskaya poroda loshadey. Alma-Ata, 1981. 184 p.

209. Murgiano L., Waluk D.P., Towers R., Wiedemar N., Dietrich J., Jagannathan V., Drögemüller M., Balmer P., Druet T., Galichet A., Penedo M.C., Müller E.J., Roosje P., Welle M.M., Leeb T. (2016). An Intronic MBTPS2 Variant Results in a Splicing Defect in Horses with Brindle Coat Texture. *G3*. Sept; 6(9): 2963–2970.

210. Murphy J., Arkins S. Facial Hair whorls (trichoglyphs) and the incidence of motor laterality in the horse (2008). *Behavioral Processes*, Volume 79, Issue 1, September. P. 7-12.

211. Mursalimov V.S., Satiyev B.Kh. Bashkirskaya loshad'. Ufa, 1989. 156 p.

212. Naumova A. Frantsuzskaya verkhovaya (2010). *Konnyi Mir*, № 4. P. 44-51.

213. Nekrasova A. Ostorozhno: masti! Part 1 (2010). *Nevzorov Haute Ecole*, № 1. P. 44-51.

214. Nielsen L.L. Why Are People Allergic to Horses? (2007) Available on: http://ichopage.weebly.com/allergies.html

215. Nikishov A.A., Blokhin G.I., Santuryan F.E. Vosproizvoditelnaya sposobnost' sobolinyh norok pastelevoy okraski. Moscow, 1985. 8 p.

216. Nikolayeva A.A. Sovremennoye sostoyaniye budyonnovskoy porody loshadey. Nauka o konevodstve na rubezhe vekov. Divovo, 2005. P. 228-247.

217. Nikolayeva A., Kibort M. Imeni Budyonnogo (2008). Konnyi Mir, № 12. P. 34-40.

218. Nikonova A.I. Itogi i perspektivy raboty s novoaltayskoy porodoy loshadey. Nauka o konevodstve na rubezhe vekov. Divovo, 2005. P. 213-221.

219. Normanskaya Y.V. Tsvetooboznacheniya v drevnegrecheskom yazyke. Naimenovaniya tsveta v indoyevropeyskih yazykah: Sistemniy i istoricheskiy analiz. Edited by A.P. Vasilevich. Moscow, 2007. P. 54-65.

220. Norodd Nes, Einar J. Einarsson, Outi Lohi Beautiful Fur Animals and Their Colour Genetics. Hillerod: Scientifur, 1998. 271 p.

221. Nunnery C., Pickett J.P., Zimmerman K.L. (2005) Congenital stationary night blindness in a Thoroughbred and a Paso Fino. Veterinary Ophthalmology. Nov-Dec; 8(6):415-9.

222. Obolenskiy V.I. Osnovy konnzavodstva i lechebnik loshadi. Moscow, 1904. 486 p.

223. Oborotova Y. Vozvrashcheniye mezenki (2007). Konnyi Mir, № 2. P. 44-48.

224. Odintsov G.F. K istorii russkih gippologicheskih tsvetooboznacheniy. Issledovaniya po slovoobrazovaniyu i leksikologii drevnerusskogo yazyka. Moscow, 1978. P. 172-221.

225. Oke S. Mutation Causing Lavender Foal Syndrome Identified, May 19, 2010, available on: http://www.thehorse.com/ViewArticle.aspx?ID=16377

226. Overton R. By a hair (2004). Paint Horse Journal, March. P. 144-150.

227. Overton R. In the Genes (2004). Quarter Horse News, December 15. P. 24-27.

228. Overton R. Positively perlino (2001). Paint Horse Journal, February. P. 72-78.

229. Overton R. The White Stuff (2002). Paint Horse Journal, January. P. 106-111.

230. Paklina N., Orden C. van Povorot sud'by (2008). Konnyi Mir, № 9. P. 72-74.

231. Pankova T. Zagadka loshadey Zabaikalya (2008). Konnyi Mir, № 5. P. 48-51.

232. Pankova T.Y., Vinogradov I.I. K voporosy istorii zabaikalskoy loshadi. Strategiya vedeniya ovtsevodstva, kozovodstva, konevodstva i drugih traditsionnyh otrasley zhivotnovodstva Sibiri v sovremennyh ekonomicheskih usloviyah. Chita, 2005. P. 102-111.

233. Parfyonov V.A. Loshadi. Moscow, 2002. 192 p.

234. Parfyonov V. Orlovskiy rysak – 225 let pobed! (2001) Konnyi Mir, № 6. P. 10-16.

235. Parfyonov V. Russkaya verkhovaya: nazvaniye obyazyvayet (2004). Konnyi Mir, № 4. P. 32-37.

236. Parfyonov V., Politova M. Legenda Karachaya (2005). Konnyi Mir, № 1. P. 38-42.

237. Pavlikhina O. Zavitki i otmetiny (2008). Alpha Kentavra, № 1. P. 36-41.

238. Pavlyuchenko S.V. Izmenchivost' i nasledovaniye okraski ostevyh i pukhovyh volos soboley. Doctoral Thesis (agriculture). Moscow, 1981. 23 p.

239. Peters A. A Roan by Any Other Name is a Roan (2002). Thoroughbred Times, May 4, available on: http://www.thoroughbredtimes.com/weekly-feature-articles/2002/may/04/a-roan-by-any-other-name-is-a-roan.aspx

240. Pielberg G. Molecular Coat Color Genetics. Dominant White in Pigs and Greying with Age in Horses. Doctoral thesis. Uppsala, 2004. 34 p.

241. Pielberg G., Golovko A., Sundström E., Curik I., Lennartsson J., Seltenhammer M.H., Druml T., Binns M., Fitzsimmons C., Lindgren G., Sandberg K., Baumung G., Vetterlein M., Strömberg S., Grabherr M., Wade C., Lindblad-Toh K., Pontén F., Heldin C.H., Sölkner J., Andersson L. A cis-acting regulatory mutation causes premature hair graying and susceptibility to melanoma in the horse (2008). Nature Genetics, August, 40(8).

242. Pikuła R., Gronet D. Wykorzystanie polimorfizmu białek krwi do charakterystyki struktury genetycznej populacji koni półkrwi w zależności od ich umaszczenia (2002). Zootechnica, 1(1-2). S. 121-128.

243. Pikuła R., Tomaszewska-Guszkiewicz K., Smugała M., Stępień J. Relationship between the genetic polymorphism of blood proteins and the coat colour in horses (1997). Animal Science Papers and reports, vol. 15, № 1. P. 15-21.

244. Pilsworth R.C., Knottenbelt D.C. Coat colour changes (2005). Equine veterinary education, № 4. P. 172-174.

245. Podkorytov A.T., Zaborskih P.V., Zaborskih Y.Y. Zootehnicheskaya kharakteristika altayskoy loshadi na sovremennom etape razvitiya. Nauchnoye obespecheniye konkurentosposobnosti plemennogo sportivnogo i produktivnogo konevodstva v Rossii i stranah SNG. Nauchno-prakticheskaya konferentsiya, posv. 70-letiyu prof. S.S. Sergiyenko. Divovo, 2007. P. 50-56.

246. Politova M. Bavarskaya polykrovnaya (2009). Konnyi Mir, № 12. P. 36-41.

247. Politova M. Vestfalskiy variant kachestva (2008). Konnyi Mir, № 10. P. 40-46.

248. Politova M. Rodom iz Golshtinii (2007). Konnyi Mir, № 6. P. 40-45.

249. Politova M., Reissmann M. Vvedeniye v genetiku masti loshadey. Moscow, 2006. 62 p.

250. Politova M.A., Reissmann M., Vagner H.J. Vliyaniye genotipa v lokuse MC1R (Extension) i ASIP (AGOUTI) na rabotosposobnost' i plodovitost' loshadey russkoy verkhovoy porody. Moscow, 2003. P. 476-479.

251. Polzunova A. Franstsuzkiy fenomen (2002). Konnyi Mir, № 5. P. 46-51.

252. Pruvost M., Bellone R., Benecke N., Sandoval-Castellanos E., Cieslak M., Kuznetsova T., Morales-Muñiz A., O'Connor T., Reissmann M., Hofreiter M., Ludwig A. Genotypes of predomestic horses match phenotypes painted in Paleolithic works of cave art. Proceedings of the National Academy of Sciences of the United States of America, November 7, 2011.

253. Radjabli H., Volkova Y. Pitomets rezvyi Karabakha (2009). *Konnyi Mir, № 6*. P. 42-47.

254. Reissmann M. Uvidet' chernoye v belom (2009). *Konnyi Mir, № 10*. P. 52-57.

255. Reissmann M., Bierwolf J., Brockmann G.A. Two SNPs in the SILV gene are associated with silver coat colour in ponies (2007). *Animal Genetics*, vol. 36, issue 1. P. 1-6.

256. Rendo F., Iriondo M., Manzano C., Estonba A. Identification of horse chestnut coat color genotype using SnaPshot (2009). BMC Research Notes, 2:255.

257. Rieder S., Hagger C., Obexer-Ruff G., Leeb T., Poncet P.A. Genetic analysis of white facial and leg markings in the Swiss Franches-Montagnes Horse Breed (2008). *Journal of Heredity*, March-April, 99(2):130-6.

258. Rieder S., Stricker C., Joerg H., Dummer R., Stranzinger G. A comparative genetic approach for the investigation of ageing grey horse melanoma (2000). *Journal of Animal Breeding and Genetics*, vol. 117(2). P.73-82.

259. Rieder S., Taourit S., Mariat D., Langlois B., Guérin G. Mutations in the agouti (ASIP), the extension (MC1R), and the brown (TYRP1) loci and their association to the coat color phenotypes in horses (Equus caballus) (2001). *Mammalian Genome*, 12. P. 450-455.

260. Robinson R. Genetika okrasov sobak. Moscow, 1995. 88 p.

261. Rong R., Chandley A.C., Song J., McBeath S., Tan P.P., Bai Q., Speed R.M. A fertile mule and hinny in China (1988). *Cytogenetics and Cell Genetics*, 47(3). P. 134-139.

262. Ryabova Y.V. Sovershenstvovaniye selektsioniruyemyh priznakov u loshadey russkoy verkhovoy porody. Sbornik nauchnyh trudov Mezhdunarodnoy nauchno-prakticheskoy konferentsii "Agrotekhnologii XXI veka". Moscow, 2007. P. 326-328.

263. Ryabova T.N., Ustyantseva A.V. Analiticheskaya spravka. Akhal-tekinskaya poroda v 2008 godu. Ryazan', 2009. 78 p.

264. Ryder O.A., Chemnick L.G., Bowling A.T., Benirschke K. Male mule foal qualifies as the offspring of a female mule and jack donkey (1985). *Journal of Heredity*, September-October, 76(5). P. 379-381.

265. Sanagayeva A.V. Fenotipicheskiye osobennosti loshadey vladimirskoy porody Gavrilovo-Posadskogo konnogo zavoda (2009). *Izvestiya Sankt-Peterburgskogo Gosudarstvennogo agrarnogo universiteta, № 14*. P. 103-107.

266. Sandmeyer L.S. Equine Recurrent Uveitis (2008), July, available on: http://www.appaloosaproject.info/index.php?module=pagemaster&PAGE_user_op=view_page&PAGE_id=40&MMN_position=68:68

267. Sandmeyer L.S., Breaux C.B., Archer S., Grahn B.H. Clinical and electroretinographic characteristics of congenital stationary night blindness in the Appaloosa and the association with the leopard complex (2007). *Veterinary Ophtalmology*, November-December; 10(6):368-75.

268. Santschi E.M., Vrotsos Paul D., Purdy A.K., Mickelson J.R. Incidence of the endothelin receptor B mutation that causes lethal white foal syndrome in white-patterned horses (2001). *American Journal of Veterinary Research, № 1*. P. 97-103.

269. Schmutz S.M., Berryere T.G., Dreger D. MITF and White Spotting in Dogs: A Population Study (2009). *Journal of Heredity*, 100 (Suppl. 1): S66-S74.

270. Scott P.W. Skin of the neck, mane and tail of the curly horse (2004). *Equine veterinary education*, Vol. 16, № 4, August. P. 201-206.

271. Schwark H.-J., Petzold P. Das Haflinger Pferd. – 2, neubearb. Aufl. – Wittenberg Lutherstadt: Ziemsen, 1986.

272. Shchapova O. KWPN – znachit pobeda (2008). *Konnyi Mir, № 7*. P. 50-55.

273. Shepard C. The Barlink Factor. Possible New Dilution Gene in Paint Horses (2006), http://www.new-dilutions.com/pearl/American/peaches.htm

274. Shepard C. Champagne Delusion: Champagne Look-Alike Dilutions (2003). *Champagne Horse Journal*, Fall.

275. Shimbo F. The Akhal-Teke Glow (1998). *Akhal-Teke Quarterly, № 12*, January.

276. Shustrova I. "Raspisniye" loshadi (2002). *Konnyi Mir, № 3*. P. 34-37.

277. Silva P. da Posledniye iz mogikan Sorrayi (2003). *Konnyi Mir, № 2*. P. 42-46.

278. Simonov L., Merder I. Loshadi. Konskiye porody. Moscow, 2008. 189 p.

279. Slawik C. Blondiny s vostochnym obayaniyem (2006). *Konnyi Mir, № 3*. P. 48-51.

280. Slawik C. Koroli pushty (2006). *Konnyi Mir, № 5*. P. 44-47.

281. Slawik C. Noriker: istoriya dlinoy v 2000 let (2006). *Konnyi Mir, № 9*. P. 50-53.

282. Slawik C. Tsyganskoye pegoye schastye (2006). *Konnyi Mir, № 12*. P. 32-35.

283. Solopov A.I. Tsvetooboznacheniya v latinskom yazyke. Naimenovaniya tsveta v indoyevropeyskih yazykah: Sistemniy i istoricheskiy analiz. Edited by A.P. Vasilevich. Moscow, 2007. P. 66-76.

284. Sorokina I., Milko O., Ignatyeva Y. V podvodu i pod voyevody (2002). *Konnyi Mir, № 6*. P. 44-49.

285. Sotskaya M.N. Genetika okrasov i sherstnogo pokrova sobak. Moscow, 2010. 318 p.

286. Sponenberg D.P. 1996. *Equine Color Genetics*, Iowa State University Press. 156 p.

287. Sponenberg D.P. 2003. *Equine Color Genetics*, 2nd ed. Ames, Iowa: Iowa University Press. 215 p.

288. Sponenberg D.P. 2009. *Equine Color Genetics*, 3rd ed. Wiley-Blackwell. 277 p.

289. Sponenberg D.P. The inheritance of leopard spotting in the Noriker horse (1982). *Journal of Heredity*, 73(5):357-359.

290. Sponenberg D.P., Carr G., Simak E. The Inheritance of the Leopard Complex of Spotting Patterns in Horses (1990). *The Journal of Heredity*, № 4.

291. Sponenberg D.P., Weiss M.C. Dominant black in horses (1997). *Genetic Selection Evolution*, 29. P. 403-408.

292. Stachurska A.M. Inheritance or primitive markings in horses (2000). *Journal of Animal Breeding and Genetics*, vol. 117(2). P.29-38.

293. Stachurska A., Brodacki A. Genetic structure of Małopolski horse population with respect to basic coat colours (2000). *Annals of Animal Science*, № 2. P. 9-19.

294. Stachurska A., Brodacki A., Sochaczewska M. Dziedziczenie odcieni maści gniadej u koni (2002). Roczniki naukowe zootechniki, Kraków, t. 29 z. 1. S.19-31.

295. Stachurska A., Bruśniak A., Kolstrung R. Frekwencja genów odpowiedzialnych za umaszczenie w populacji kuców felińskich (2002). Roczniki naukowe zootechniki, Kraków, t. 29 z. 1. S.243-251.

296. Stachurska A., Pięta M., Jaworski Z., Ussing A.P., Bruśniak A., Florek M. Colour variation in blue dun Polish Konik and Biłgoraj horses (2004). *Livestock Production Science*, Volume 90, Issues 2-3, November. P. 201-209.

297. Stachurska A., Ussing A.P., Nestaas T. Maści rozjaśnione na przykładzie koni fiordskich (2001). *Medycyna weterynaryjna*, № 12. S. 876-879.

298. Stachurska A., Ussing A.P. Maść tarantowata – najbardziej różnorodny wzór białej sierści u koni (2001). *Przegląd Hodowlany*, № 12. S. 13-14.

299. Stamatelakys I. Believe in Brown (2010). *Paint Horse Journal*, April. P. 58-64.

300. Stamatelakys I. The Science of Sabino (2007). *Paint Horse Journal*, August. P. 62-69.

301. Starodumov M. On – russkiy amerikanets (2007). *Konnyi Mir*, № 4. P. 30-36.

302. Stegacheva S.P. Zolotistiye i serebristiye akhaltekintsy (2010). *Konevodstvo i Konniy Sport*, № 2. P. 33.

303. Stegacheva S. Rasprostraneniye metallicheskogo bleska shersti v akhaltekinskoy porode (2011). *Akhal-Teke Inform*. P. 184-185.

304. Stolnaya Y. Samaya sovershennaya (2005). *Konnyi Mir*, № 3. P. 34-41.

305. Sukhodolskaya I. Krylatiye tabuny bashkirskoy zemli (2006). *Konnyi Mir*, № 1. P. 54-58.

306. Swinburne J.S., Hopkins A., Binns M.M. Assignment of the horse grey coat colour gene to ECA25 using whole genome scanning (2002). *Animal Genetics*, № 5. P. 338-342.

307. Sydney's Illustrated "The Book of the Horse", 1875. Available on: http://www.newdilutions.com/RHC/index.htm

308. Śląska B., Rozempolska-Rucińska I., Jeżewska-Witkowska G. Variation in some reproductive traits of mink (neovison vison) according to their coat colour (2009). *Annals of Animal Science*, Vol. 9, № 3, Kraków. P. 281-297.

309. Tellington-Johns L., Taylor S. Kak pravil'no vybrat' i vospitat' loshad'. Ttouch – novyi metod vozdeystviya na loshad'. Moscow, 2004. 224 p.

310. Terry R.B., Archer S., Brooks S., Bernoco D., Bailey E. Assignment of the appaloosa coat colour gene (LP) to equine chromosome 1 (2004). *Animal Genetics*, Volume 35, Issue 2, April. P. 134-137.

311. Tesio F. Razvedeniye skakovyh loshadey. Edited by D. Balakshin, T. Tikhonova. Moscow, 2007. 192 p.

312. *The Horse in Celtic Culture. Medieval Welsh Perspectives*, edited by Sioned Davies and Nerys Ann Jones, Cardiff: University of Wales Press, 1997. 190 p.

313. Tolkovyi slovar' zhivogo velikorusskogo yazyka V.I. Dalya, republication based on the 2nd edition (1880-1882), available on: http://vidahl.agava.ru/

314. Toth Z., Kaps M., Sölkner J., Bodo I., Curik I. Quantitative genetic aspects of coat color in horses (2006). *Journal of Animal Science*. 84. P. 2623-2628.

315. Trommershausen-Smith A., Suzuki Y., Stormont C. Use of Blood Typing to Confirm Principles of Coat-Color Genetics in Horses (1976). *The Journal of Heredity*, № 1. P. 6-10.

316. Tsyganok I. Percheron – bogatyr' iz Frantsii (2001). *Konnyi Mir*, № 5. P. 6-11.

317. Tsyganok I. Frantsuzy, pokorivshiye mir (2009). *Konnyi Mir*, № 1-2. P. 60-66.

318. Urusov S.P. Kniga o loshadi. Nastol'naya kniga konnozavodchika, konevoda, konevladel'tsa i lyubitelya loshadi. Moscow, 2000. 1020 p.

319. Vasilevich A.P., Kuznetsova S.N., Mishchenko S.S. Tsvet i nazvaniya tsveta v russkom yazyke. Edited by A.P. Vasilevich. 2nd edition. Moscow, 2008. 216 p.

320. Vasilyeva A.P. Voroniye arabskiye loshadi i perspektivy ih ispol'zovaniya v plemennoy rabote s porodoy (2010). *Konevodstvo i Konniy Sport*, №1. P. 8-10.

321. Vdovina N.V., Yuryeva I.B. Mezenskaya loshad'. Itogi raboty s porodoi. Sostoyaniye i perspektivy razvitiya nauchnogo obespecheniya selskokhozyaystvennogo proizvodstva na Severe. Syktyvkar, 2007. P. 127-132.

322. Vinogradov I.I., Pankova T.Y. Sovremennoye sostoyaniye i perspektivy razvitiya Zabaikalskoy loshadi. Strategiya vedeniya ovtsevodstva, kozovodstva, konevodstva i drugih traditsionnyh otrasley отраслей zhivotnovodstva Sibiri v sovremennyh ekonomicheskih usloviyah: Sbornik materialov. Chita, 2005. P. 96-102.

323. Vitt V.O. Loshadi i osly. Istoriya konnozavodstva. Moscow, 2003. P. 1019-1024.

324. Volkova Y. "Arabo-poni" iz Uelsa (2007). *Konnyi Mir*, № 8. P. 54-59.

325. Volkova Y. Akhaltekintsy (2000). *Konnyi Mir*, № 1. P. 8-13.

326. Volkova Y. Beliye pyatna v shersti i rodoslovnoy (2007). *Konnyi Mir*, № 4. P. 48-51.

327. Volkova Y. Bogatstvo vikingov (2007). *Konnyi Mir, №* 5. P. 40-43.

328. Volkova Y. Bol'shoye sokrovishche malen'kogo grafstva (2002). *Konnyi Mir, №*1. P. 6-11.

329. Volkova Y. Gnediye iz Klivlenda (2008). *Konnyi Mir, №* 4. P. 42-47.

330. Volkova Y. Gordost' Luzitanii (2006). *Konnyi Mir, №* 6. P. 48-52.

331. Volkova Y. Zoloto Kinskih (2005). *Konnyi Mir, №*1. P. 34-37.

332. Volkova Y. Islandskaya saga (2004). *Konnyi Mir, №* 3. P. 46-50.

333. Volkova Y. Karabkhskiye loshadi. K istorii porody (2000). *Konnyi Mir, №* 2. P. 4-7.

334. Volkova Y. Koloss angliyskyi (2004). *Konnyi Mir, №* 6. P. 45-51.

335. Volkova Y. O chyom rasskazhet mast' konya (1998). *Zolotoy Mustang, №* 5.

336. Volkova Y. Ot Tsezarya do nashih dney (2007). *Konnyi Mir, №* 3. P. 34-38.

337. Volkova Y. Posledniye iz "Korsyeri" (2003). *Konnyi Mir, №* 6. P. 44-49.

338. Volkova Y. Pro pyatna I nesapyatnannuyu reputatsiyu (2006). *Konnyi Mir, №* 2. P. 50-54.

339. Volkova Y. Rozhdyonniye yuzhnym vetrom (2001). *Konnyi mir, №* 3. P. 4-9.

340. Volkova Y. Sokrovishcha imperii (2008). *Konnyi Mir, №* 2. P. 42-50.

341. Volkova Y. S plantatsii na show-ring (2006). *Konnyi Mir, №* 7. P. 40-47.

342. Volkova Y. Chernyi zhemchug Frislandii (2003). *Konnyi Mir, №* 1. P. 38-45.

343. Volkova Y. Shokoladnyi nabor (2006). *Konnyi Mir, №* 4. P. 44-51.

344. Volkova Y., Silva P. da Syn za otsa ne otvechaet, esli papa ... osyol (2003). *Konnyi Mir, №* 3. P. 58-61.

345. Vorobyova I. Estonskaya krov' (2010). *Konnyi Mir, №* 6. P. 48-52.

346. Vorobyova I. Pochemu ghibridy bespolodny? (2010) *Konnyi Mir, №* 1. P. 54-55.

347. Vostochno-prusskiye pegiye loshadi trakenenskogo proiskhozhdeniya (2007). *RusTrakehner, №* 1. P. 34-37.

348. Wahler B. Arabian Coat Color Patterns (2011), available on: http://www.arabianhorses.org/education/genetic/docs/11Genetic_Coat_Color_Patterns.pdf

349. Westfall Danielle, Dr. Tuhela-Reuning Laura metallic Sheen as Observed in Individuals of the Akhal-Teke Breed, available on: http://cgakhaltekes.com/index_Page2110.htm

350. Wiersema J.K., Riessen H.A. van Het Paard In Zijn Kleurenrijkdom. - Zuidgroep, 1978. 251 p.

351. Willis M.B. Genetika sobak. Moscow, 2000. 607 p.

352. Woolf C.M. Multifactorial Inheritance of Common White Markings in the Arabian Horse (1990). *The Journal of Heredity, №* 4. P. 250-256.

353. Woolf C.M., Swafford J.R. Evidence for Eumelanin and Pheomelanin Producing Genotypes in the Arabian Horse (1988). *The Journal of Heredity, №* 2. P. 100-106.

354. Xiao X., Jia X., Guo X., Li S., Yang Z., Zhang Q. CSNB1 in Chinese families associated with novel mutations in NYX (2006). *Journal of Human Genetics;* 51(7):634-40.

355. Yanova Y.Y. Geneticheskoye determinirovaniye masti i otmetin u loshadey. Doctoral Thesis (agriculture). Rostov-on-Don, 2003. 117 p.

356. Yanova Y.Y. Zakonomernosti nasledovaniya belyh otmetin u loshadey. Novye selektsionniye, fiziologicheskiye, biotehnologicheskiye metody v konevodstve. *Divovo,* 1999. P. 283-297.

357. Yanova Y.Y. O nasledovanii mastey pri skreshchivanii donskoy i akhaltekinskoy porod. Nauchniye osnovy sokhraneniya i sovershenstvovaniya porod loshadey. *Divovo,* 2002. P. 250-254.

358. Yanova Y. O chem rasskazhet beliy volos (2002). *Konevodstvo i Konniy Sport, №*6. P. 30-31.

359. Yelizarenkova T.Y. Slova i veshchi v Rigvede. Moscow, 1999. 240 p.

360. Yuferev A.A. Istoriya i sovremennoye sostoyanie populatsii vyatskoy loshadi v Ydmurtii. Problemy i nauchnoe obespecheniye otrasli konevodstva Yevropeyskogo Severa RF: Materialy mezhdunarodnoy nauchno-prakticheskoy konferentsii, posvyashchennoy 10-letiyu vozrozhdeniya mezenskoy loshadi. Arkhangelsk, 2003. P. 39-46.

361. Yuldashbayev Y.A., Kolesnikova N. Svoystva volosyanogo pokrova okhotnichyih sobak porody angliyskiy koker-spaniel' raznogo okrasa. Sokhraneniye raznoobraziya zhivotnyh i okhotnichye khozyaystvo Rossii: Materialy 3 Mezhdunarodnoy nauchno-prakticheskoy konferentsii. Moscow, 2009. P. 294-300.

362. Yurasov N.A. Konevodstvo. Moscow, 1939. 410 p.

363. Yuryeva I.B. Osnovniye napravleniya deyatelnosti po vosstanovleniyu i sovershenstvovaniyu populyatsii mezenskoy loshadi. Problemy i nauchnoye obespecheniye otrasli konevodstva Yevropeyskogo Severa RF: Materialy mezhdunarodnoy nauchno-prakticheskoy konferentsii, posvyashchennoy 10-letiyu vozrozhdeniya mezenskoy loshadi. Arkhangelsk, 2003. P. 25-32.

364. Zaborskih Y.Y. Istoricheskiy analiz razvitiyaUlaganskoy populyatsii altayskoy loshadi v XX veke i zootehnicheskaya kharakteristika porody na sovremennom etape. Aktualniye problemy selskogo khozyaistva gornyh territoriy: materialy Mezhdunarodnoy nauchno-prakticheskoy konferentsii. Gorno-Altaysk, 2007. P. 150-156.

365. Zaborskih Y.Y. Opyt sohraneniya aborigennoy porody lokalnogo rasprostraneniya v sovremennyh rynochnyh usloviyah na primere altayskoy loshadi. Materialy mezhdunarodnoy nauchno-prakticheskoy konferentsii "Problemy konevodstva". Novosibirsk, 2008. P. 141-147.

366. Zaborskih Y., Zaborskih P. Loshad' Zolotyh gor (2007). *Konnyi Mir, №* 7. P. 36-40.

367. Zaitsev A., Adamkovskaya M. Mustangi ozera Manych (2007). *Konnyi Mir,* № 3. P. 50-51.

368. Zaitsev A.M., Khrabrova L.A. Gheneticheskiye osobennosti allelofonda vyatskoy loshadi. Problemy i nauchnoye obespecheniye otrasli konevodstva Yevropeyskogo Severa RF: Materialy mezhdunarodnoy nauchno-prakticheskoy konferentsii, posvyashchennoy 10-letiyu vozrozhdeniya mezenskoy loshadi. Arkhangelsk, 2003. P. 76-81.

369. Zeynullin A. Kushumskaya poroda loshadey. Nauchnoye obespecheniye konkurentosposobnosti plemennogo sportivnogo i produktivnogo konevodstva v Rossii i stranah SNG. Nauchno-prakticheskaya konferentsiya, posv. 70-letiyu prof. S.S. Sergiyenko: sbornik nauchnyh trudov. *Divovo,* 2007. P. 95-97.

370. Zharikov Y.A., Khozyainov G.N. Kharakteristika sovremennoy populyatsii pechorskih loshadey v Ust'-Tsilemskom rayone Respubliki Komi. Sostoyaniye i perspektivy razvitiya nauchnogo obespecheniya selskohozyaystvennogo proizvodsnva na Severe. Syktyvkar, 2007. P. 156-162.

371. Zhukovskaya Y. O terskoy porode zamolvite slovo (2002). *Konnyi Mir,* №2. P. 6-11.

Index

Photos and associated captions are indicated
by photo number and in *italics*. Tables are indicated by *t*.